Sign language

The study of deaf people and their language

J.G. KYLE and B. WOLL

School of Education Research Unit
University of Bristol

with G. PULLEN and F. MADDIX

CAMBRIDGE
UNIVERSITY PRESS

Published by the Press Syndicate of the University of Cambridge
The Pitt Building, Trumpington Street, Cambridge CB2 1RP
40 West 20th Street, New York, NY 10011-4211, USA
10 Stamford Road, Oakleigh, Melbourne 3166, Australia

© Text, Cambridge University Press 1985
© Illustrations of BSL signs, Bernard Quinn 1985

First published 1985
Reprinted 1986, 1987
First paperback edition 1988
Reprinted 1988, 1989, 1991, 1993, 1994, 1995

Printed in Great Britain by Woolnough Bookbinding Ltd,
Irthlingborough, Northamptonshire

Library of Congress catalogue number: 84-14265

British Library cataloguing in publication data
Kyle, J.
Sign language.
1. Deaf – Means of communication. 2. Sign language.
3. Psycholinguistics.
I. Title II. Woll, B. III. Pullen G.
IV. Maddix, F.
419   HV2474

ISBN 0 521 26075 2 hardback
ISBN 0 521 35717 9 paperback

CN A19
AN 59035

Sign language

CANCELLED
THE NORTHERN COLLEGE
LIBRARY
BARNSLEY

Northern College
Library

NC03196

Contents

Acknowledgements

Sitting down to consider the amount of help we have had at every stage of the preparation of this book, it is clear that it would be impossible to thank adequately all those who made a contribution. It has taken about three years from beginning to end and in that time there has been a great amount of support for the research projects which provide the basis of our work in this field. In the first instance we wish to thank the Department of Health and Social Security for the project 'Sign language learning and use' (JR 212/8), the Nuffield Foundation for 'Deaf people and the community' (VNAF 31), Leverhulme Foundation for 'Change in BSL', UNESCO, the European Commission Ministry for Disabled People and the European Cultural Foundation for the work on international comparisons of sign languages, and most recently the Medical Research Council for the project 'Young deaf people in employment' (G.8117792). Without the financial support and encouragement of these bodies our research activities could not have been possible.

A large number of deaf people worked with us at various times, transcribed tapes and helped to explain to us the meaning of sign language: they include Jennifer Ackerman and Linda Day. Two people in particular had a major impact, since they worked full time with us and contributed very directly to the information we have collected. Lorna Allsop interviewed all the deaf people mentioned in the first chapter and set out much of what we know about the deaf community. Gloria Pullen has been with us throughout the work in this book; she has contributed at every level as a sign language teacher, a consultant and a key investigator in the projects listed; she collected the material and set out appendix 1 and has supported us through every stage of our work.

Of the hearing people who have worked with us the principal contribution has been that of Peter Llewellyn-Jones. He first involved us in sign language work and then became a colleague in the university. He made chapters 9 and 11 possible by his thorough knowledge of sign language users in the UK; for his efforts we are deeply indebted. Two students who worked closely with us on the development of the notation system were Maggie Carter and John Coleman. Frank Maddix was responsible for the computerisation of the system and

Acknowledgements

provided appendix 3. Additionally we had support, co-operation and encouragement from a wide range of people of whom we would particularly like to thank Dr R. Conrad from Oxford, and Professor Peter Robinson in Bristol.

In the final analysis, of course, despite the research work, the final product could not have appeared without the wholehearted effort of those who prepared the manuscripts over and over again. We want to thank Eileen Nash and Maureen Devoy who typed early parts of the book, but particularly those associated with the research projects themselves. Jenny Mills-Roberts and Liz Young worked tirelessly to keep us on the right tracks in every sense; they made our work on sign language and deaf people possible with their efficiency and commitment. Kaz Threlfall, and recently Lynn Houlton, have had the final task of putting together the whole manuscript again and again. With Liz, their work in the last few months has been vital and for their cheerfulness and involvement throughout we are forever grateful.

Bernard Quinn of the British Deaf Association illustrated the many signs in the book. Mike George of Bristol University took the photographs. Without their work we would not have satisfactorily got through the final stages.

Our last vote of thanks goes to our families who have supported us over the past few years and through the long research days. Our grateful thanks to all.

JIM KYLE   BENCIE WOLL

Introduction

It is not at all surprising to find that the eventual form of a book on a new field such as sign language has greatly altered in writing. The requirements of the field in terms of the community of deaf people, the body of educators of deaf children, the parents and all of the professionals concerned with deaf people have combined to pull the content in several different directions at once. In the end we decided to concentrate on those topics that were most central to our own professional backgrounds in psychology and linguistics and to try to provide a link between these different fields. It has been impossible to meet all the needs of everyone we hope will read this book, and some of the chapters can only be considered introductory accounts; we are, however, happy if this book is seen as an introduction to sign language, since it would be false to pretend we have discovered even most of the answers. It is still premature to believe that sign language grammar is fully accessible to hearing researchers. What we have tried to do is to set down a framework on which other researchers might build and from which professionals may be able to develop a coherent practice for their work with deaf people. We hope we have largely avoided the dogmatic presentation of 'truth' which has blighted work with the deaf, and particularly with deaf children, for so many years. It is not our intention to prescribe methods for solving deaf people's 'problems' but rather to highlight the richness and value of deaf people's lives and language so that the professional approach can be made more meaningful and respectful.

Dignity is perhaps the key word. It is this feature which has been denied deaf people in the rush for success in speaking or educational achievement. The most important value must be integration and involvement in society, but this cannot be achieved by pressure to succeed. It must be a sharing and an offering which takes into account the dignity of deaf people. Two aspects seem critically important and have been greatly undervalued. They are, firstly, the need for *access to information* and, secondly, *the right to choose*. Even those deaf people who have left school without 'society's valued spoken language' retain a basic right to access to society's information. In addition, they have the right to choose their means of access to this information. It can be through sign language or

1

spoken language or through some mixture, and the deaf child must be given the range of provision from which this latter choice can be made. To view sign language in this political sense is a rather strange idea for most people and really only understandable in the context of the history of deafness. The understanding of sign language and its users is the first step to breaking down barriers for all those in the deaf world.

Our intentions in writing this book are reflected by the four sections into which it can be roughly divided. In the first (chapters 1–4) we wish to introduce the reader to deaf people and their language in a way which is accessible to all those interested. Chapter 1 describes the community of language users and examines their relationships with the hearing society in which they live. Not only can we see how sign language has been developed and used by deaf people in all their interactions, but we can also see why the situation of hearing people has tended to work against their access to the deaf community. Chapter 2 focuses on the language itself and sets out some of the factors which confirm the language status of British Sign Language (BSL); this is a general introduction and most of the issues raised are tackled more fully in later chapters. Chapter 3 explores the history of sign language and its use; previous books have concentrated on education and methods, but here we have tried to focus on the writings which deal directly with deaf people and their language. Chapter 4 deals with the issues surrounding the language acquisition of deaf children; in the past, this has only been examined in spoken language terms, but increasingly researchers have looked at sign language acquisition. This section shows how gesture and sign are different and explores the relationships between early acquisition of words, signs and gestures in both deaf children and hearing children. In addition, it is in this period that we see the early development of the language skills central to our study of BSL.

In the second section (chapters 5–8) we describe in detail what we know of BSL as a language. BSL has only recently been the subject of linguistic analysis, but already a great many features of the language have been described which were previously unrecognised. Research on other sign languages has contributed to these discoveries and we also discuss that work in these chapters. Most importantly, we refer frequently to features of spoken language to help our explanation of sign language features. We do this for two reasons: firstly to help non-specialists to relate the discussion of sign language structure to what they know of their own language and, secondly, because any understanding of how sign languages work must be constructed upon features of spoken language which have already been well researched. Linguists in the past have been at such great pains to show that forms of language such as writing are subsidiary to spoken language, that sign language has been ignored or misunderstood;

however, despite the striking differences between signed and spoken languages in channels of communication and articulators used, they show remarkable similarities. It is by looking at these similarities and differences that we can gain a better understanding of language generally.

In chapter 5 we present the elements which are found in sign language and compare them to the elements of spoken language. A way of writing down signs is introduced as a preliminary to the discussion of sign form. In chapter 6 the discussion centres on signs themselves, how they come into existence, change over time, and alter their meanings. The role of fingerspelling and other loan signs is also described. Chapter 7 is devoted to a preliminary description of the morphology (the grammatical processes which individual signs undergo). Morphology and syntax together make up the grammar of a language, and it is in the description of BSL grammar that we can see the role of non-manual as well as manual elements in greatest detail. Chapter 8 describes the comparative study of different sign languages. Just as spoken languages form related families, so also do sign languages, and these relationships are presented along with discussion of the question of language universality.

In the third section (chapters 9 and 10) we draw on psychological techniques to examine sign language. Chapter 9 uses data from a large study of hearing people's use of BSL to compare spoken and sign language learning. Theories already in existence go a long way towards explaining the poor levels of sign language learning and use, and raise questions as to the validity of current sign language training techniques in the UK. A linked appendix (appendix 2) elaborates an alternative approach to sign language teaching. Chapter 10 tackles a core issue for psychologists: the question of internal representation when the form cannot easily be based in speech. The developments in the field of cognitive psychology have in recent years considered how speech-based codes provide the means for the learning and memory processes. If deaf people use a different type of code, i.e. a sign-based code, and still achieve effective functioning, then many of the psychological theories have to be re-examined.

A significant aspect of sign language is how it is to be used in bridging the gap between deaf and hearing communities and this is the focus of the fourth section. Chapter 11 tackles sign language interpreting, and chapters 12 and 13 deal with education. Not surprisingly, in view of the learning problem seen in chapter 9, we have discovered major problems in sign language interpreting, particularly from BSL into English. The task of the interpreter in spoken language situations is compared with that of a BSL interpreter. We can see that lack of training facilities and the peculiar requirements of the situation reduce the effectiveness of the BSL interpreter's performance. In dealing with education in chapters 12 and 13 we enter a difficult world where different views are strongly held and often strongly expressed. Our review tries to match up the methodologies propounded with the actual results obtained and finds that very rarely has effective research been done. The choice of method, in the face of deaf children's poor achievement in English learning, has been, and still is, a matter of belief and commitment rather than informed questioning. Our examination leads us to the conclusion that BSL knowledge is critical to the teacher's functioning, but that methods can be developed by the bilingual teacher which vary in their emphasis on speech, sign and written English, according to the priorities of the situation.

In the final brief chapter we bring together the views which have developed from our original starting point. The status of BSL allows a meaningful co-operation with deaf people in education and communication, and recognition of this provides us with hope for the future.

Finally, there should be a brief explanation of terminology. The term *sign language* is used to refer to the language of deaf people, parallel to *spoken language* of hearing people. Where a specific national language is referred to, capitals are used, e.g. *British Sign Language* (BSL) or *American Sign Language* (ASL), in the same way as we use capitals for the spoken languages English, French, Japanese, and so on. We also talk about learning *sign* as we would talk about learning a spoken language; the practice of this is *signing*, equivalent to *speaking*. When discussing a specific lexical item we refer to *a sign* which is the equivalent of *a word*.

In relation to the systems of signing current in the UK the generic term is *signed English* though this is not a precisely formulated approach as are those systems which appear in the USA, such as Signing Exact English or Seeing Essential English or even Signed English. The term to cover all these approaches, both in the UK and elsewhere, is *Manually Coded English* (MCE). Whenever these are used with speech simultaneously it is likely that a *Total Communication* approach is being used.

In practice these terms should not conflict though, like any attempt at regularising a still developing terminology, they will initially seem overly complex. Just as we need these distinctions in talking about spoken language we also need them for sign language.

In writing down signs we have used a well recognised convention of capitalising the sign glosses or translations to English as in GIVE or GIVE-REPEATEDLY, where the hyphen indicates that there is only one sign. For fingerspelling we have used lower case separated by dots as in j·o·a·n·n·a. The full notation system used is described in appendix 3 and for the complete description the reader can consult this section.

1. The deaf community

British Sign Language is a language of movement and space, of the hands and of the eyes, of abstract communication as well as iconic story-telling, but most important of all, it is the language of the deaf community in the UK. It is not a new language nor is it a system recently developed by hearing people; rather it is a naturally occurring form of communication among people who do not hear. It is a language which until recently has been ignored and therefore completely underestimated in its potential. It is different, often strikingly so, from English, but it shares features and grammatical processes with many other spoken languages. Increasingly, linguists have come to analyse it as a true natural language. It differs from other languages in one major respect of its features: it does not rely on spoken words.

Since one of the primary concerns of all education has been the acquisition of spoken communication as the most acceptable means of interaction, people who are unable to communicate through speech are regarded in some measure as inferior. When they go on to develop their own means of communication, which is usually not that of their parents, then the majority of the community tend to ostracise them and may ascribe to them levels of competence well below that of the rest of the community. Deaf people are one such group, set apart from the hearing community. It is perhaps not surprising that their language is only now coming into the open. A major reason for this is probably a growing international concern for, and recognition of the rights of, minority groups. The idea that deaf people can form such a group rather than be considered educational failures within the mainstream is a relatively new possibility for educators and researchers alike. The nature of this group of people and their communication is the focus of this book.

Adequate statements of what the deaf community consists of have proved to be notably elusive for students of the literature. The term 'community' to some extent identifies a separateness of existence and mode of operation which people have found difficult to use to describe deaf people. The way in which the deaf community is defined is by and large a product of the understanding, or lack of it, by society as a whole. There seem to be two extremes of attitude which highlight this: the first is a view that the principal characteristic of deafness is the *lack* of something, i.e. hearing and/or communication ability; the second is the acceptance of an identity of deafness which stresses the group feelings of deaf people and the effectiveness of their communication.

Associated with the first position are attitudes such as those found by Bunting (1981) and Kohl (1966):

Forty-seven per cent of the public thought that one half or more of deaf people try to hide their deafness largely because they do not want to appear different . . . most people accepted that the deaf were isolated and had difficulties getting on with people at work . . . (Bunting, 1981: 1–2)

Myklebust (1964) claims that there is a qualitative difference in the behavior and personality of deaf individuals. He attributes this to the qualitative difference in experience the deaf have, and shows as a descriptive basis that the deaf are socially immature as compared to the hearing and even to individuals who are hard of hearing. (Kohl, 1966: 9)

In practice, as Baker and Cokely (1980) point out, these are views from 'the outside', but might be seen more kindly as simply statements arising from society's values and level of understanding at that time. Baker and Padden (1978) express views somewhere between the two:

The deaf community comprises those deaf and hard of hearing individuals who share a common language, common experiences and values and a common way of interacting with each other and with hearing people. The most basic factor determining who is a member of the deaf community seems to be what is called 'attitudinal deafness'. This occurs when a person identifies him/herself as a member of the deaf community and other members accept that person as part of the community. (Baker and Padden, 1978: 4)

In effect, this too raises a number of issues. It includes everyone who has a hearing loss, even the hard of hearing. It also seems circular – 'those who share' are the community; to join you have to want to share. However, the evidence would need to show the degree of commonality of language, experience and values. The key is probably in the concept of 'attitudinal deafness' whereby the individual expresses himself/herself through identification with a group with whom communication is shared. As will be described later in this chapter, deaf people do not form the same sort of geographical or historical community as is associated with, say, migrant groups, but the identity of deafness and the strength of belief in its language form seem just as strong. Perhaps this can be most effectively described by those who are deaf:

It is the pleasure gained from mixing with other deaf people that makes one remain a member of the deaf 'in-group' – the British deaf community. So powerful is the attraction of social interaction with deaf people that others, on making contact with the deaf but who have not skill in BSL, learn to sign and become members of the community. These latecomers are the post-lingually deaf, orally educated deaf and deaf people who are educated in schools for the hearing. (Lawson, 1981: 166–7)

In these four quotations one can see the clear distinctions which Baker and Cokely (1980) recognise in the approaches to understanding the society of deaf people: *the clinical-pathological* (usually views of the hearing community and often based on psychological or educational data), and the *cultural* (usually views of the deaf people themselves and linguists, primarily couched in terms of the unifying factor of shared sign language). Baker and Cokely (1980) point out, quite rightly, that these are not simply differences of attitude: they have profound implications for the way deaf people are treated. The first approach emphasises what is lacking in deaf people and makes as its top priority the 'normalisation' of deaf people, while the second implies acceptance (though not always understanding) of deaf people as a separate group with their own organisation and traditions.

Unfortunately, this discussion does not bring us much closer to defining the community as such. One can see the educational view as being very powerful. Deaf people may be identified as those who have gone to deaf schools or who have had special provision made because of their hearing problems; in addition educational examination will show them to have specific problems with many of the standard subjects in school. The fact that we do know a good deal about deafness in school children has tended to create the basis for the clinical-pathological framework. The assumption that deaf people find similar problems in adult life has been easily made by many hearing people but:

It is not true, as it is often assumed, that all deaf people need the constant support and assistance of the social work services. Most deaf people manage their personal, domestic and working lives as well as other members of the community. (BDA working party, 1974)

In fact, Lawson's (1981) deaf 'in-group' would claim to have virtually no need for social services geared to the handicapped.

The definition of the deaf community is thus not greatly helped by an examination of school performance, nor can it be seen simply in terms of hearing loss, which is the other base for the clinical-pathological framework. Not all deaf people wish to be associated with the deaf population and many of them choose to work and socialise with hearing people rather than simply withdraw into isolation. However, the fact remains that all members of deaf 'in-groups' have a measurable hearing loss (thus hearing people in deaf groups may aspire to the status of 'friends of the deaf' rather than members of a deaf community, according to Markowicz and Woodward, 1975). The degree of this loss may be variable over a wide range because of the changing policies concerning

7

diagnosis and provision of hearing aids. Older people may have had a relatively minor hearing loss but because of lack of hearing aid provision when they were young may see their identity as deaf. Fifty per cent of the 41–65-year-old pre-lingually deaf population 'never' wear a hearing aid, and this is primarily because they were not available in their youth (Kyle and Allsop, 1982b). There are, therefore, specific difficulties in seeing hearing loss as the determiner of deaf community membership.

Higgins (1980) perhaps unravels the strands most effectively. He sees 'belonging to the deaf community' as arising from a conscious choice to identify with the deaf world and from participation in its activities, though both are complemented by hearing loss. Many writers have gone further and see sign language as the core and principal criterion for membership (Markowicz and Woodward, 1975; Lawson, 1981). While this may be emerging as the identifier in the USA, deaf people in Britain may see it as a less strong determiner although an extremely important component in community life (Kyle and Allsop, 1982b). Language is a much more complex factor than it appears in other ethnic groups and the linguistic insecurity about BSL that we have described suggests that its use is not a simple criterion for membership (Kyle *et al.*, 1984).

Baker and Cokely (1980) perhaps present the most satisfactory view, in that they see centrality of membership of the community as determined by a number of overlapping criteria with no one factor sufficient in itself. These determiners are audiological (having a hearing loss), linguistic (understanding and using sign language), social (participation in deaf social life) and political (influence in the organisation of the community). Within each component centrality is measured by the strength of positive attitude. The core members are those who do not feel deafness itself is a problem, who have early facility and pride in signing, who are seen constantly at social gatherings of deaf people and who enjoy the confidence of their peers and therefore are consulted or elected as leaders in the organisation of deaf activities. Central members are often deaf people whose parents are deaf and who naturally view their peers in relation to the deaf club. These need not be leaders in the sense of academic or employment success. Lawson's (1981) picture of the community emphasises the same points, at least structurally, with deaf people of deaf parents as central figures and hearing people, by and large, only peripherally involved.

These seem to be the most consistent of the theoretical views of the community and it remains in this chapter to detail the practicalities of community life. Much of the theory is based on knowledge of the American deaf community and, as can be seen from Loncke (1983) on the Flemish deaf community, the basis for the theories may not be universal. However, the understanding of the 'community' as set out above gives support to Freeman, Carbin and Boese (1981) in their statements on the importance of deaf culture. In their usage, culture is distinct from community in that it includes the knowledge, belief, art, morals, and law as well as the practices of members of the community. These are mainly mediated by language, so deaf culture, like all cultures, is carried through the language.

Freeman, Carbin and Boese's view is that involvement in deaf culture (for example, reading deaf magazines, seeing deaf theatre groups) is essential to an understanding of the community. This culture is not in any way sinister nor is it based on handicap: it exists because of a natural need for identity. In the USA Deafpride is an organisation set up specifically to maintain, and give an understanding of, the culture and heritage of deaf people. Freeman, Carbin and Boese propose that this cultural acceptance is vital to the well-being of deaf children and to the bi-cultural, bilingual experience which may be the best approach in education and development.

In the UK, while these views are shared, the structure and characteristics of the community may be different from those in the USA. Most notably there is no higher educational centre (such as Gallaudet College in the USA) where deaf people may come together. The learning and experience generated in these formative years of college tuition in the USA may have to be gained rather differently and the community is different as a result.

Berger and Luckman's (1966) views on how cultures construct their reality are particularly useful here. The hearing view of people who cannot hear may be counterproductive in evaluating what is meaningful to deaf people. Just as in any group separated in some way, deaf people through their language negotiate and agree on a construction of reality. This reality need not be identical with hearing people's views. We have frequently had the experience that deaf people questioned about such and such a happening will simply shake their head and say 'it's the deaf way'. They are very clear in the division between what deaf people accept and what a hearing person will understand. Layne (1982) examines this specific interview situation in the USA and Seidel (1982) extends the theory. The implication is simple: there is a need to understand the deaf community at a deeper level through its language. This can only be attempted in preliminary form in this book since we are not yet able to share the constructions of knowledge available to deaf people. Our purpose is therefore to describe some aspects of the British deaf community in terms of the structure we can observe and its characteristics, as examined in a series of interviews by a deaf interviewer (Kyle and Allsop, 1982b).

The British deaf community: structures

The community of deaf people is unusual in many respects, since it does not form a geographical nucleus. Deaf people do not live in the same street or area of town. They do not all work in the same places. They are not usually found in jobs where communication with other members of the community is essential and they may not have direct access to the media controlled by the larger community. In some parts of the UK they meet only once or twice a week and they spend most of their time in a hearing world. This produces a community pattern which is rather fragmented in the time spent together but extremely closely bonded in the friendship of the members.

It is a complex sociological group which is greatly strengthened by the tendency to marry other community members. Schein and Delk (1974) maintain that more deaf than hearing people remain single, but of those who marry, over 80 per cent marry other deaf people. Kyle and Allsop (1982b), in a personal interview study of the deaf population in an English county, found 35 per cent of deaf people were single (in comparison to 25 per cent of the hearing population), but of those who married, 92 per cent married another deaf person. This inevitably affects the type of communication at home, as single people living with relatives are more likely to use speech and lip-reading. Even this difference makes generalisation about the community very difficult. However, it is possible to examine individually some of the key structures or groups important in the maintenance of community life. These areas will be considered under the headings: the deaf social club; the mobility of deaf people, i.e. inter-club activity; the professionals who work with the community – social workers, teachers, parents and interpreters.

The deaf social club and its role

The role of the deaf social club has varied greatly over time, almost certainly as a function of hearing society's interest. Batson and Bergman (1976) noted striking developments in references to deaf people in literary works. Views have varied from that of the 'simple deaf individual isolated from the world and its evils' – something of an idealised picture of silent nobility – through the 'social failure and handicapped person' to a more accepting view in current literature, where the linguistic structure aspects of the deaf community's sign language are emphasised. Very few authors, deaf or hearing, have identified themselves as members of the deaf community and so even some deaf authors may not provide a wholly accurate description of the deaf world. Accepting even a weak principle of language relativity, it is an almost impossible task adequately to explain the principles of organisation and values of the deaf community in written English. Nevertheless it is possible to examine at some level the functioning of the deaf community in the UK. As one might expect, the central environments for deaf interaction are the social clubs which exist throughout the UK.

The history of the setting up of centres for the deaf (Lysons, 1977–8) shows the great religious influence on early meetings of deaf people. The founding of a society for the deaf was usually the result of pressure from deaf people themselves who turned either to the schools for the deaf or to the church to provide premises and tutors or preachers. Lysons (1977–8) describes early developments in these centres and shows how the running of the centres and missions was gradually taken over by hearing people. The same pattern can be discerned in the setting up of national organisations for deaf people. The first attempt to co-ordinate the efforts of individual missions came in 1877, when 20 deaf people from different centres met in Manchester to form the National Deaf and Dumb Society which aimed to develop provision for the adult deaf community. By 1885 the Society had disappeared but by 1890 it was replaced by what is now the British Deaf Association. The BDA had its origins in a charity funded by hearing persons to aid poor and sick aged deaf people. Perhaps inevitably, and as can be seen in the other national bodies concerned with deafness, the role of hearing people quickly became a dominant one.

Despite over-reliance on the hearing missioner the deaf community was never totally eclipsed, since most organisations, and certainly most centres for the deaf, maintained a separate function or section designated as a sports and/or social club. This area has been dominated by deaf people themselves and it is probably within the workings of the social club that the use of sign language is most evident. The function of the social club is to allow members to interact in a relaxed setting where there is no pressure for spoken language use and comprehension and where sign language provides the common communication medium. For these reasons (its non-academic nature and its lack of emphasis on English) the deaf social club has been viewed by hearing people as epitomising the failing deaf person. The stigma of deafness tends to be attached to the social gathering of deaf people. It has resulted in pressure from teachers and parents to keep deaf children away from these social clubs. The situation is quite understandable from a hearing point of view: success has to be linked to interaction with the community at large through speech and so a group which meets and uses a language which is not speech, and which is unlikely to be understood by hearing people without effort, constitutes an 'out-group'. The fact that 29 per cent of profoundly deaf people (in our study) rarely go to the deaf social club must be partly attributable to this underlying feeling of stigma.

The activities of social clubs are, as one would expect, determined by the interests, nature and number of the members. Small clubs in rural areas may meet as infrequently as once a month while city clubs are open every evening. This is very similar to Baker and Cokely's (1980) description of deaf clubs in the USA, though we cannot confirm their belief that the deaf club's social role is declining.

The deaf community

Traditionally there is strong emphasis on sporting activities and most clubs will enter teams in local deaf and hearing leagues. The organisation of the majority of activities will proceed wholly under the control of the deaf committees until there is a meeting of the official body (controlled by hearing people), where an interpreter is required.

It is frequently reported that there are strong differences within the deaf club between the older and younger members. Higgins (1980) reports these differences of attitude and interest in his sample in the USA. It is, however, difficult to establish whether these are simply generation differences, such as one normally finds also within the hearing community, or whether there is a more significant factor implicated in the reported disputes. Certainly the deaf community has a different age structure from any hearing society. A similar hearing group would have members of more than one generation contributing to the functioning of the community and would therefore have some degree of understanding of the younger members since they are part of the same family; this is less likely in the deaf community. Deaf married couples mainly have hearing children (90 per cent according to Schein, 1979) who are primarily members of hearing society; the young deaf people at the deaf club will have hearing parents and will therefore be new members of the community. So, in addition to all the difficulties which arise because of a generation gap, there is a lack of continuity from generation to generation. The deaf population is small overall and a deaf club with 200 registered members is considered a large one. It is therefore understandable that there is some degree of interaction among different clubs.

The mobility of deaf people

Schein and Delk (1974) indicate that deaf people who have jobs are more poorly paid than hearing people, and this is confirmed for the UK. Kyle and Allsop (1982b) found that 45 per cent of deaf people over 25 years of age work in factories. In this section of the hearing population one would expect low mobility and therefore one must expect deaf people to lack opportunity for travel. However, deaf people do appear to meet other deaf people in other areas of the country rather less often than hearing people meet. Meeting other deaf people 50 miles away was an infrequent event (less than once a year) for 54 per cent of deaf people in our study, whereas only 5 per cent of hearing people met so rarely. Deaf people also report that they have difficulty in following the signs of the other groups, so accent and dialect differences are at least noticeable, although we must distinguish between reports of difficulty in communicating and actual difficulties observed when deaf people are in contact with each other.

The differences in signs which deaf people report are matters of concern in many countries, so much so that often hearing-controlled committees are set up to provide some standard for language use. These committees aim to provide standard signs for school use, to provide a common vocabulary across a country, and to enrich the 'poor' vocabulary of the native sign language. This approach ignores a number of important factors. One problem arises in a mismatch between hearing persons' use of the word 'language' and deaf people's concept of 'signing'. A question about 'language' differences is often interpreted as a question about 'sign' differences, and signs do themselves differ to a greater or lesser extent in different parts of the country.

The nearest to 'sign language' we get in BSL is a sign glossed perhaps as SIGNING. Specific queries make deaf people comment on signs and as a result the confirmation of differences in different parts of the country is in the vocabulary. Hearing people in Britain, while well aware of accent differences in speech in different parts of the country, have the concept available of a standard written language, and thus their responses to such a question are not comparable with deaf people's responses. Kyle *et al.* (1984) discuss this question in relation to actual data. The whole of this is an argument for greater interaction among deaf people to confirm their language knowledge. The social club has therefore a very important role in extending the experience of its members and allowing access to the process of interaction which produces a standard language.

Since schooling is organised on a regional basis, deaf young people may initially be isolated within their school groups. Young people from different schools may therefore need a period of acclimatisation. It is only by inter-club activity that such differences are likely to be altered. The experience of signing in different schools is identifiable by older members of the community, and the variations between signers from different schools may help or hinder acceptance within the community, depending on the background of the other members.

Interaction at a regional or national level very often follows the local pattern of social or sports meetings, the only difference being one of scale. However, there is a further dimension in that there are often regional committee meetings or meetings of deaf organisations with a strong hearing presence. In these settings deaf people with good oral skills are more in evidence, and certainly the variety of signing used by both hearing and deaf representatives will be directed to this oral skills group rather than to the profoundly deaf users of BSL. The explanation of the tendency to see English or signed English as a more official language than BSL is discussed further in later chapters, but generally, this biases interpreters to the use of signs in English word order, and this can gradually reduce the participation of profoundly deaf people in the national committees. The representatives of the deaf community in the eyes of the hearing world become those who can communicate in speech or those who can sign in English word order. Llewellyn-Jones, Kyle and Woll (1979) showed how signed English and BSL versions of the same text result in a higher status rating for signed English style than for BSL style.

Lawson's (1981) view, that deaf people have not yet adjusted to BSL as a language for formal meetings, strengthens the need for interaction among different social clubs. The growing awareness of the linguistic status of BSL will correspondingly strengthen the linguistic component of Baker and Cokely's (1980) model. The ability of workers with the deaf to adjust to this is also of some importance.

The professionals

The social worker. Generally speaking, it is social workers who are responsible for the daily management of the deaf centre and for the organisation of the social work services for deaf people. Their role can therefore be seen as community-based, facilitating the activities of the social club, and as pastoral, dealing with the immediate problems of deaf people and their families, often with an emphasis on older deaf people. It is possible, though perhaps surprising to readers, for a person to become a social worker for the deaf in the UK without being able to communicate fluently with deaf people. This is partly as a function of a newer, more broad view of social work and partly because of a tradition that BSL, instead of being a prerequisite, could be learned on the job. Unfortunately this leads to a rather difficult situation in relation to the deaf community when a social worker enters the deaf club. The examination of skills in BSL will be taken up in a later chapter and so it will not be pursued here except to say that the evaluation of the social worker's signing skills is a primary focus for deaf people.

In the past, in many communities, either the hearing committee of the deaf centre has been responsible for appointing social workers, or the hearing committee of the local social services department has determined the staff responsible for the needs of deaf people. The degree to which deaf people are themselves involved in the selection procedure is variable throughout the UK but it seems that there probably is a trend towards giving members of the deaf community more power in deciding the appointment of at least community social workers. Nevertheless problems arise because of difficulties in defining the social work role. The most obvious confusion arises because of the conflict between the advisory role of a social worker and the role of the interpreter in literal representation of the deaf person's communication. Social workers traditionally accompany deaf people to job interviews and instances have been reported when the employer has interviewed the social worker rather than the deaf person. The social worker may feel that he can answer simple questions more efficiently than his client, or may put himself in the position of evaluating the suitability of the job for his client. Transcripts of deaf people's views (Kyle and Allsop, 1982b) confirm this problem of interpreting ethics, and it almost certainly explains the relatively low figure of only 27 per cent in our study who said their normal interpreter was a social worker.

The experienced social worker is also often asked to act as a teacher for members of the public who wish to learn sign language. The vast majority of sign language classes in the UK are organised in this way, by hearing people who have no training in teaching (Kyle, Woll and Llewellyn-Jones, 1981). Only a small proportion of classes have deaf tutors and clearly any weakness in the sign language knowledge of a hearing tutor will be compounded in the performance of his students. There is now a move towards greater involvement of deaf people in the process, with direct initiatives by the British Deaf Association in support.

A number of social workers are considered to be within the deaf community, usually because they have deaf parents. They and the majority of social workers are seen as facilitators for the development of the deaf community. They are generally cast in the role of defenders of the deaf community and are most commonly the proponents of sign language for education and for families of deaf children.

Parents and teachers. While in certain respects it is unfair to cast parents in the same light as teachers, both groups are united by a deep educational and developmental concern for the needs of deaf people. Both are usually seen only on the fringes of the deaf community, although when the educational system began in the UK deaf people were themselves greatly involved in the educational process as teachers, and hearing teachers often occupied the social work role, particularly with regard to interpreting. The traditional link of teachers and community has become weakened in recent times, to the extent that contact with those deaf parents who have deaf children may be only in school-focused meetings. Realistically of course, it is unusual for teachers in any branch of education to have long-lasting ties to the community of the children they teach, but less contact means deaf adults have little influence on education. The recent trend towards deaf advisers in schools for the deaf (e.g. Cox *et al.*, 1979) has begun to have an effect on the signing used in school, though this is not comparable with access to the deaf community.

Parents often have the same conflict and the same feelings in relation to the deaf community as do the teachers. For a long time parents have been presented with the sign language option as the final recognition that their child cannot be integrated into the world at large (e.g. *TALK*, 1982). When this option becomes reality, because their child chooses to interact with other deaf people in the evenings, they may see their collaboration as further evidence that they have failed in their child-rearing. Just as with teachers, of course, there is little precedent in the hearing world for parents accompanying their children into the society with which they choose to associate. The difference between the home and the deaf club is that the society which their child joins is one where communication is flowing, and the home setting may become simply another hearing world setting in which there is little communication and considerable experience of unsatisfactory relationships. This can hasten the break between parents and a young deaf person.

Interpreters. It is obvious that the role of interpreter is a critical one for deaf people, and it is one which has caused the greatest degree of concern among those working with deaf adults in the UK and the USA. Llewellyn-Jones (1981a) has suggested that the change in the nature of training for social work has led to a particular concern about the level of interpreting standards. This has resulted in the UK in a co-ordinated attempt to provide an interpreter register of people with recognised skill and a proposal to assess all those who wish to act as interpreters for the deaf in any formal setting (Simpson, 1981). While there is a prior need for training (see chapter 9) the provision of sign language interpreters in the UK has long been out of step with most other developed countries. Most notable has been the complete lack of provision of interpreters for educational settings; deaf people have no statutory right to sign language interpreters for any sort of educational course even at university. Since in the USA it is within the education setting that the pressure for interpreters and their training has been strongest, it is clear that the sign language interpreter in the British deaf community occupies a rather different position.

The job of interpreting in courts, at meetings and in job interviews falls most often to the local social worker for the deaf. Except in the case of courts of law, the onus of finding an interpreter rests with the deaf person himself; he must approach the interpreter to 'ask a favour'. While this service is usually gladly given by social workers it makes it very difficult for the deaf person to be anything other than grateful for the service, even when the interpreter has failed to understand the content of a meeting or when the deaf person's statements have been inaccurately represented in English. When a BSL interpreter works efficiently and accurately, on the other hand, there is a danger that the deaf person may seek to use the interpreter as a social worker, soliciting advice because of confidence in the interpreter's language skill. Without official standing or standardised training the BSL interpreter engages in a very difficult task. His position in relation to the deaf community is not clear and it is not obvious as to how the task of interpreting can be made more acceptable to both the hearing and deaf communities.

Given many of these structural features of their community life, deaf people may have considerable difficulty in making a contribution to society as a whole unless they can achieve bilingualism. The fact that only a relatively small number of deaf people find themselves in that position makes it all the more important that hearing people understand the characteristics of the deaf community.

The British deaf community: characteristics

Many of the characteristics of deaf people are shared across different countries. The study reported by Schein and Delk (1974) remains a definitive profile of adult deaf people in the USA. Since then, Higgins (1980) has broadened the view to include the feelings and attitudes of deaf adults. More recently, two large studies in the UK have evaluated the characteristics of the deaf population: as viewed by hearing people (Bunting, 1981) and as expressed by deaf people to a deaf interviewer (Kyle and Allsop, 1982b: the Avon Study). Both studies dealt with a global view of deaf people. In Bunting's case, pre-lingually deaf people were not clearly separated from those with acquired deafness, in the Avon Study, those who infrequently attended the deaf club were involved in interviews, though their responses can be analysed separately from those whose involvement in social activities is much more pronounced. In the Avon Study the target population was profoundly deaf and 175 lengthy interviews were completed in BSL (this constitutes 1 in 2,500 of the total population of the county).

The centrality of this group, the profoundly deaf, in relation to Baker and Cokely's (1980) model can be debated, but the purpose of the Avon Study was to construct a picture of deaf people and their views and from this perhaps to draw contour lines around the central part of the community. In the event, all interviewees shared basic features of the community: they all had a serious hearing loss (79 per cent were profoundly deaf) and nearly all (95 per cent) had access to sign though many did not use it at home or at work.

The main characteristics of the interviewed group are detailed in table 1.1. The total population of this area in the 15–64-year-old age group is 569,090 and the county is a mixture of rural and urban communities. There is nothing to suggest that this area is atypical of the UK in relation to deafness. The deaf population follows a pattern more or less as one would predict from previous studies, with younger people more likely to use hearing aids and more likely to have attended a Unit attached to a hearing school.

In employment there are similar patterns to those suggested by Schein and

Table 1.1. *Characteristics of the deaf population (Kyle and Allsop, 1982b)*

Age	%
16–25 years	30.8
26–45 years	46.6
46–65 years	22.6
mean	34 years, 6 months
Onset of deafness	
birth	72.6
up to 2 years	13.1
3–5 years	8.6
over 5 years	6.8
mean	1 year, 1 week
Cause of deafness	
don't know	54.9
family	5.1
rubella	5.1
illness	28.6
accident	3.4
difficult birth	2.3
ear disease	0.6
Sex	
males	48
females	52
Use of hearing aid	
always	35
sometimes	37
never	27
Age learned to sign	
0–4 years	26
5–7 years	40
8–11 years	19
over 12 years	15
mean	7 years, 1 month

Delk (1974) for the USA and by Montgomery and Miller (1977) and Storer (1977) for the UK. Deaf people are likely to have factory jobs, be supervised by hearing people and have considerably less chance of promotion than hearing people. Bunting's (1981) investigation of hearing people's views coincides with this: 41 per cent of her sample suggested deaf people had different types of job from hearing people and thought that deaf people should have jobs with no contact with people or jobs which involved manual work. This represents what actually happens: deaf people mainly work with large numbers of hearing people in lower-paid jobs. However, deaf people do not avoid contact with hearing people even though they acknowledge communication problems: 63 per cent claim to talk to hearing workmates at coffee breaks, and the primary means of communication are speech and lip-reading.

One can therefore dismiss the view that deaf people form a community separate and isolated from the world, since in practice one can see that at work (around half of the waking hours) deaf people use or accept the use of speech and lip-reading. The fact that community members choose to adopt a language in leisure hours which they describe as more relaxing does not diminish the achievement of integration which may have been so difficult at school. In addition, deaf people claim to be happy at work (71 per cent) and few dislike their work surroundings (6 per cent). Studies of job satisfaction amongst hearing people generally indicate that people are satisfied with their employment (Warr, Cook and Wall, 1979) and the contrasting view of deaf people as totally frustrated in their employment is not upheld in this simplistic form. It seems much more likely that people who become deaf in mid-career are the group whose dissatisfaction with employment is most obvious. This is supported by Kyle and Wood (1983) in their study of acquired deafness. When asked questions about employment which would be consistent with an isolationist community view, deaf people in the Avon Study generally were positive in their desire to work with the hearing community. Only 32 per cent felt deaf people could not work with hearing people, and 30 per cent wanted factories to themselves (as exist in Russia and China). The principal theme was that there was greater need for understanding at work and that interpreters should be available at the work place.

If members of the deaf community are not separated from hearing people at work, it is possible that home and social life reflect the choice of deaf identity in the sense of Baker and Cokely's (1980) model. By and large this turns out to be the case, though there are particularly interesting problems of language use which remain and particular difficulties in access to the media, which make the community more complex. As Schein (1979) points out, the 90 per cent statistic is crucial, 90 per cent of deaf people having hearing parents and siblings and 90 per cent of deaf parents having hearing children. Home life still, therefore, requires contact with the hearing community.

In the Avon Study, 61 per cent lived with a husband or wife, while 26 per cent lived with one or both parents. Of those living with parents, 76 per cent used speech and lip-reading as their main means of communication while of those living with a spouse, 92 per cent used communication forms which were either signing alone or signing and speech. If most communication was with parents there was likely to be less interaction. In effect, it implies that if the language is a core feature of the community, as Lawson (1981) states, then deaf people almost have to 'marry into' the community identity.

The other aspect of home life, contact with the media, seems to be the major problem for deaf people (Kyle and Allsop, 1982a). Deaf people have considerable contact with nearly every aspect of the mass media, television, newspapers and books. 77 per cent read a newspaper every day, 50 per cent watch television every night and 58 per cent said that at least sometimes they read books. However, they seem to get much less out of this than hearing people. Thirty-five per cent said they could not understand the television programmes they watch, 74 per cent said the newspapers were too difficult for deaf people and when pressed about books, 52 per cent could not remember the type of book (i.e. thriller, romance) which they had last read.

This is a crucial finding in relation to understanding the values of the community. While deaf people are happy to work with hearing people, at home they may find those closest to them unable to communicate satisfactorily (with interaction lessened as a result), and they may be denied access to the visual medium of information which, at least theoretically, would be of most use in understanding the hearing world. The 'attraction of social interaction' which Lawson (1981) highlights must be greatly heightened by the problems arising from attempts at interaction with the hearing community. This is not to suggest that the deaf community is a refuge from hearing home life but rather that community feeling is based on shared access to information as well as shared beliefs (as Freeman, Carbin and Boese, 1981, claim). The access to information implies shared communication and this then becomes an identifying feature of the community.

Attendance at the deaf club or constant deaf social interaction is therefore rather less relevant in our study of the community. Deaf people, because they work with hearing people and often live with hearing people, have limited time for attending a deaf club. It cannot therefore be seen, as oralists have often suggested, as a place for people who reject hearing society, but must exist because deaf people choose to meet. In the Avon Study, 58 per cent of deaf people went to the deaf club once a week or more, although, as if to emphasise the 'natural choice' element, 70 per cent of men but only 48 per cent of women went as regularly as this. Presumably this is because the wife is more likely to stay at home with children while the husband goes out.

In questions about the nature of those who attend the deaf club there is general rejection of the view that they are somehow handicapped. Statements which imply acceptance of deaf community life ('are proud to be deaf' or 'are treated normally there') are readily agreed with, and fit the image of deaf people

Table 1.2. *Membership of the deaf community (Kyle and Allsop, 1982b)*

Do you agree that the following can be members of the deaf community?

	% agree
Hearing people	44
Deaf people who cannot sign	58
Deaf people who prefer mixing with hearing people	39
Deaf people who went to partial-hearing unit (PHU)	70
Deaf people who went to a hearing school	40
People who *became* deaf	74

united by a desire to interact easily and normally in a social setting. In contrast to Bunting's (1981) finding that 52 per cent of hearing people thought deaf people socialised less than hearing people, our study found that 78 per cent of deaf people felt their social life was the same or better than hearing people's.

At each step of this analysis then, it is possible to consider the Baker and Cokely model and it is evident that its applicability is not to be assessed in terms of a population driven together by lack of some skill (such as speech or hearing) but rather, one brought together by a conscious desire to interact meaningfully and to share information and (perhaps as a direct result) to share experience and belief. It is very unusual for deaf people to discuss 'being deaf' unless it is for the benefit of a hearing member of the group, nor is it typical for deaf people to sit around complaining about the hearing world. One can see therefore that the centrality measurement which comes out of the Baker and Cokely model, i.e. 'attitudinal deafness', does not quite apply in this British deaf community.The expression of choice within the community, or need to share information and communication, is not 'I want to be deaf' but rather 'I am a person and wish to be in contact with other people who can share my language'.

When one asks deaf people themselves directly about the community then the answer is probably rather similar to one which would be given by hearing people when asked about the hearing community: 'What community do you mean?' There is no single sign for 'community' in BSL and obviously the neat sociological definition of community is not what is perceived by deaf people. Table 1.2 presents a view of which groups are possible members of the deaf community. The principal exclusions are seen to be those deaf people with a 'hearing attitude'. Even lack of BSL is not seen as an excluding factor on its own. In effect it seems quite clear that membership, in so far as it exists, can be interpreted only in a multifactorial way. The interpretation must, however, also take into account a strength factor based on attitude towards interaction with other deaf people.

A slight adaptation of Baker and Cokely's (1980) model may suffice to make this point (fig. 1.1). In this model the audiological, linguistic, social and political definitions serve to provide a description of an individual in the eyes of the community, but the vertical dimension is needed to show an individual's commitment to the community and it is this which determines acceptance by deaf people. In practice, the two planes interact: the more typical the description (i.e. greater hearing loss, better skills in BSL, etc.) the more likely that attitudes will strengthen participation, but it is probably the commitment and sharing which represents the membership criterion, not the deafness nor even the language, *per se*.

In this model we can do no more than acknowledge the truth of our opening statement that there are severe difficulties in adequately characterising the deaf community. It involves a shared language; it involves hearing loss; it involves social interaction and political relations; but all of these inter-relate and interact with attitudes towards other deaf people. The choice to communicate and share information with other people must be seen as a primary feature, and because of the language used by members of the community this communication will generally be restricted to other deaf people. Whether or not we can show sign language to be the central, defining feature of the community, it is nevertheless the medium through which deaf people interact and anyone who seeks to understand the community of deaf people must interpret the data through its language. There are considerable grounds for acknowledging the desire of deaf

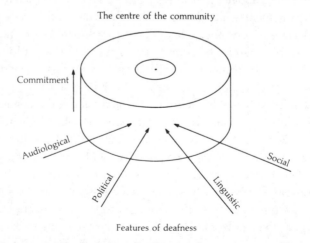

Fig. 1.1   Factors contributing to centrality of community membership.

people to be together as a 'community', though the use of the term does not in itself provide an explanation of the structure and characteristic attitudes of the deaf population. There is clearly a deaf culture in the UK though this is not as visible to hearing people as it is, for example, in the USA. Deaf people work with hearing people but relax with other deaf people. They do not reject hearing society nor are they themselves failures. Their desire to be together is the strength of their community and our study here will concern the outcome of this community life — their language.

2. British Sign Language

An introduction to deaf people and their community was given in chapter 1; we can now discuss the language itself. Since the book as a whole will present a detailed description of the language, we wish in this chapter only to introduce British Sign Language (BSL). Numerous questions arise when there is discussion of sign language, and we will raise the preliminary issues in this section before moving on to a more detailed analysis of the structure of sign language and its use by deaf and hearing people.

Sign Language and its origins

People often ask the question: is this a new language which has been developed by hearing people for deaf people? Sometimes even deaf people themselves are suspicious of the term British Sign Language, or BSL. The simple answer is that BSL is the language of deaf people in the UK and has been so since there have been reports from those who have worked with deaf people. (Hodgson, 1954, suggests the existence of sign languages in Greek times.) Of course, BSL has changed in time, just as English has.

Signs have often been viewed as an international gesture language; the philosophers of the 18th century considered sign as a possible basis for an international language of communication. This belief implies that signs share characteristics across different cultures. But at the same time, signs in the UK have often been said to vary dramatically from town to town, and sign language has been viewed by educators as so variable from place to place as to be simply an invented language by a group of non-speaking people in one local area.

The truth as usual lies somewhere in between these two claims. Sign languages are not the same across cultures, and there are differences between the vocabulary of BSL and that of American Sign Language (ASL) even though there are strong cultural and spoken language similarities between the two countries. Nevertheless, as has become apparent at international meetings, deaf people do communicate effectively across language boundaries. Sometimes it is claimed by deaf people themselves that they are simply using mime, but since hearing people do not follow this sign 'interlanguage' very well (as they would do if it were simply mime) it is more likely that at least some grammatical processes used in the visual medium are shared across cultures despite differences in vocabulary. Once some basic vocabulary items are negotiated, conversation can flow since people use similar means of putting signs together. This particular issue will be expanded considerably in chapter 8, where we make direct comparisons of a number of different sign languages.

In relation to the parochial aspect of BSL, there are regional variations but these are not as great as the international differences mentioned above. Just as hearing people have some difficulties in areas of the UK in attuning themselves to the way of speaking, deaf people will also complain about the regional variation. In our experience there is no situation where this variation threatens the assumption that there is a single language, BSL, in the UK.

BSL is therefore a dynamic language, developed and passed on within a community, rather than a poor gesture system. There is one major factor, however, which has always distinguished sign language transmission across generations from spoken language transmission. Ninety per cent of deaf children are born into families where their parents are hearing, and where there is usually no prior experience of deafness (Meadow, 1980). The parents view the child as different – usually as handicapped – and consequently their goal is normalisation. As one would expect, this normalisation must include use of the language of the community, i.e. the spoken language. Teachers have mostly supported this view. Until recently, therefore, they have used only speech with deaf children. Deaf children at school have had no adult model of the language they may come to use among their peers. The language is therefore carried to a large measure by those children with a link to the deaf community: by those with deaf parents, and by those old enough to attend the deaf club. It has not always been so, and in early deaf education in almost all countries there were deaf teachers of the deaf. While that tradition continues in some countries, notably in the USA and Scandinavia, for deaf children in the UK there is only limited (though now increasing) access to the language of deaf adults. The fact that the language has continued to be used indicates something of its naturalness for deaf people and the effectiveness of the visual medium for communication.

Sign language and imagery

By its nature, BSL must be visual at least from the point of view of the receiver. It is therefore very tempting to adopt a hearing evaluation of the visual medium which sees it as a world of pictures (sometimes moving, sometimes static) of concrete objects and actions rather than abstractions, and of gestures which crudely represent these objects and actions. Hearing people have often been unable to view the language of deaf people as anything other than a crude system of gestures, iconic in nature and consisting of communication tied to the objects of 'the here and now'. If this were so, of course, hearing people as sharers in the visual world would be instantly able to understand BSL – but they cannot. The speed and manner with which the signs are put together as well as their form, do not allow a simple visual explanation of their derivations or meanings. If signs were simply gestures or direct visual representations of the world, then the hearing community would have no difficulty in using the language to communicate more effectively with deaf people.

BSL is made up of images and arbitrary symbols. It exists in a visual-spatial mode, with iconic signs such as GIVE (fig. 2.1) and FOOD (fig. 2.2), but there are also signs like EASY (fig. 2.3) and ALLOW (fig. 2.4) which have no clear iconic origins. While stories in sign language often have pictorial characteristics or use mime they are not transparent, and mime is used to enhance the story-telling rather than give the meaning. These devices are also used in story-telling in a spoken language through intonation and other non-verbal devices. The core of the signed story is therefore conveyed in a systematic linguistic way.

A further problem in the hearing person's view of the nature of signing has been the belief that only the movement of the hands conveys the message. As has been pointed out by Siple (1978) for ASL, and is apparent in our videotapes of deaf people signing, the focus of the receiver's gaze is not on the hands but on the face, with the same changing focus from eyes to mouth that hearing people use. Signs, even with iconic bases, are only perceived in the periphery of vision. This is unlikely to be enough for high level communication. It would seem that interaction in sign is as complex as the behaviour of hearing people in speech. Particularly noteworthy is the discovery of gaze localised on the face and lips, where the information being communicated is neither gesture nor always a reflection of the spoken word. Vogt-Svendsen (1983) and Baker (1980) have remarked on the importance of the distinctive lip patterns which constitute components of the signing, and this is an aspect of sign which will be examined in considerable detail later.

One of the measures of a language's abstractness is when it can be used to describe and analyse itself (Hockett, 1960). As greater numbers of deaf people enter the field of research, there is a growing incidence of academic research papers being presented wholly in the native sign language of the presenter. The linguistic sophistication of papers presented by Lawson (1983) and Ulfsparre (1979) suggests the level of abstractness possible in sign language to be little different from that of speech, even though the channels used are so different.

The views of hearing communities on the nature of sign language have

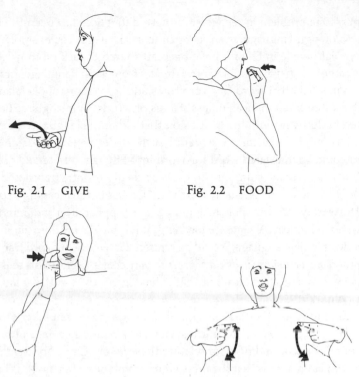

Fig. 2.1   GIVE   Fig. 2.2   FOOD

Fig. 2.3   EASY   Fig. 2.4   ALLOW

usually underestimated its complexity. While it is easy to counter the arguments concerning the gestural-concrete nature of sign language and to highlight its effectiveness, we are still only in the initial stages of understanding its grammatical structure.

Sign language and grammar

Since hearing writers on deafness have traditionally seen sign language as a collection of gestures, it is not surprising to find that it has been claimed that sign language has no grammar at all. In effect, the suggestion is that signing is simply a loose collection of hand movements with no fixed sequence. Unfortunately, just as hearing people have difficulty in answering questions about the way they use speech, deaf people, by being unwilling or unable to identify the principles of sign when questioned by hearing researchers, have sometimes contributed to this view of sign language.

Sign language certainly has a grammar, but it is unlike the grammar of English although many features of sign language structures are found in other spoken languages. One problem in recognising these differences has been the lack of awareness of sign language as an independent language. For example, errors made by deaf people in English have been attributed to lack of knowledge of English rather than to possible interference from sign language grammar. Although it is clear that word-for-word translations from one spoken language to another often result in meaningless strings of words, sign language has been translated in this way, with the conclusion that either the language is deficient, or that it is 'ungrammatical'. A sentence such as the French *Est-ce qu'il vient d'arriver?* could be translated word-for-word into English as *Is it that he comes to arrive?* but whatever meaning this suggests, it clearly is not a translation of the meaning of the sentence 'Has he just arrived?' Certainly the meaning expressed straightforwardly in other spoken languages may appear utterly different from those found in English. A sentence meaning 'It has plenty of room' in Shawnee (an American Indian language) would be rendered in word-for-word translation as *Figure of room, occupancy in a field of general space occurs.* Clearly this tells us not that Shawnee is ungrammatical but that it has a very different grammar from English (Whorf, 1956).

According to Hockett (1958) all natural languages share a number of 'design features'. These include a grammatical system, a semantic system, a phonological (or sound) system, and rules for relating these levels. One important feature of all spoken languages is that the units which combine to form words have no meaning in themselves, apart from the context in which they appear. That is, in a word such as English *pin*, no meaning can be attached to the sounds themselves, represented by *p, i* and *n*. They are just building blocks which combine to form a word. Sign language clearly has its own grammatical system and its own semantic system (in the form of signs instead of words). We cannot expect a *sound* system, but we can look for the building blocks in the manual channel. Here we can identify components smaller than signs. Stokoe (1960) described three parameters for American Sign Language (ASL): the location of the sign in space (the Tab), the handshape used in making the sign (the Dez) and the type of movement made by the hand or hands (the Sig). For our examination of the manual aspect of BSL signs in chapter 5 we have added a fourth component, which is the orientation of the hand relative to the body (the Ori). Each of these components derives its importance from the existence of 'minimal pairs' where the meaning of the sign is altered by change in only one of the components. The discussion in chapter 5 centres on the relation of these components and their incidence in the language, so here it suffices to point to their existence.

There are, however, further components in the articulation of a sign which have only recently been recognised as building blocks of signs. These are the features of *facial expression, lip patterns* (mentioned earlier as one focal point of a deaf receiver's gaze – these are not always related to spoken word patterns, see, for example, Vogt-Svendsen, 1983), *signer's eye-gaze* (a complex system of pronouns in BSL is based on eye-gaze and position in space), *the body-posture, the shoulders* and *the head* (each of these is used in spoken language communication, but can have a much more formal relation to the articulation and meaning of a sign). Just as spoken words can be broken into component parts, so signs can be shown to have similar complex components.

This leads us to the obvious question of how these components re-combine, and how signs themselves combine to provide the richness and complexity which other languages display. This is the question which occupies the rest of this book, but here we may introduce certain topics within which such questions can be considered. Four aspects which are of particular interest in sign are: modification of signs; simultaneity in signs; use of space in signing; sign order.

Modification of signs in BSL

In contrast to English, where information about tense and plurality is largely given by the use of suffixes, signs often express this information through modification of the base sign. Bellugi (1980), in discussing ASL, describes some fifty different derivational and inflectional forms. As our work on BSL unfolds we are beginning to find the same degree of richness in BSL. For example, the sign LOOK (fig. 2.5) can be altered to mean YOU-LOOK-AT-ME (fig. 2.6), LOOK-AT-EACH-OTHER (fig. 2.7) or KEEP-LOOKING-AT-ONE-ANOTHER (fig. 2.8). Because these modifications cannot be simply described in English, BSL translators have often ascribed only one basic concept to each of these different meanings and thus have unconsciously contributed to the notion that BSL has a very small vocabulary. Instead, the range of modifications available results in a large number of meanings available to signers.

Fig. 2.5   LOOK   Fig. 2.6   YOU-LOOK-AT-ME

Fig. 2.7   Fig. 2.8   KEEP-LOOKING-AT
LOOK-AT-EACH-OTHER   ONE-ANOTHER

Simultaneity of signs in BSL

Occasionally very strong claims have been made about the different nature of spoken and signed language. Lane (1977) suggests that spoken language is essentially sequential while sign is predominantly parallel because of the simultaneity of the visual medium. The building blocks of signs are articulated simultaneously, but this is also true of spoken languages, particularly 'tone' languages where pitch occurring simultaneously with articulation determines the meaning of a word. More remarkable is the situation where two whole meaning units can be presented simultaneously: in this type of structure two separate signs are articulated at the same time with different hands. These are frequent in informal settings, appearing in phrases such as BORN/DEAF (fig. 2.9), or LITTLE/BOY (fig. 2.10).

Fig. 2.9   BORN/DEAF   Fig. 2.10   LITTLE/BOY

Use of space in signing

A further feature of BSL is the use of locations in signing space to designate reference points for people, objects and concepts. These can be used throughout a conversation by referring to that point in space as a way of indicating that topic. There is also frequent use of space in story-telling, with changes of reference points where the story-teller adopts a different posture or orientation to indicate a change of speaker or perspective – though this is a stylistic rather than a grammatical device. Points in space may also be used to designate time: Brennan (1983) has discovered a number of 'time-lines'. The fact that there are a number of dimensions available indicates the complexity of the use of space for temporal marking in BSL. Placement might therefore be used as a general term for the exploitation of space in BSL, where it identifies referents which can be returned to later in the conversation.

Sign order in BSL

The order of BSL signs is very often different from English, using primarily a topic–comment structure (see chapter 7). Carter (1980b), in an examination of noun phrase modification, concludes that there are four types of modification available to BSL users: 'pre-modification' (in English: *red wine*); 'post-modification' (in French: *vin rouge*); 'simultaneous modification', where the modifier is incorporated into the articulation of the sign, as in LONG-HAIR or WIDE-SMILE; and finally, 'suspended modification' where the noun is articulated with one hand and held, while the other hand articulates a series of modifications. Her comments on the complexities of this sort of study are echoed by Stokoe, referring to similar examples in ASL: 'The point . . . is that Sign, far from having no grammar, has such interesting structure and so unusual a system that it challenges all theories of grammar' (1980: 138).

It can be seen from the hints above, and from the relatively advanced research work on ASL, that the languages of deaf people should no longer be considered inferior collections of badly made and inconsistent gestures. The whole area of study of BSL is very new, but already many of our earlier concepts about sign language must be revised. Virtually all the features of BSL we have discovered can be found in spoken languages, even if they are not found in English.

Sign language and education

Educators in the UK have, by and large, never accepted sign language as a *method* in their classrooms. In fact, sign language should not be considered

59035

simply as a method but as a means of communication – a language. This means that its use does not solve the problems of educating children. What it can do is open up a channel of communication, and provide a vehicle for the curriculum. The idea of sign as the panacea overcoming all the difficulties that deaf children have in learning, is certainly mistaken. Equally, the view that the deaf child does not 'need' sign language or that 'we do not have to resort to signs here' is mistaken in its understanding of the function of a language. That teachers and pupils must share a means of communication which is equally accessible to both parties is a fundamental principle of all education. When communication exists between teacher and pupil, then education can begin. Sign language can be such a shared language, but then the skill of the teacher is required to provide the knowledge which the child needs as part of growing up.

In most schools for the deaf, even where teachers do not use sign, there is a recognisable form of BSL used by the children. Deaf adults often talk about 'school signing', the style of which may be governed by the necessity of avoiding the teachers' detection of the use of the hands, or even 'school signs' where children in the absence of contact with adult BSL users develop individual signs distinct from those used by the deaf community. Kyle and Allsop (1982a), in interviewing deaf young people and adults, show how these signs may change in the process of integration with the community. Without a detailed examination of deaf children's BSL it is difficult to say how 'school signing' relates to adult forms of BSL. Cokely and Gawlik (1974) claimed that deaf children in the USA use a different language variety from ASL, and were concerned that teachers should understand this form and offer alternative adult forms. Nevertheless, at least in the UK, it seems that deaf children do graduate quickly to adult signing and claim to have learned this before leaving school (Kyle and Allsop, 1982a).

Signs can often be used within a teaching method to teach a specific skill: for example, signs can be used to train speech or to teach reading. Systems of sign have come to be developed for the specific purpose of allowing speech and sign to be presented together. The philosophy of Total Communication which now predominates in most countries specifies the use of signs *and* speech together in classroom activities. Usually it requires sign use in spoken language word order, and it is claimed to be a particularly powerful tool in achieving a learning environment in the school.

Evans (1981) discusses in some detail the considerations of using sign and speech and outlines the main concepts in this form of education. The use of sign and speech together opens up a whole series of possibilities for educators and allows a much fuller participation in group activity by deaf and hearing people together. However it is not easier than, nor a substitute for, a knowledge of BSL.

A study of social workers for the deaf in the UK indicates weaknesses in knowledge of BSL which carry over into simultaneous sign and speech (Kyle, Woll and Llewellyn-Jones, 1981), and it is therefore important that use of sign and speech together is based on a knowledge of both languages. Our experience, and this is reflected in other countries, notably Sweden, (Ahlgren, 1982), has been that teachers using Total Communication without any BSL background have begun to request courses for a fuller understanding of the language even though in the end their target form for teaching is a signed English variety.

The inter-connection between BSL, signed English and speech arises from the needs of educators to teach the language of the hearing community. The complex issues involved in this inter-relationship will be examined in some detail in chapter 12. This has been a traditional minefield for workers in the field of deafness. It suffices to say here that one can see from Hansen (1980) and Ahlgren (1982) in Scandinavia, and Savage, Evans and Savage (1981) in the UK that there is a role for different forms of language use in deaf education.

Sign language and sign systems

We have said that BSL is a language which has a complex structure and is valued by its users. What does complicate the picture is the existence of artificial systems of signing which may be closely related to the signs used by deaf people (e.g. Makaton Vocabulary in the UK, Signing Exact English in the USA and Signed Swedish in Sweden), or which may have only a slight concordance with sign language (e.g. the Paget-Gorman Sign System in the UK). These are described in more detail in Peter and Barnes (1982), but it is important simply to discriminate them from the naturally occurring languages of deaf people. They have all been constructed for a particular purpose, usually educational, and generally have the goal of producing better spoken and written language in the user.

The Makaton Vocabulary (Walker, 1976), is a graded system of word–sign translations arranged in a vocabulary acquisition sequence:

Makaton is the applied use of a specific developmental vocabulary. It has been designed to provide a controlled method of teaching approximately 350 signs to mentally-handicapped children and adults and other language-handicapped people, in order to provide a basic means of communication; to encourage expressive speech where possible; to develop an understanding of language through the visual medium of the signs and the logical structure of the sign language. (Walker and Armfield, 1982: 16)

Makaton has been used primarily with mentally-handicapped people, and has gained widespread popularity in the UK. It is often misleadingly referred to in the literature as 'British Sign Language', but it is not a claim made by the originators, who quite clearly present the system as a valuable aid to communication in a special school or hospital setting. This aid to communication has often been demonstrated to be a critically important step towards interaction and to spoken language use.

Bornstein (1979) reviews the systems of signing used with deaf children which draw their inspiration from the language of adult deaf people. Signing Exact English (Gustason, Pfetzing and Zawolkow, 1975) and Signed Swedish (Bergman, 1979) are examples of these systems, where the aim is primarily to support the learning of the majority language. The systems resemble each other in that they use adult deaf signs supplemented whenever necessary by signs developed by the originators. These supplementary signs are used to provide a particular grammatical device or feature which is not present in a sign language. For English-based systems these include extra markers for tense, for the verb 'to be', and for 'the' and 'a'. There are a range of systems currently used in the USA; but in Sweden Signed Swedish has been replaced by a greater use of the natural sign language of deaf people. Savage, Evans and Savage (1981) describe the specific use of fingerspelling to represent English in an educational setting. The role of fingerspelling and its relation to sign language is dealt with more extensively later in this book.

The Paget-Gorman sign system (Rowe, 1982) was developed as a systematic sign system which follows structured and logical rules for its grammatical and semantic processes. The signs were constructed to allow easily the combination of a basic concept and a qualifier to designate an actual word meaning. Thus the sign for 'cats' consists of a base designating an animal, plus a simultaneous marker for a property of the specific animal (in this case, cat's whiskers), followed by another marker to pluralise the sign. This system is used in a number of schools in the UK, with a degree of success (Fenn and Rowe, 1975). However, it does not relate to BSL to any marked degree and Rowe points out that it was designed to avoid BSL structures: 'to portray the grammatical features of the English language in order to help deaf children to develop English structure and abandon the 'word salad' commonly produced' (1982: 13).

All these systems are new, though the idea of their construction is old. Scott (1870) discussed the structured use of signs to support English skills, and also highlighted a feature which is common to all the systems: they are designed to be used simultaneously with the spoken language.

BSL, in contrast to the educational systems discussed above, is a language which has no conscious derivation. It is a language rich in variation throughout the UK, much of such variation deriving from the traditional separateness of the deaf schools and the low degree of mobility of the deaf community. It does not have the grammatical features of English found in artificial sign systems, having its own grammatical markers and word order. Most importantly, it exploits the medium of vision and space in a systematic way, and thereby uses a whole range of 'articulators' from eye-gaze to body-posture. The theoretical basis for these artificial systems will be examined further in chapter 12.

Attitudes towards sign language

There is no doubt that awareness and use of sign language within deaf education is greatly on the increase, not only in the USA but also in Europe (Tervoort, 1983), and that this awareness is based on the existence in various countries of systematic research programmes which study the language of deaf people. There are numerous arguments concerning the nature of BSL which this research can begin to resolve. Often a major block to the encouragement of BSL in young deaf people is that it is believed to be a language which the general community does not use or understand, and that it is virtually impossible for hearing people to learn. At present there are about a thousand people at any specific time attending sign classes in the UK (Kyle, Woll and Llewellyn-Jones, 1981). Given that this is not a formal provision, and that the courses usually last about ten weeks, if we extend these figures to a yearly total there is evidence of a great desire by the public to learn to communicate with the deaf. In addition, when we monitored an experiment by our local television company to have sign language interpretation of the news, the most favourable responses came from the hearing community, and hearing people were learning signs from watching it. Further, there is little to suggest that sign language is physically any more difficult to learn than any other language (Stokoe, 1980). Our perceptions in the past may have misled us into a false view that BSL consists of a few signs which can be learned very easily and which will produce fluent communication with all deaf people. We now recognise that nearly all of the principles of learning foreign languages apply to the learning of a sign language, and none more so than the principle of contact with native users of the language. Access to deaf people in the learning stage is essential to fluent use of sign language. However, there is a general problem in attitudes towards deaf people's signing, which are similar to the attitudes towards other sub-cultures within the population. Stokoe comments:

The commonly held belief that the 'mother tongue' is the sole repository of 'normal grammatical structure' is a concept well known to anthropologists, who call it ethnocentrism. When it is used to deny that some other language is 'systematic' and to impute to the out-group who use that other language a deficiency of mental functioning, this notion comes perilously near racism. The study of the grammatical systems of sign languages as well as their semantic systems is the best way to replace such superstition and prejudice with useful knowledge. (1980: 145)

The view that the use of signs in the classroom will interfere with the correct order of English has been another frequently voiced argument for the ineffectiveness of sign language in the classroom. However, as we come to understand the differences between BSL and English we can begin to use signing constructively in a way which does not negatively affect English use. There is no reason to state that pupils who use a foreign language at home, or even in the playground, cannot learn the language of their teacher; it is usually the case that both languages are recognised.

The understanding and acceptance of sign language in education becomes a case for bilingualism in BSL and English. Again, this concept of two fluent languages in one child is one which has not always been accepted in the UK, and the Warnock Report (1978), surveying the field of special education and setting down proposals for its future in the UK, was at pains to emphasise the importance of linguistic minorities. It is perhaps not surprising that the countries which have been most accepting of the language of deaf people (e.g. the USA) are those where there are large or respected minority groups or where there is a very strong positive approach to the learning of foreign languages (for example, in Scandinavia). In Denmark parents of deaf children have a statutory entitlement to training in communication in sign language (Hansen, 1980). Generally speaking, our attitudes may have clouded our judgement in relation to the status of sign language. In the case of BSL the research is only at a very elementary stage of development, and the following chapters are an attempt to set down what we do know positively of it at the present time.

3. Historical aspects of BSL

There are relatively few early records of sign language with which we can compare its current form. In addition, there are few commentaries by or about deaf people which might provide insight into the development of sign as a language among deaf people. Virtually all our historical accounts deal with education and cover similar ground (Moores, 1978; Flint, 1979; Savage, Evans and Savage, 1981). They deal with children insofar as their needs have had to be met by the schools, but they offer little basis for an understanding of deaf people in general. Our purpose in this chapter is to try to interpret these historical accounts of education in the light of our own discoveries of texts relating to deaf people. What we know of sign and the deaf community in earlier centuries is now presented as a base for understanding BSL as it exists today.

Developing education

Hodgson's (1954) history begins in Greek times with references to signs among the deaf and dumb, though many other accounts present the case of a dumb man cured by St John of Beverley as the earliest record within the UK of the treatment of deafness. Unfortunately there is actually no reference to deafness in this miraculous cure described by the Venerable Bede.

Most modern accounts see the systematic education of deaf people as having started in the 16th century (Savage, Evans and Savage, 1981) and as becoming a subject for discussion at least in England during the 17th century. Digby (1644) mentions lip-reading and Bulwer in the same year describes gesture as an international communication system. John Bulwer and George Dalgarno are the two writers of the 17th century who show the greatest understanding of the basis of sign language.

Most writers never put their ideas into practice with deaf people and their interest was mainly in whether language might exist without speech. Dalgarno (1661) was one of the important figures during this period. He devised a means of communication through fingerspelling which was well argued as the ideal way to teach deaf people. Nevertheless, his ideas were hardly known at the time and it was left to Dugald Stewart, the Scottish philosopher, to rediscover him in 1815. Stewart felt Dalgarno's work had been almost deliberately overlooked, particularly by Wallis who was famed as a teacher of deaf people in the late 17th century. Stewart compares Dalgarno in importance to Sicard in France, whose theories of sign and education have had a profound influence in deaf education.

Wallis and Holder were two of the first teachers of speech to the deaf. Holder preferred a purely articulatory method, and there is some measure of disagreement as to which of the two was the more effective teacher. In some respects this was the precursor to the great debate which began formally in the next century. Baker in 1720 follows the chronology from Wallis, but major progress was not until 1760 when Thomas Braidwood began to teach deaf pupils in Scotland. At almost the same time de l'Epée began teaching through sign in Paris, while Heinicke in Leipzig emphasised the strict oral approach where only speech was used with, and accepted from, pupils. Conflict arose between the German (Heinicke) and French (de l'Epée) systems when Heinicke declared all other methods to be useless and pernicious and no less than 'folly, fraud and nonsense' (according to Scott, 1870).

Braidwood's fame is based on his success in developing speech in his pupils, not all of whom were deaf; but the tradition deriving from him, later to be known as the English method, was something of an intermediate between the German and the French methods. Savage, Evans and Savage (1981) claim that the perceived total oralism of Braidwood is something of a myth, and consider that Watson's account (1809), which describes the uses of sign in education, reflects Braidwood's original approach. The Royal Commission (1889) made a similar claim in setting out the history of deafness: 'The first school for the deaf and dumb in Great Britain was started on the combined system in 1760 by Braidwood in Edinburgh.'

This 'combined' system was the English one of speech *and* signs. Green testifies that signing was in existence in the original Braidwood school:

observing that he [his son] was inclined in company to converse with one of his school fellows by the tacit finger language, I asked him why he did not speak to him with his mouth? To this his answer was as pertinent as it was concise: 'He is deaf'. (Green, 1783)

A summary of the perceived methods of Braidwood is provided in Arnot's *History of Edinburgh* (1779), quoted in Kerr-Love and Addison (1896):

He begins with learning [teaching] the deaf articulation or the use of their vocal organs; and at the same time teaches them to write the characters and compose words of them. He next shows them the use of words in expressing visible objects and their qualities. After this he proceeds to instruct them in the proper arrangement of words or grammatical construction of language.

The deaf (Mr Braidwood observes) find great difficulty in attaining pronunciation but still more in acquiring a proper knowledge of written language. Their only method of conversing is by signs and gestures. Their ideas are few, being entirely confined to visible objects and to the passions and senses . . . . The connection between our ideas and written language being purely arbitrary, it is a very hard task to give the deaf any notion of that mode of conversing, their being only hieroglyphical.

When we visited this academy we found that the boys not only could converse by the help of the artificial alphabet they learned by putting the fingers into certain positions, but they understood us, although perfect strangers to them, by the motion of our lips.

Braidwood himself did not produce an account of his method or theories. Braidwood moved to London in 1783 and the first charitable school for the deaf opened in 1792 with Watson, Braidwood's nephew, in charge. In 1810 a school in Edinburgh opened with one of Braidwood's grandsons as head, and in 1812 a further school in Birmingham opened with Braidwood's other grandson as head teacher. The approach attributed to Braidwood, of developing articulation, therefore pervaded the early education of the deaf in the UK.

The method was proving very effective, at least superficially, since at one of the anniversary receptions of the London school the *Times* could report:

For these poor children, totally deaf . . . have through the benevolence of this society been taught not only to speak, read, write and cypher but also to comprehend the meaning and grammatical arrangement of words whereby they are enabled to hold converse with those about them and with each other. (4 May 1798)

This type of evaluation of the school's effectiveness, by display of the pupils' talents and acquired skills, was a notable feature of deaf schools throughout the 19th century.

Watson describes the teaching of spoken and written language through the use of signs:

In order to bring (the deaf learner) acquainted with (sounds and words) we must proceed by the most obvious and simple methods, depending upon what has been termed natural language (gesture, feature etc). (1809. 75)

Everyone who would undertake the arduous task of successfully teaching the deaf and dumb, should closely turn his attention to the study of that language termed *natural* (1809: 81)

He also claims that deaf people 'from most distant parts' can understand each other through signs. An account of Clerc's visit to Watson's school in 1814 supports this claim:

As soon as Clerc beheld this sight [the children at dinner] his face became animated; he was as agitated as a traveller of sensibility would be on meeting all of a sudden in distant regions, a colony of his countrymen . . . Clerc approached them. He made signs and they answered him by signs. This unexpected communication caused a most delicious sensation in them and for us was a scene of expression and sensibility that gave us the most heartfelt satisfaction. (de Ladebat, 1815)

The first half of the 19th century saw the rapid advancement of provision for deaf school children throughout the UK. Most major cities opened schools in this period, so that there were 22 by 1870. In the early part of the century the methods used were mainly the combined system with an emphasis on articulation and speech, though this gradually gave way by mid-century to an almost total reliance on sign as the mode of communication, and on written language as the means of access to English. Most of these schools had very long periods of stability under one headmaster: Kinniburgh in Edinburgh, Baker in Doncaster, Scott in Exeter, Neill in Newcastle, Anderson and later Addison in Glasgow, and Barnes-Smith in Bristol. It seems likely that these periods of extended stewardship led the schools into the 'disrepair' highlighted by Hodgson (1954). When the time came for change it was probably as much a rejection of an older generation as of the older methods.

Although we can say that from 1800 until the 1880s the method of teaching used the combined system, in the middle of this period there was a concentration on written language. Tuckfield (1839) proposed the development of children's language through signs and fingerspelling, her method drawing largely on that used in Paris. Dickens (1865) describes the teaching of reading through signs. The most lucid description of signs used in class to teach English is provided by Scott; his views on sign language are simple enough:

Sign language then is used by teachers because it is the only common ground on which they can meet their pupils and where they can both understand each other so that one can communicate and the other receive the knowledge to be conveyed. But when it can be abandoned for alphabetic language it is so and it is never considered other than a *means* in deaf-mute instruction. (1870: 118)

However, he strongly defended sign language from those who claimed it was degrading. Scott described two classes of signs, each with two subdivisions: 'natural', to include *truly natural signs* (used by hearing people as well, effectively non-verbal communication) and *descriptive or imitative signs* (such signs as are currently available in BSL: EAT, SLEEP etc.); and 'artificial', to include *methodical signs* (signs made up to provide word–sign direct equivalents as used in the French method) and *arbitrary signs* (where the sign form may be indicative of a concept).

Scott discussed fingerspelling and its role, as well as speech and lip-reading. The latter is seen as most useful for those who become deaf and for those who are partially deaf. He agreed that, in theory, deaf people should be taught to speak, but considered that undue emphasis on speech for the congenitally deaf would be 'one of the greatest calamities that could befall the deaf-mute, if our modes of instruction were to take a retrograde movement in this direction' (p. 158).

Scott believed that emphasis on oralism had re-opened a debate which had been laid to rest by trial in the schools. Oralist views had returned as a function of wider opportunities for educators to travel to other schools, especially those in Germany. Travellers then returned:

full of wonderment at what they considered a new and marvellous achievement − teaching the dumb to speak. It is remarkable that people generally are much more anxious to have their wonder excited than their intelligence exercised. They have often come back with greatly exaggerated accounts of what was done and in this, as in many other things, have believed more in what they saw abroad than what they found at home. (1870: 163–4)

He claimed that those pupils who were successful had already been selected for their intelligence and partial or previous hearing. In his view deaf education had to concentrate on written language, but Scott was part of an establishment which was coming to be challenged.

Milan and after

Thomas Arnold was almost certainly the first purely oral teacher of the deaf in the UK in the 19th century. Following his training in sign language at Doncaster he set up his own school in 1868 using an oral only approach. Just at that time another school opened in London which brought Van Praagh from Holland to instil the new method from the continent. The founding of the Association for the Oral Instruction of the Deaf and Dumb followed in 1870. The Association began training teachers in 1872 and Ackers, a parent of a deaf child, founded the Society for Training Teachers of the Deaf and the Diffusion of the German System.

It is clear that a significant mood of change had arrived in the 1870s and many schools had begun to employ oral teachers and were trying out these methods with selected pupils. In schools in Europe the movement had gone further, and even in France there were no strong advocates of the use of sign in school. Only in the USA was there still recognised support for the sign language view. Even there the scene was being set for the oral–manual dispute, with Alexander Graham Bell and Edward Gallaudet the best-known protagonists.

It was in this atmosphere that the International Congress on the Education of the Deaf was held in Milan in 1880. Before the start of the conference delegates were allowed to visit the schools for the deaf in the area to see for themselves the achievements of the oral method. The demonstrations were the by now traditional ones of deaf and dumb people speaking and lip-reading effectively and also giving their own opinions on how much they owed to the method. The *Times* correspondent was so impressed that he wrote: (13 September 1880) 'Deafness, as I have already intimated, is practically abolished.'

The first session of the congress was swift and proceeded to a vote, carried by a large majority, that the method of oral teaching was by far superior to that of using signs and that it should be the preferred method in all schools for the deaf. The fact that on the following day the meaning of the motion had to be discussed indicated the hasty nature of the debate. Ackers, in a crusading paper (1880), highlighted the problems of inverted order in sign language and affirmed his view that articulation should be used throughout each lesson. Gallaudet seems to have been the principal defender of the combined system. Nevertheless, the congress vote strengthened the belief of oral educators throughout Europe.

The national conference in the UK in the following year discussed at length the implications of Milan. Elliott (1882) opened the discussion with a plea for moderation and careful consideration of the facts. He presented a series of points which he felt weakened the resolution of Milan:

(a) The provisions made for interpreting were very inefficient insofar as English was concerned, to the extent that English speakers were neither effectively heard nor able to understand significant parts of the proceedings. English was understood by probably no more than about two people other than the English and American representatives.

(b) There was an imbalance in the voting according to the experience of those voting: i.e. oralists tended to have less experience: 'The great majority of the following members we are told were connected with the schools in Milan and who represented a total of children fewer than half of those I myself represented at the Congress, could certainly know little or nothing of the opposite system. Therefore, the 'incontestable superiority' of speech over signs for the purpose named, they must have taken on trust' (Elliott, 1882: 10).

(c) The congress was not in any sense ecumenical or international: 53 per cent of members were from Italy, 34 per cent from France, 7 per cent from England and America and there was one representative from Germany, with none from Belgium or Switzerland.

(d) There was some question as to the background of the pupils giving demonstrations at the schools during the previous week. According to general Italian figures, only 15 per cent of deaf children were 'semi-mute' (i.e. adventitiously deaf), but in 1880 63 per cent of pupils at the Royal School in Milan had acquired deafness. Elliott also extends these figures to all of Italy to show a disproportionate provision for those with acquired deafness, on whom the decisions for oralism had been based. On the basis of the figures provided by the congress, Elliott concludes that Italian schools did not 'educate a fair proportion of the born deaf pupils'.

Despite this negative view, Elliott's recommendation to the conference was that his school should experiment with the oral system so that it could be judged properly in the UK.

However, at the conference in 1881, Arnold, Schontheil, Van Praagh and Ackers rejected most of Elliott's criticisms of Milan and the proposed experiment in Elliott's school where, it was claimed, the teachers were not sufficiently trained in the method. Arnold explained his background:

In 1840, as a teacher of the deaf and dumb in the Yorkshire Institution, I trained a youth, congenitally deaf, to speak. He was publicly examined at Wakefield . . . and answered many questions distinctly. In 1860, I brought a youth from Australia, whose speech I restored. He had almost lost it through scarlet fever. He became able to converse freely with others, and happily his hearing afterwards returned. I may say he was the occasion of my taking up and developing the oral method of teaching. I had no assistance from any other teacher. (1882: 140)

Scott Hutton, despite support for the use of sign language, perceives very clearly the value of the regeneration of deaf education:

For my part I rejoice at this [the great oral controversy]. I believe the cause of the deaf owes a debt of gratitude to the advocates of the oral method whose zeal and devotion put to shame the apparent lukewarmness and lethargy of those who profess to be following 'a more excellent way. (1882: 45)

There was an inevitability about the ascendency of the new method.

It is quite clear that Milan, although it became the focus of change in deaf education, was by no means the cause, since the most active educators of that time had begun to look for change and amongst their principles were the advantages of speech and lip-reading over signs. Schontheil sums up the approach and emphasises:

Rarely write, never gesticulate, always speak. Do not cut up your words and sentences, and let emphasis clearly mark the chief sounds, radical syllables and the most important words. Lip reading will then be easy, the voice will sound naturally, speech will come forth spontaneously and the double affliction of being deaf and dumb will undoubtedly be overcome.' (1882: 45)

From this point on, the oral method began to take hold of the administration. The Royal Commission set up in 1885 reported in 1889. As well as legislating for the education of all deaf children by local authorities they set out a directive for the oral method:

Recommendation 9: That every child who is deaf should have full opportunity of being educated on the pure oral system. In all schools receiving government grants whether conducted on the oral, sign and manual or combined system, all children should for the first year at least be instructed on the oral system and after the first year they should be taught to speak and lip-read on the pure oral system unless they are physically and mentally disqualified. (Royal Commission, 1889)

Unfortunately this produced the circular argument still voiced today (e.g. Van Uden, 1981) that if deaf children use signs or do not succeed with oralism, they must *therefore* be mentally or physically handicapped even if this handicap is not visible. However, Ackers (a member of the Commission) was not satisfied even with this and tabled a reservation (1890) to the 1890 Act: 'Also there are not any deaf children "physically or mentally disqualified" and so schools on any other system than the Pure Oral are not required.'

Wherever local authorities set up their own schools then the oral approach began to dominate. Those who used sign became failures. In Bristol, from 1894 when the Act was implemented, till 1907, the local authority school (oral) competed with the charitable school (sign) and it is clear throughout this period that there was increasing opposition to the sign method. This was mainly on the part of the school inspectorate and Eicholz in particular, who pursued the oral philosophy with zeal. The retirement of the head coincided with the end of the signing school.

Much the same was happening elsewhere. In 1881 the governors of the Glasgow school investigated the oral method, examined the experiment in oralism in Elliott's school, but decided against change. Addison in Glasgow in 1899 was still using sign language:

The system of instruction is that generally known as the combined system . . . Speech, writing, the manual alphabet and signs are all used in the instruction of children; the idea being to adapt the method to the capability of the child rather than to force the pupil into a groove for which he is unsuited. (Addison, 1899)

Inevitably, the outspoken advocacy of oralism produced opposition among deaf people. The British Deaf and Dumb Association was founded in 1890 and resolved at the first gathering:

That this Congress of the British Deaf and Dumb Association . . . indignantly protests against the imputation . . . that the finger and signed language is barbarous. We consider such a mode of exchanging our ideas as most natural and indispensable and that the combined system of education is by far preferable to the so-called Pure Oral.

This position helped confirm the rift between missioners for the deaf, who dealt with deaf adults, and the schools; it is not until 1907 that there is some evidence of an attempt to come together again. Nevertheless, discussion of methods was not allowed and the series of talks at the conference was rather unsatisfactory. Elliott (1907) at the international conference on the education of the deaf, in Edinburgh, was able to comment in detail on the developments in deaf education since the Act and looked on them with some satisfaction. By 1904 there were 2,200 deaf children in boarding schools and 1,100 in day schools in England, of whom 2,600 were educated orally. Elliott's views by then were more in line with oral philosophy and although not all children learned to speak properly: 'imperfect speech is easier to follow by the uninitiated than signing or spelling on the fingers, both of which require more practice than most people are able to give' (Elliott, 1907: 13).

Elliott's principal worry was the lack of recognised teacher training and by 1912 this pressure led to the setting up at Manchester University of what is now the Department of Audiology and Education of the Deaf. Under the guidance of Sir Alexander and Lady Ewing this department dominated the education of deaf children, not only in the UK but in many parts of the Commonwealth, almost to this day. The fact that training was exclusively oral severed any possibility of a link between deaf adults using sign and the education of deaf children. All through this period motions have been unanimously passed at BDA conferences decrying the use of pure oralism and effectively widening the gap between teachers and the deaf community.

Until the last 10–15 years the publications and texts available to teachers were almost solely oralist in philosophy. Story (1905), Haycock (1933) and Ewing and Ewing (1938) were among the influential texts which rejected sign language. The Ewings' view is summed up in two basic tenets: The 2–3-year-old child uses gestures a great deal and though it might be his 'mental salvation' it is also the 'greatest threat to his future mental life'; and 'without the use of words thinking must be both hindered and limited'. The increasing knowledge about hearing and the gradual provision of hearing aids supported the oral approach, though its philosophy had scarcely changed since Arnold's first pronouncements fifty years earlier. The question of whether it was better technology or better use of the oral method which helped deaf children was a matter which bubbled under the surface from time to time.

Swayne (1934) from Margate school expressed concern at standards and suggested that these might be not as good as before the oral method was introduced. The question of methodised signs (English-based signs) began to be raised again. A letter in the *Teacher of the Deaf* magazine from an unnamed head teacher was emphatic in its concern for deaf education:

Unless we can do something about the blind attitude of speech teachers, Oralism will be utterly discredited . . . To me the saddest sight in this connection is a party of deaf children walking out. Forbidden to sign or fingerspell, they move along in chains. It must

45

be wrong. Speech and lip-reading are not practicable in the playground, the road and under many other conditions. Now you can go further and suggest accepted methodized signs in step with the language medium for those who can think but cannot yet grasp language as it is spoken or finger-spelt. Agree and please let us drop this excuse of 'parents' wishes'. The parents are pitifully in the hands of teachers and they have been woefully misled. (*Teacher of the Deaf*, 1946: 50)

Increasing concern, despite the now wide availability of hearing aids, led to the Lewis Report (1968) which discovered that although British schools for the deaf preferred pure oralism, this was not the practice. Of 45 schools for the deaf, three-quarters used manual communication in some context, though this was on the whole unsystematic. Savage, Evans and Savage (1981) trace the growth in signing in schools in the UK since 1968 to this report and to the growing claims made for Total Communication as a philosophy. Newcastle school and many schools in Scotland had begun by this time to create opportunities for research and had made acceptable the involvement of profoundly deaf people in schools. The efforts of Allan Hayhurst of the BDA in this must be recognised, and though the British deaf community has not yet begun to be seen as having a significant role in education, the research and interest generated has allowed a re-evaluation by teachers of the needs of deaf people (Brennan and Hayhurst, 1981).

The fact that this has produced an alternative cry for the return to days of 'natural oralism' (Braybrook and Powell, 1980) as so clearly summarised by Schontheil (1882) (see quotation on p.43) is almost as inevitable as it is unnecessary. As Kyle and Allsop (1982a) point out, deaf people view speech and lip-reading as essential skills, as well as wishing to use sign language for learning. Deaf adults and children do not view the use of signing and speaking as opposed. Conrad (1981) suggests that children should 'choose' the method to be used, by their own progress under a range of approaches. The fact that parents' and teachers' organisations have begun to consider this offers a hopeful base for the future.

Developing sign

Language skills

Virtually every major philosopher has considered the problem of how language came into being. By the 18th century it had become something of an obsession. Speech as the overt expression of language was believed to be the element of behaviour which made people human and language related directly to man's capability for thought. The argument over whether thinking could exist without language ran in parallel to the simple dispute about whether speech or gesture came first in man.

The gestural theory of language origins is that gestures were the first mode of communication among men and that these broadened to non-verbal cues such as facial expression and then to cries. As the system became refined cries were formed into words and then eventually into sentences. The alternative view is that speech developed much more directly and that gesture is independent of, or at best subject to, the meanings expressed in speech. Obviously, the argument is not easily resolved and any comments made in the space available here will seem rather simplistic. There is some relevance for our discussion, however, in that philosophers began to look at deaf people and their use of sign language as a test case.

Accounts such as that of the Wild Boy of Aveyron (Itard, 1821 – discussed in Lane, 1977) suggested that spoken language was not completely natural in the sense that it would develop on its own without adult or other models. Itard demonstrated that Victor (the boy discovered in the forests of Aveyron living wild with no contact with other humans) was capable of thought and learning but never aspired to the development of speech. A similar situation has been described more recently with the well-documented case of Genie (Curtiss, 1977), where a child deprived of speech and language stimulation was discovered at the age of 13 years with no natural speech. Like Victor, Genie's speech has been slow to develop and this has been used to reinforce an argument for a critical period of language development, after which language learning is very difficult.

However, the major dispute in the 18th century concerned the theorising of philosophers such as Condillac (1746, reprinted 1971). His view was that images (which were the basis of thought) were not always representable in speech and were more directly related to gestures. Because sounds were added to gestures in early evolution, a series of spoken words was often needed to represent what had previously been a single gesture. This then presented a misleading view of thought whereby the ideas existed in sequential sentence-like strings.

Diderot (1751) set out, in a 'Letter on the deaf and dumb', a case for considering their sign language as a way to study the natural order. Hewes (1976) has especially linked the evolved present-day sign language of deaf people to this more gestural origin. Speculation on the topic reached such a peak in the 19th century that the Paris Société de Linguistique finally banned all communications on language origins. However, interest continued. Tylor, the British anthropologist, in setting out a classic work on the origins of mankind (1874), discussed at length the structure of sign language and its role in the deaf community. He saw signs as a more primitive language form, albeit a very complex one. He identified points concerning the object–subject–verb order of signs and even discussed the role of artificial sign systems.

Stout, in his *Manual of psychology* (1899), considered the relation of language and thought and described how signs develop from iconic representations to cognitive symbols which gradually form a language. Like Tylor, he saw sign as a more primitive language form which those who develop speech tend to leave behind. However, again we find the status of sign language elevated to a tool for thinking which functions effectively for the 'deaf mute'.

This argument has by and large been lost in the 20th century, where knowledge of sign language has been ignored in favour of a view which has seen deaf people as handicapped, with a world consisting of concrete objects and gestures which can only reflect the present. These gestures do not allow thinking at all but only a crude form of communication which latterly has become forbidden in schools for the deaf. Linguists, too, have lost sight of the philosophers' and anthropologists' work, as Hewes points out:

Impressed by the apparent arbitrariness of most spoken languages, it has been argued that such arbitrariness is an essential criterion for language or that a high degree of iconicity would interfere with understanding. The sign languages of the deaf are dismissed as crude, rudimentary and if their users are unable to communicate except in such languages they display various serious cognitive handicaps. (1976: 489)

While linguists had a limited view of sign language, it seems equally the case that philosophers had little real knowledge of deaf people and tended to be of the armchair speculation variety, even though some of this speculation was very illuminating. Very few of those concerned with the problems of deafness had actually dealt with deaf people. There is no evidence, for example, that Dalgarno ever tried out any of his ideas with deaf people. However, the few records we have allow us to put together some picture of deaf people, their community, their language and how they were viewed.

Sign language

The sign language of deaf people is not at all well documented until the 19th century, and since we have no evidence from the past about the existence of deaf communities there is very little to work on. Green (1783) mentions finger language as it was used in Braidwood's school, but in considering the use of signs among adult deaf people it is not till 1817 that there is documentation. Bulwer's two books, *Chirologia* (1644) and *Philocophus: or the deafe and dumbe man's friend* (1648), are the first two books published in English giving any insight into sign language. Both these books, however, introduce a common belief that signs or gestures are natural and international. This belief is found in

Table 3.1. *Some gestures recorded in Bulwer's 'Chirologia' (1644)*

Gesture	Meaning
Stretching out of the hands	Impart, request, sue, solicit, beseech
Wring the hands	Weeping
Throw the hands up to heaven	Amazement
Clap right fist in left palm	Chide, insult
Interlock fingers	Sluggish, melancholy
Show and shake bunched fist	Threaten, anger, challenge
Hold out hand hollowed	Crave, beg, covet
Put forth right hand spread	Fee, heart, bounty
Shake hand	Have not
Hand to the face	Shame
Hold up hand hollow above shoulder and shake it by turning and returning the wrist	Encourage, embolden
Finger in the eye	Crying
Hold up thumb	Assent
Hold up both thumbs	Transcendency of praise
Give with two fingers	Pinch penny
Begin with first finger on left hand and tell on to last on right	Counting
Extend little finger from fist	Contempt
Suck on finger in mouth	Envy
Forefinger raised	Adore, thanks
Grip the left hand, clutching the thumb	Avarice, miserly
Lifting index finger towards face	Invitation

virtually every text on the subject published up to this century. The most serious problem this belief poses for the historical linguist is the resulting descriptions of signs as, for example, the 'natural gesture of eating'. Whether this gesture might consist of a mime of chewing, a mime of putting food in the mouth, a mime of cutting food with a knife and fork or any combination of these is rarely made explicit. Bulwer, however, although believing gesture to be 'the onlye speech and generall language of human nature' was clearly in contact with the deaf and aware of signs as forming a complex system: 'A notable argument we have of this discoursing facilitie of the hand is . . . that wonder of necessity which nature worketh in men that are borne deafe and dumbe; who can argue and dispute rhetorically by signs . . .' (1644: 5).

Bulwer goes on, in *Chirologia* to describe hundreds of gestures of the hands and fingers, some of which are listed in table 3.1. As we can see, some of the gestures are still in general use with the meanings described, both in sign language and in speech. Others, however, are not in use by the general population. We therefore may have in *Chirologia* the first description of BSL signs of the 17th century. Support for this comes from Bulwer's second book, *Philocophus*, published in 1648 and dedicated to Sir Edward Gostwick, Bart. and William Gostwick, his brother, both of whom were deaf. In the dedication, Bulwer states:

What though you cannot express your minds in those verball contrivances of man's invention; yet you want not *speeche*, who have your *whole body* for a *tongue*, having a language more naturall and significant, which is common to you with us, to wit, *gesture*, the general and *universall language* of *human nature* . . .

you already can expresse yourselves so truly by signes, from a habit you have gotten by using always signes, as we do speech: Nature also recompensing your want of speeche, in the invention of signes to expresse your conceptions.

Bulwer, in passing, also provides two other details about deaf communication which have found echoes in recent work on non-manual components of sign:

The deaf are natural phisiognomers. For as concerning the notes of the affections, affections which appear in men's faces, by instinct they know and disclose them readier than we can.

They will seem discontented and angry, if in your relations to them, among other manners and signes you make unto them, you do not therewithall use the motions of speech which are made with the mouth; as if you defraud them of the means of understanding you.

While Bulwer makes brief reference to 'arthrologie' — the alphabet on the joints of the fingers and the 'drawing of letters on the arm with the finger', the first description of a manual alphabet is found in Dalgarno. He is also the first to state clearly the distance between sign language and spoken language:

The deaf man has no teacher at all and though necessity may put him upon continuing and using a few signs, yet those have no affinity to the language by which they that are about him do converse amongst themselves. (1661: 3)

Dalgarno's alphabet in 'dactylology' appears to be based on the same principle as the 'arthrologie' of Bulwer: using the joints of the fingers to symbolise the letters of the alphabet. Dalgarno's alphabet (fig. 3.1) uses the right index finger to point to vowels, and the right thumb to point to consonants at specific locations on the left hand.

While Dalgarno's alphabet was soon superseded by one which required fewer fine distinctions of location, his insight into the processes of production and

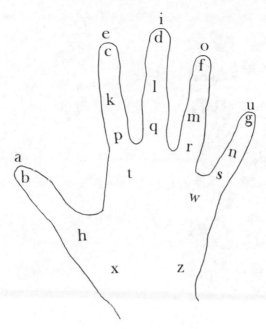

Fig. 3.1   Dalgarno's alphabet.

reception of fingerspelling is extremely important, and still only imperfectly understood:

if we compare words written with printing, this is still not only more simple and therefore more easily apprehended, but also it is as easy to represent a word as one compositum with a confined action of the hand, though there be many distinct pointings, as to make one word by an aggregate of many distinct letters. (1661: 25)

Dalgarno describes other alphabets he has considered but rejected, such as one formed by drawing letters on the hand, and an alphabet which forms letters 'symbolically', i.e. iconically. Examples he gives of this second alphabet include letters such as *x* formed by crossing index fingers, *m* and *n* by presenting three fingers and two fingers joined respectively. He claims that such an alphabet is problematic because some letters cannot be expressed iconically and it is generally too laborious, but the alphabet currently used in Britain is based on just such principles and derives from an alphabet published in 1680 in an anonymous pamphlet *Digiti lingua*. The alphabet in *Digiti lingua* preserves the feature of the Dalgarno alphabet where the tips of fingers of the left hand indicate the vowels *a,e,i,o,u*. The remainder of the letters are formed on Dalgarno's rejected 'symbolic' system. The configuration of the hands indicates some visual feature of the written letter. Although the alphabet in current use deviates in some ways

51

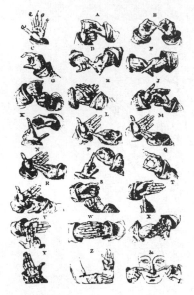

18th century

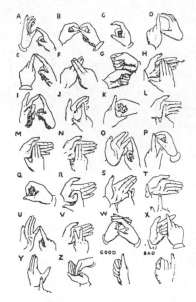

19th century

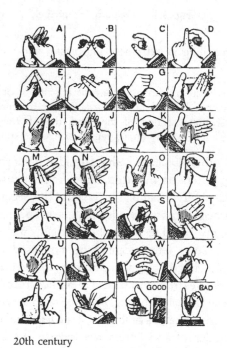

20th century

Fig. 3.2   Evolution of the British two-handed alphabet.

from the *Digiti lingua* alphabet, the two are clearly very closely related. We can see this by comparing the modern alphabet with two others, one from the 18th and one from the 19th century, which show a number of intermediate features (fig. 3.2).

In fig. 3.3 three examples of letters in *Digiti lingua* are compared with their modern form.

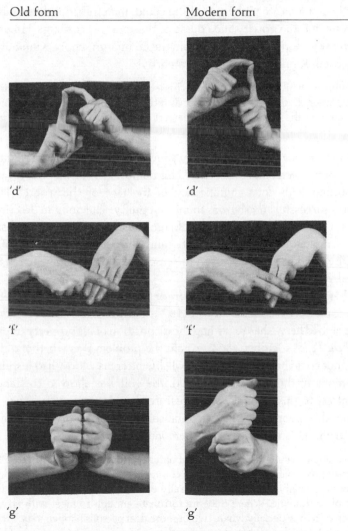

Old form   Modern form

'd'   'd'

'f'   'f'

'g'   'g'

Fig. 3.3   Some letters in *Digiti lingua* and their modern form.

Thinking and reasoning

Green (1783) mentions finger language as it was used in Braidwood's school, and Watson describes some processes of new sign formation (1809), but in considering the use of signs among the deaf, it is not until 1817 that there is firm documentation. Jean Campbell, deaf and dumb from birth, was accused of drowning her child by throwing him into the river from a bridge in Glasgow. Since there was no school for the deaf in Glasgow she had not been educated. Her solicitor therefore put up the defence that she could not be tried since he could not communicate with her and she could, therefore, not distinguish right from wrong, nor the gravity and course of the court proceedings. However, an interpreter was found, the principal from the Edinburgh school, Kinniburgh, and she was tried. Kinniburgh communicated by:

making figure with his handkerchief across his left arm in imitation of a child lying there, and having afterwards made a sign to her as if throwing the child over the bar . . . she made a sign and the witness said for her 'not guilty, my lord'. (*Glasgow Herald*, 26 September 1817)

According to Hume (1829) 'she had by signs and gestures very intelligibly told her story' of the accidental drowning. 'This dumb show she indeed repeated and went through with equal significancy in the face of the Court.' This was apparently successful and she was found not guilty. The point in describing the case is that it showed the capability of sign to convey meaning as abstract as moral discriminations in the case of guilt. Brown, the professor of Moral Philosophy in Edinburgh, discussed the case in detail at the time (cited in Kerr-Love and Addison, 1896).

Another example of the recognition of signing as a legally valid form of communication is described by Tylor (1874) in the case of the will of a deaf man who had signed his wishes regarding the disposition of his property (reported in *Justice of the Peace*, October 1864). Again the problem was whether a deaf and dumb signer could have made a valid will, but after his widow had testified as to the meanings of the signs he had used, the will was allowed to stand.

In contrast to this 'natural' use of gesture by a deaf person without contact with other deaf people in an educational setting, Watson describes the formation of 'artificial' language by deaf persons in contact:

It is in this simple manner [i.e. by the use of natural gestures] that two or more deaf and dumb persons are enabled to hold instant converse with each other . . . Thus far these signs may be termed *natural* but the naturally deaf do not always stop here with this language of pantomime. Where they are fortunate enough to meet with an attentive companion or two, especially where two or more deaf persons happen to be brought up together, it is astonishing what approaches they will make towards the construction of an artificial language. I mean that by an arbitrary sign, fixed by common consent, or accidentally hit upon, they will designate a person or a thing, and only that person or thing, by that sign . . . (1809: 78)

While signs were often regarded as an indication of mental weakness, Sicard (1803), Watson (1809) and Scott (1870) all recognised that deaf people were the creators of signs:

As a foreigner is not fit to teach a Frenchman French, so the speaking man has no business to meddle with the invention of signs, giving them abstract values. (Sicard, 1803)

Never let anything so chimerical be thought of as an attempt to turn master to the deaf and dumb in the art of signing. Whatever others might say, I own, I have always found it best to become, in some measure, a learner instead of a teacher, of this mode of expression. (Watson, 1809: 82–3)

Tylor (1874) cites Kruse, an educated deaf-mute teacher, as providing insight into how the signs originate:

What strikes him most or what . . . makes a distinction to him between one thing and another, such distinctive signs of objects are at once signs by which he knows these objects and knows them again; they become tokens of things. And whilst he silently elaborates the signs he has found for single objects . . . he develops for himself suitable signs to represent ideas . . . and thus he makes himself a language . . . a way for thought is already broken and with this thought as it now opens out the language cultivates and forms itself further and further. (Kruse, 1853; quoted by Tylor, 1874: 51)

Unlike previous authors, Tylor had considerable experience of deaf adults and deaf children, and was particularly interested in the nature of the language. The descriptions of individual signs he sets out are particularly illuminating, but his knowledge of the grammar of sign is exceptional and makes it quite obvious that linguists have been only rediscovering the structure of BSL over the last ten years. In line with Scott, Tylor separated the methodised artificial signs invented by hearing people from natural sign language, and felt there was little to sustain the former:

So far as I can learn, few or none of the fictitious grammatical signs will bear even the short journey from the schoolroom to the playground, where there is no longer any verb 'to be', where the abstract conjunctions are unknown and where mere position, quality and action may serve to describe substantive and adjective alike. (1874: 23)

Although Tylor felt the 'gesture-language' had no grammar as such and was independent of spoken language, he described very accurately the consistencies of order in signing. This usually meant topic-prominence, where the primary idea came first. He also showed the contextual effects necessary to distinguish passive and active sentences in sign, but most important was his realisation of the richness of sign language which is lost when only the glosses are written down. In consultation with a deaf man he presented the natural order as:

1. object; 2. subject; 3. action; illustrating it by the gestures 'door key open' to express 'the key opens the door' . . . it must always be borne in mind that the intelligibility of a gesture-sentence depends on the whole forming a dramatic picture, while this dramatic effect is very imperfectly represented by translating signs into words and placing these one after another. Thus when Mr Hebden expressed in gestures 'I found a pipe on the road' the order of the signs was written down as 'road pipe I-find' . . . but what the gestures actually expressed went far beyond this, for he made the spectator realize him as walking along the road and suddenly catching sight of a pipe lying on the ground. (1874: 27)

It is obvious that Tylor had considerable insight into sign language, which might have been of great value to educators and linguists alike if his publications had not been overtaken by the changes of attitude and philosophy which occurred around the time of the Milan Congress.

But the view that signs were important for thought was held even by the most ardent oralists. Bell (cited by Kerr-Love and Addison, 1896) claimed that no language would reach the mind of a deaf child like the language of signs. In effect it was accepted as a form of internal representation, though not a language. So Story (1905) can claim that signs interfere with the acquisition of language, 'interposing an additional and unnecessary representation between idea and word'. Of course, this returns to the idea held at the beginning of the previous century that signs are a form of concrete, non-English representation. Elizabeth (c. 1830) presents the deaf English of a boy describing his illness: 'cough much now, pain bad; soon no cough; no pain'. The difficulty is, of course, as Tylor (1878) pointed out, that sign is far richer than these glossing of signs into English would suggest. The problem then becomes one of how to use the representation that sign allows. Sadly we are probably no closer to understanding the nature of sign-like English sentences in deaf children's written work (Dawson, 1981).

Nevertheless, all through the 19th century there was consistent and repeated expression of the value of signs to the mental life of deaf people. At the same time deaf people identified more closely with their schools: teachers acted as interpreters; the religious care of deaf people arose usually from spontaneous calls by deaf people on their old schools to provide them with a meeting place. It is therefore among those who had this deep concern with the beginnings of the deaf community and among deaf writers themselves (as shown by Batson and Bergman, 1976) that we find this adherence to sign for learning and thinking.

Stewart (1815) in his case study of James Mitchell, who had a visual handicap as well as deafness, shows the considerable level of thought which is available without speech. Mitchell used sign and understood the signs of his sister through touch. Stewart believed Mitchell was unique and quotes Sicard at length on how, if such a person were found, the principles of deaf-blind education might be carried out in sign. Although Mitchell was deaf and blind, Stewart used his case to consider and criticise educators of the deaf for confounding 'the gift of speech with the gift of reason' and therefore concentrating on articulation. These are again indications that philosophers saw deaf people as just as capable as hearing people of adequate thought.

But what was not clear, as Jean Campbell's case illustrates, was whether thinking could take place without education in contact with other deaf people. Ray (1848) considered this problem and supplied some evidence on the nature of thinking, but it related to basic emotional responses to natural phenomena such as lightning or the stars. His view was that these recollections of deaf people revealed a primitive ignorance but a remarkable reflective power.

Booth (1878) was content to point out that deaf people do not think only in signs or gestures but may well use words in memory. Payne (1903) however, argued that it is necessary to separate the question of word or sign in order to consider the mental development of the child and that this development of thought is most easily achieved through signed information. Educators however had decided on this subject (Eicholz, 1932, rejected signs as a shorthand method for expressing ideas) and psychologists had lost interest in internal representation and thought in the pursuit of a science of behaviour. The discussion of the implications of sign language as a vehicle for thought has only recently been re-opened and perhaps experiments in the near future will cast light on this area of interest.

Sign language has existed for a long time and philosophers have generally seen thought as independent of language. To the extent that speech complements thinking, sign may also. Our understanding of basic structures in sign language should, therefore, be an important priority of our work in this field, and the fact that there appear to be changes in sign over time may provide information on the changing conditions of sign language use.

4. Sign language acquisition

Any attempt to present language development in a single chapter would seem to most readers at least rather foolhardy; the extent of the field, the diversity of influences and the vast proliferation of research in recent years, make it much too dynamic a study to be encapsulated so easily in one chapter. We can therefore say from the outset that we wish only to give an introduction to this field of work insofar as it can be directly related to sign language. In this, of course, we will be able to show not only that sign language acquisition research follows child language research paradigms, but also that it complements, and at times significantly extends, what we know of the development of language. The issues which arise here have implications throughout the rest of the book and are particularly important to our considerations of 'applying sign language' in education. We can hope, therefore, to provide some basis for understanding how deaf children come to learn their language.

The first major question is 'what is their language?' When we discussed the community in chapter 1, we claimed both that BSL was the language of deaf people in the UK and that 90 per cent of deaf children were born to hearing parents. In this there lies a difficulty. The child's first language is usually the language of his parents. For most of the 90 per cent of deaf children with hearing parents, as for hearing children in Britain, the parents' language is English. The question is simple: do children who cannot hear effectively acquire, through lip-reading and residual hearing, their parents' spoken language or the language of their peers as a first language? If one is a believer in the oralist philosophy then the answer is the former, and if one is a profoundly deaf person the answer is the latter. Tervoort (1979), in a study of the problem of which is the first language of deaf children, came to the conclusion that although it could not be fully specified it at least involved signing. The facts, however, do not allow support for any simple viewpoint on the development of language in deaf children. It is these 'facts' which we need to examine insofar as they affect general achievement levels in the target language of education: spoken language; the communicative environment itself: the home and family; and the development of sign language.

There is a great deal of confusion both in concepts and terminology regarding language development in deaf children. The first source of confusion is that many approaches do not distinguish carefully between terms such as *speech, verbal communication, talk, language,* and *linguistic communication.* We take the view that *language* is an abstract concept, referring to ways humans have, both innate and learned, of structuring concepts and relations between them. Through interaction a child learns specific linguistic knowledge, shared by an individual with other members of the language community. By linguistic, or verbal knowledge, we refer to specific types of symbolisation, involving meaningful elements and the combination of those elements. The representation of these elements in communication is not restricted to speaking words; language may be either spoken or signed. We will therefore specifically refer in this chapter to both *spoken language* and *signed (sign) language* as coming under the heading *language. Speech* (in speech production) refers to the motor skills involved in converting the linguistic or verbal knowledge into a communicative form articulated in the oral/aural channels. *Sign* is used as a parallel term to represent the same skills in the visual/manual channels. The terms *verbal knowledge* and *verbal communication* are therefore used for both spoken language and signed language. *Non-verbal communication,* on the other hand, should be restricted to those communications, in either the oral/aural or manual/visual channels, which do not involve linguistic knowledge. Writers on deafness have often shown a lamentable lack of clarity in the use of these terms.

This new book is about modern scientific techniques of teaching hearing-impaired children to talk intelligibly, which necessarily relates to the development of their capacity to communicate effectively in spoken language in real-life situations. It is more than ever true that, as Gray and Wise wrote in 1959, 'the actual human voice . . . is still the universal medium of social exchange'. In his book *Psychology of deafness* (1960), Myklebust has stated, 'an important consideration is that only through a verbal language can we expect the human being to attain to his highest potential'. (Ewing and Ewing, 1964: 1)

Here we see confusion between the role of the 'human voice' and 'verbal language': table 4.1 illustrates the contrasts and the levels at which they occur.

Achieving society's language

The expectation for hearing children with hearing parents is that they will learn the spoken language of their parents and of their society. The tradition of deaf education has worked diligently towards this goal. The fact that education for deaf children begins at the age of 3 years or earlier means that language progress may depend to some extent on success in schooling, since their early placement in school shortens the pre-school, family interaction period. This not only

Table 4.1. *Sign and spoken languages compared*

	Spoken language	Sign language
Instrument	Air, larynx, tongue, etc.	Hands, body, etc.
Production	Articulated speech phonemes of a language	Articulated signing cheremes of a language
Reception	Ears	Eyes
Units	Morphemes, words, etc.	Morphemes, signs etc.
Combination	Grammar of a given spoken language	Grammar of a given sign language
Universal features	Only certain types of structures occur. Each spoken language uses a subset of these structures. Features also occur in sign languages.	Only certain types of structures occur. Each sign language uses a subset of these structures. Features also occur in spoken languages

undermines some of the direct comparisons we would wish to make between deaf and hearing children's language after the age of 3, but the issue of language acquisition is clouded by competing philosophies in educational programmes. Our purpose in this chapter is to look at language development rather than education, and therefore, in setting out the achievements of deaf children in language we are not, for the moment, concerned with the merits or faults of particular school methods. In chapter 12 we will examine how signing may be fitted to school practice and at that stage comment will be more relevant.

Certain features, in addition to the shortening of the pre-school period mentioned above, differentiate deaf children from their hearing peers. During the first year of life, parents will often be in a stage of uncertainty as to the degree of their child's deafness. The diagnosis of deafness, although more easily made now, is generally unconfirmed to the parents till after the child's first birthday. There will be many people around, well-wishers and professionals, who will encourage the state of uncertainty. The parents may be given the most optimistic view that normal language development is possible, or be told that medical intervention may be possible or, better still, that technology can solve the problems.

Language development begins with the earliest communications between the infant and his mother; the work of Bates, Camaioni and Volterra (1975), for example, relates early gesture in hearing children to their language progress; all of this in the first year. The relevance of pre-linguistic communication to the development of language has been recognised only within the last decade: earlier work on child language, based as it was on the acquisition of syntax, rarely concerned itself with the pre-verbal period.

Deaf children are different for at least these reasons and, not surprisingly, their spoken language development is different. It is this difference which makes special education necessary, but it is a difference which has not been fully described. Early methods used to train deaf children most closely resembled a speech remediation programme, i.e. they were based on a view that speech organs had to be made to function. This rigid approach, entailing vast amounts of repetitive drill with devices to maximise the child's residual hearing, is rather less in evidence now and has given way to a recognition that speech drills do not lead directly into language and communication. This realisation has resulted in a more natural approach to the teaching of spoken language (Powell and Braybrook, 1981), promoting the use of natural conversation wherever possible with simultaneous optimisation of hearing through, for example, radio hearing aids. Certainly this is an approach which has been in use for a considerable time, although Powell and Braybrook are the only authors who specifically discuss its features.

Much of current philosophy is based on the premise that deaf children arrive at school linguistically inept and require careful tutoring by trained teachers in order to begin to learn language. In fact, this suggests that the 'natural language' approach used by all parents is of limited value with deaf children, despite its obvious situational and emotional relevance. This is something which would now be disputed by many parents' organisations. However, children who have followed a programme of activities set out by peripatetic or pre-school staff still arrive at school with very low levels of linguistic knowledge. Schlesinger and Meadow (1972) found that 75 per cent of their American deaf pre-schoolers (average age 44 months) had a language age of 28 months or less. Meadow (1980) attributes this to the 'inappropriate reactions and non-selective reinforcement from others' when deaf children attempt to vocalise. In other words, emphasis on the *teaching* of language, as opposed to its communication value, may limit the child's willingness to 'try out' language. Deaf children, of course, do vocalise from infancy. Meadow (1980) reports on the generally accepted observation that deaf babies babble and coo normally from birth until about 9 months, when these behaviours diminish and disappear. Whether this is because the child gets little feedback on his own behaviour and loses interest in vocalising, or whether early babbling is unconnected to the development of language, it is clear that early diagnosis of hearing loss is critically important.

Even given this advantage we are not well placed to estimate spoken language potential and evaluate language skills in deaf children. One important problem, for example, is distinguishing between language development and speech development, as discussed above. We will first discuss studies of deaf children's speech, then go on to studies of language. It is important to bear in mind, however, that many studies confuse them. There is no straightforward approach to measurement, only a range of alternatives.

Speech

In the area of speech assessment one can look at articulation measures which consider the clarity of speech based on phonetically balanced samples or one can examine intelligibility – the degree to which independent listeners can understand the speech. In addition, one must decide whether to examine words, phrases or sentences as basic units; one can choose to elicit spontaneous speech or collect samples of prepared or read text. The final possibility, of course, is a simple rating by teachers of the child's overall ability, without reference to specific criteria.

No matter which method is used there is a strong positive relation between amount of hearing and clarity of speech (Jensema, Karchmer and Trybus, 1978) and a minimal relation with intelligence (Markides, 1970). The consideration of what is acceptable speech is a problem; both Swisher (1976) for United States subjects and Conrad (1979) for a vast sample of UK school leavers consider the level of speech attainment for profoundly deaf children to be discouragingly low. Conrad's (1979) results indicate over 60 per cent of profoundly deaf children as having unintelligible speech or speech which is very difficult to understand by people not directly involved in deaf education. In addition, the low ratings by teachers of Conrad's 16-year-olds turn out to be very similar to the findings of a European survey of 8-year-olds (CEC, 1979). So the often repeated claim that these poor results are for a sample of children now overtaken by technological advances (e.g. Powell and Braybrook, 1981), and therefore unrepresentative of current achievement, is neither a new one (as Bergman, 1979 points out), nor one supported by research on those children benefitting from these new hearing aids and other technology. Kyle (1981c) reports a study where speech ratings for children aged 6 to 11 years were collected from teachers over a three-year-period. There were no significant improvements as the children got older; differences between children were accounted for by degree of hearing loss, and not amount or type of speech training. There is no evidence that the general results of poor speech performance discovered by earlier researchers can be discounted, nor are there grounds for suggesting that there is a new generation of deaf children without speech problems.

This lack of improvement in speech with age is not an uncommon finding.

Babbini and Quigley (1970) and Jensema, Karchmer and Trybus (1978) also report this. Conrad (1979) did consider the possible assistance offered by technological aids such as visible speech machines, and points out that Alexander Graham Bell in 1874 used pictures of speech wave forms to train deaf speakers. Conrad's prognosis is cautious rather than optimistic:

We have also seen the indisputable dependence of speech quality on degree of deafness. We are confronted here with an inflexible chain between deafness and oral language which continues to defy technological assault. (1979: 241)

Perhaps not surprisingly, a very similar pattern emerges for lip-reading or speech comprehension. Conrad (1977) indicated that deaf children's lip-reading after 12 years of training and experience is no better than hearing children deprived of sound for the experiment. The usual finding is that even under the best circumstances lip-reading is difficult. Problems of assessment, as with speech assessment, revolve around methodology. In a controlled environment where language knowledge could be assessed, Conrad (1979) could still show that there is a significant hearing loss effect on speech comprehension. However, lip-reading ability does relate positively to intelligence. In effect, lip-reading is easily confirmed as a very difficult skill to acquire. Discussion of deaf children's oracy repeatedly returns to this question of degree of hearing loss. The degree to which we are able to overcome this is at least very unpredictable, with the success of some children in speech and lip-reading inexplicable.

Spoken language

The picture for spoken language development is only marginally more optimistic than that for speech. Gregory and Mogford (1981), in a study of spoken language development in six severely deaf children, indicate significant degrees of progress in the acquisition of words, but conclude that the language development of deaf children is fundamentally different in quality, speed of development and in the actual type of utterances produced. In their longitudinal study of milestones in word acquisition by severely deaf children aged from 15–18 months to 4 years they found the first word appearing at an average age of 16 months, ten words at 23 months, 50 words at 29 months and 100 words at 34 months (in comparison with norms for hearing children of 11, 12, 19 and 20 months respectively). The age at which the deaf children reached each of these stages was significantly correlated with hearing loss. They also found, as in Nelson's (1973) study of hearing children, that the children's two-word utterances started at around the 50-word stage, but on average the deaf children were much older than hearing children at this developmental stage (33 months for the deaf children, rather than the 18 months that Nelson found). In terms of the actual vocabulary acquired, deaf children learned different words from those used by hearing children, using more modifiers and 'control' words like *no* and *thank you*; but Gregory and Mogford relate this to the child's actual developmental level, that is, the deaf children were older at comparable stages of development and so used behaviour appropriate to older children. Nevertheless, the picture is of significantly later development. Schlesinger and Meadow (1972) relate this delay in language development to later speech intelligibility, and other problems by referring to the concept of a 'critical period' for language development (McNeil, 1966). The notion of critical period is that children must learn a language (any language) during the rather brief period of the first two or three years of life. If a first language is learned later, there will be problems in developing a full linguistic system. When a first language is not learned in this period by children unable to hear, the result is a poor prognosis for successful training of speech in the later stages of education.

The other comment one returns to frequently is best expressed by Gregory and Mogford:

Sounds approximating to words do not exist in the interaction of deaf children with their mothers for several months before the true word is formed. Although they do vocalise and these vocalisations have functions within the interaction there is no impression that the vocalisation may be words. The first words of the deaf child are deliberately elicited and trained. (1981: 225)

That is, there is no feeling of natural growth in deaf children's spoken language: it is worked at and learned sound by sound, syllable by syllable, often at the expense of disruption of natural communication flow. The more deaf the child the harder this work becomes and the less related to normal language development. The major question can be seen as whether *language* can be acquired in this way or whether the over-riding environmental characteristics ensure that only a 'communication phrase book' is made available to the child. It is just as dangerous to offer a simple answer to this as to all the previous key questions on deaf children. To approach it, however, we can examine some of the factors in the language environment and then examine a language situation which does seem to work for deaf children.

Language environment

Many of the problems of spoken language development for the deaf child are attributed to the family situation and the behavioural and emotional problems encountered. Gregory (1976) observes that while the amount of hearing children's interaction with care-givers accelerates beyond the age of 2 years, deaf children's interactions actually decrease. This probably results from the lack of satisfactory interchange and leads to increasing frustration and emotional stress for all members of the family. We can see this if we consider the changes in interaction which take place as a hearing child grows and communication develops. When interacting with a baby it is normal to attribute interaction to the baby's vocalisations, and, in effect, 'speak for the child':

Mother and baby aged 6 months

Baby: (gurgling sounds)

Mother: You like that, don't you?

This behaviour would be inappropriate, however, with a child of 3 years, even if the child were deaf. What happens is that mothers reduce their interactions to ones which are still appropriate, instead of expanding communication in other contexts. There is no doubt that hearing families with deaf children experience nearly all the problems attributed to them by writers on the subject. From the point of diagnosis until the young adult becomes independent, families may see themselves in a constant struggle to normalise, and thereby socialise, the deaf person. Meadow (1980) provides an excellent review of the work in this field under the headings of 'social and psychological development, behaviour problems and the developmental environment' and we want to do no more here than try to distil the salient issues as they apply in our context.

There are reviews of the development of deaf children socially and emotionally (e.g. Myklebust, 1964; Bradford and Hardy, 1979), and in nearly every case the authors present evidence from studies showing deaf children as immature (Remvig, 1969), disassociated or aloof (Myklebust, 1964), impulsive or lacking in insight (Rainer and Altshuler, 1968), and lacking in self-confidence or initiative (Lewis, 1968). Schlesinger and Meadow (1972), in a comparison of deaf and hearing children on the Vineland Social Maturity Scale, found lower maturity in deaf children and found degree of maturity correlated with communicative competence. Deaf children of deaf parents, however, were rated more highly than those of hearing parents.

One can suggest that deaf children's lack of language is indicative of general lack of interactive competence; or one can assume that deaf children's lack of spoken language makes the communication of behavioural and social norms impossible for parents; or one can claim that lack of shared communication deprives the deaf child of access to the knowledge required for maturity. No matter which of these shades of explanation we choose, there is no doubt that the family environment is significantly altered by deafness and that specific pressures on the parents, particularly the mother, result. Schlesinger and

Meadow (1972) found 'the mothers of deaf pre-school children to be less permissive, more intrusive, more didactic, less creative, less flexible and showing less approval of their children in comparison with the mothers of hearing pre-school children' (comment by Meadow, 1980: 80). Wood (1981) describes the same intrusive behaviours in teachers of deaf children.

For the 90 per cent of deaf children with hearing parents the language environment is already altered by these pressures, over and above the lack of hearing. Inevitably, the incidence of other problems is then higher. Denmark *et al.* (1979), in a study of 75 deaf adolescents and their families, report that over 85 per cent of parents encountered behaviour problems (attributed to the effect of deafness) in the pre-school period, over 60 per cent reported problems at home during schooling, and over 70 per cent of parents found post-school behaviour problems which could be attributed to deafness. Denmark (1981) relates this finding directly to the commonly found problem of frustration, and this is a view with which most people would agree. Meadow (1980) found that 69 per cent of parents of normal 4-year-olds deprived their children of sweets or television as punishment, while only 5 per cent of parents of deaf children did. Presumably they were unable to explain the purpose of the deprivation and to enforce the deprivation would provoke tantrums and bad behaviour arising from the frustration caused. In these circumstances the gap in communication is large and the pressure on the parents, both social and psychological, is immense.

Nevertheless, the majority of deaf children develop cognitively, and have capabilities similar to other children of their chronological age. They are perceptive, physically able and active, and as capable of dealing with the routines of the household as any other child. Their non-verbal intelligence is normal or near-normal (Vernon, 1967; Kyle, 1980b). They are able to process the information in the world around them and do interact with people at some level. Their cognitive potential is there and their basis for *language* is related to this, but it is not clear as to which language they are attaching their cognition. They are likely to be 'learners' of sign language, even if this is initially like a gestural system. The sign language which is eventually acquired might have been available for exploitation within the family much earlier.

It is clear from this brief examination of some features of the deaf child's language environment and the problems arising from it that there is a constantly repeated finding: relative to hearing norms deaf children are socially and emotionally immature, are frustrated, create behavioural difficulties for those around them and will continue to do so. There are a number of avenues of interpretation, however. The first is the traditional one: these are children failing in acquisition of spoken language (society's language) and, as a result or at the same time, their reception of society's behaviour patterns is faulty. The result is almost inevitable and, despite the effect of this behaviour on the family the method of education is claimed to be worthwhile since some speech will be acquired. A second view is that deaf children are being deprived of the chance of language by presenting them only with spoken language *via* speech, and as a result the values of society are not accessible or acceptable to them. The need is clearly for greater communication between parents and children.

Neither of these views tackles the central issue. In the past our views have been ethnocentric in their treatment of language, i.e. there has been acceptance only of English as a full and native language of deaf children. Deaf children are failures or potential failures in this key to society. The fact that their emotional development also suffers, and that their behaviour becomes deviant, has been seen as a problem of deafness. But this behavioural deviance is also a deviance from deaf society as well – it is not a characteristic of deafness as such. The extension of the period of time in which the children have access to neither a usable language nor a usable behaviour code seems set to increase the likelihood that they will be acceptable to neither deaf nor hearing society. Erting's (1982) and Lawson's (1981) claim that deaf society should be treated as an ethnic group, seems to us crucial to the understanding of the language and behaviour of deaf children. Deaf children are not the extreme of a continuum of hearing loss, somehow in danger of toppling over the edge into a sub-society, and who, unless by the struggle to preserve their hearing-like capacities, will be confined to a life of unending frustration and confusion. The society of deaf people, as we saw in chapter 1, is a structured and effective group within society as a whole, not divorced from it. The maintenance in deaf children of the condition of uncertainty as to their status is probably what is most damaging to their self-image and maturity. This is much more a question of attitude than of diagnosis, and it is perhaps what is most different in the family of deaf children with deaf parents. The question of acceptance of deaf people within society as a whole by virtue of their own cultural identity is a major issue in Freeman, Carbin and Boese's (1981) discussion. It is not a simple problem, but it is a key one underlying our interpretations of deaf children who 'fail', and it is one which does need to be tackled throughout our dealings with deaf people, sooner or later.

The clearest way into the understanding of language potential in deaf children is through the study of those with deaf parents. Although it is a relatively new field of interest it provides essential information on a subgroup of the deaf population with normal language and behavioural development.

Sign language development

Although there has been consistent concern for spoken language and speech development in deaf children, it is only in the last ten to twelve years that systematic studies of sign language development have been reported in any quantity. This can be explained partly by the sudden post-Chomsky explosion in child language research in general, and it should be pointed out that we have not yet developed adequate descriptions of language development in hearing children. The spoken language work has variously concentrated on the 'reaching of stages of development', the increasing 'mean length of utterance (MLU)', the 'grammaticality' of utterances (looking for some language generation system within the child by examination of such things as over-generalisation), and most recently on 'conversational' or 'discourse' analysis (where the model of the child's speech is expressed in the interaction between speakers). The sign language work and research on language development in deaf children has been influenced by these trends to varying degrees, though it has tended to lag behind developments in child language research.

A particular myth that can be dispelled in passing is that deaf children learning sign language at an early age are given a cognitive advantage even over hearing children (Brill, 1969). Numerous studies measuring intelligence have supported this view. Karchmer, Trybus and Paquin (1978) reported non-verbal IQs of 107.8, and Sisco and Anderson (1980) of 106.7, i.e. above the average for hearing children, although the latter did not interpret this as an effect of early signing. There is, however, a whole series of environmental, etiological and even standardisation factors which might explain the advantage. When Conrad and Weiskrantz (1981) controlled these factors by looking only at children in certain positions in families with more than one deaf child, and matched subjects carefully to hearing controls, the differences were no longer significant. In effect, a deaf child of deaf parents does not have a higher average IQ than either hearing children or deaf children of hearing parents, and therefore we cannot support the view that early signing itself, or even the environmental factors associated with early signing, produce better intelligence levels.

In terms of actual research on the emergence of language in the early period, there are surprisingly few studies of deaf children learning sign language as a first language, considering how crucial the first 18 months are thought to be for hearing children. Some of the findings in these studies are summarised in table 4.2. Only Maestas y Moores (1980) actually studied recordings of infants and only considered the language context set by parents. Generally her children were still too young to be signing, but it is apparent from her description that 'motherese' was being used and deliberate shaping of signing was found. 'Motherese' is a term first used by Catherine Snow (1972) to refer to the alterations in language use found in mothers' conversation with young children — in other words, mothers do not address children in the same way they address other adults. These modifications include simplification of syntax, altered pitch and exaggerated intonation. As the child's language develops the motherese alters, until eventually it becomes like adult–adult speech again. Maestas y Moores particularly noted how kinaesthetic information was provided to the child, both directly by the parent signing on the child's body, and by having the child in contact (e.g on the lap) while signing to another person. It is also remarkable from her data to what extent a given sign varied in form, since it could be perceived from a whole range of different perspectives by the child.

Bonvillian, Orlansky and Novak (1983), McIntire (1977) and Schlesinger and Meadow (1972) give support to the view that signs develop earlier than spoken language. Their comparisons of children (although only three out of 13 seem to have been deaf) with Nelson's (1973) hearing norms indicate significantly accelerated growth of sign language. Bonvillian, Orlansky and Novak's (1983) group had first signs at 8.6 months as compared to 11–14 months for children learning to speak, and two-sign combinations at 17 months in comparison to 18–21 months in speaking children. The differences are significant, though the representativeness of the population cannot be gauged till the children are older. A key finding, however, was that children learning to sign were beginning the process in stages III and IV of Piaget's sensorimotor period, whereas speaking usually only begins in stage VI. Schlesinger and Meadow (1972) support this by claiming sign combinations at 14 months and 100-word vocabularies at a time when hearing children have only 50-word vocabularies.

Caselli (1983) points out that this sort of comparison is not really valid unless we look at the development of gesture in hearing-speaking children as well. Her conclusions are that early deictic gestures are the first stage (i.e. pointing or otherwise indicating objects or people) in both deaf-signing and hearing-speaking children. This is then followed by the development of signs or referential gestures and words. Although Bonvillian, Orlansky and Novak (1983) relate sign combination to vocabulary size, explaining an earlier achievement in signers, Caselli (1983) claims that two-sign/word combinations occur at around the same period of 18 months in both hearing and deaf children.

The major problems with claims about relatively early acquisition of sign language as compared with the acquisition of spoken language lies with the interpretation of data. Two factors affect this. The first is the degree of interpretation of a child's behaviour as meaningful; the second is the relative discontinuity between gesture and spoken language development in hearing children in contrast to what appears to be a relative continuity in the development of gesture and sign language.

To address the first problem we can look at the extent to which adults interpret as words sounds produced by a hearing child. A common example is a hearing child's first one or two words *mama, baba, dada*. It is clear that these

Table 4.2. *Early language development studies, 0–2 years*

Researchers	No. of target children	Age (months)	Deafness		Data	Type of signing	Comments
			Parents	Child			
Maestas y Moores (1980)	7	0–16	Deaf (not clear if both were)	Some hearing, some deaf (?)	Video-recordings of interaction with parent(s) in home activities	ASL (mainly?)	Mainly deals with 'parentese' – adult's ASL fitted to deaf infants. Recorded fingerspelling to baby at 25 days. Signing while on lap. It is clear that sign language 'input' is just as diverse as spoken language input for hearing children
Bonvillian, Orlansky and Novak (1983)	11	7–	Deaf but one child had hearing father	10 hearing 1 deaf	Written and video-recordings every 6 weeks for 16 months; motor and sensori-motor skills test	ASL at home but English with relatives and neighbours	First sign at average age of 8.6 months (children produce speech at 11–14 months); 10 signs at 13.2 months (15.1 months); first combination of signs at 17 months (18–21 months). First signs usually occur in Piagetian stages III or IV, whereas for speakers it is usually in stage VI. Conclusions on accelerated growth

Study	N	Age range (months)	Child	Parents	Data	ASL?	Findings
McIntire (1977)	1	13–21	'Hearing-impaired'	'Borderline hearing loss'	Video-recordings of 4 play sessions: 20–40 minutes	ASL?	Found 85 signs at 13 months, 200+ signs at 21 months. Two-sign utterances at 10 months, question of handshapes and substitutions allows claims on the similarity of phonology acquisition in ASL and English
Schlesinger and Meadow (1972)	1	8–22	Deaf	Deaf	Video-recordings	English and ASL	First signs at 10 months; 2 signs at 12 months; first combination at 14 months: BYE SLEEP. 117 signs at 19 months. Numerous examples of holophrastic use of signs
Caselli (1983)	4	8–22	Not specified	Deaf (but no loss specified)	Video-recordings at varying intervals; no length specified. Selected samples discussed	ASL, Italian Sign Language, but not specified for parents	Lack of descriptive data weaken conclusions. Shows early emergence of deictic gesture in both deaf and hearing; followed by signs or referential gestures and words; two-sign/word combinations always around the same period — 18 months

sounds begin as babble which adults seize upon as meaningful (it is no coincidence that the words in many languages for *father* and *mother* resemble these early babbling sounds). Parents are unlikely to interpret sounds of hearing children as potential words unless they hear some phonetic resemblance to the words they represent. Parents are also unlikely to assign meaning to a large range of gestures produced by their hearing child. In contrast, deaf parents (and researchers) seek meaning in gesture rather than in vocalisation. Just as hearing parents of a hearing child give a rich interpretation of utterances which relate phonetically to real words, so too do deaf parents of a deaf child interpret gestures (and other body movements which resemble signs) as actual early signs. On the second question of continuity versus discontinuity in language development, some researchers have explained the earlier acquisition of signs as compared with words as a result of the relative continuity of sign language and gesture development in comparison with the discontinuity of gesture and spoken language development. In other words, a child (whether exposed to spoken language or sign language) develops gestures before language. If the child is learning a spoken language, then he must switch from communication in one channel to another, and this slows down his development, while a child learning a sign language need not make this channel switch. This would save time and so the child would develop language more quickly. The continuity–discontinuity issue cannot be easily resolved, but one important study (Petitto, 1983) suggests that the discontinuity between gesture and sign language may be much greater than has yet been believed.

This evidence concerns the deictic pronouns *I* and *you*. When a child learns these words in a spoken language, he must learn that their referents depend on role and not on any objective label. That is, a mother refers to a child by his name, this name is attached to the child, and not to who is being addressed. It has been frequently noted that children make errors in the use of the pronouns *I* and *you*, producing utterances such as 'Mummy give you' meaning 'Mummy give me' etc. Parents often seem to avoid this referential problem by addressing children by their names: 'Shall Mummy put Johnny's sock on?' Hearing children never make errors however in the use of pointing gestures for 'you' and 'me', since the gesture (unlike the word) must clearly indicate who is being referred to. We would expect children acquiring a sign language to have no problems with the acquisition of 'I' and 'you', since the gestures and the signs are the same. Petitto, however, has studied a deaf child learning ASL who went through the same errors as hearing children, i.e. she used the term YOU when she meant ME.

in one instance the child used YOU to indicate herself while signing to mother that she (the child) wanted to eat. Because the actual form of the child's utterance carried the meaning that *mother* should eat, mother responded by telling the child that she (mother) was not hungry and would eat later. The child, appearing disturbed over the misunderstanding, dragged her food-bag from across the room to mother's feet and repeated the sign EAT. (Petitto, 1983: 4)

This finding is important for two reasons. Firstly, it provides support for regarding sign languages as linguistic systems of the same order as spoken languages, rather than as some sort of codified gesture system. Secondly, and perhaps more importantly, it provides us with information about the nature of language itself.

There have been two major models of language development in children. The psychological model sees language as part of the child's general cognitive capacity, with its development coming from general cognitive development, rather than from some specific linguistic capacity. Language, in this view, is built up from interaction with the environment and general forms of knowledge. In the linguistic model, language emerges from specific linguistic capacities in the brain. Language, in this model, is 'qualitatively distinct' from other knowledge.

In the first model, language acquisition should derive directly from prelinguistic communication, with no discontinuities. If, on the other hand, language is separate and distinct from other types of knowledge, we should expect discontinuities and/or language development not always correlated with stages of cognitive development. Both Bonvillian, Orlansky and Novak (1983) and Petitto (1983) provide this evidence. In this way, sign language development research can make enormous contributions to our understanding of cognition generally.

Sign language research also helps illustrate issues about language development in general. One question which has concerned philosphers as well as linguists and psychologists is to what extent the development of a language depends on the kind of input. Clearly deaf children of hearing parents who only communicate orally will be receiving only restricted input or none at all. The question is whether these children can develop language, in this case sign language, without adult input. Goldin-Meadow (1977) and Feldman, Goldin-Meadow and Gleitman (1978) report development of sign language in children not exposed to it by their parents. This evidence supports the view that language is created independently of adult models. Mohay (1983) also reports this spontaneous emergence of language, including the development of two-sign combinations. She suggests that in the absence of an adult model language development occurs but is delayed. She also suggests separate development of semantic and phonological processes, with the first internally generated by the child independently of language input, and the second requiring adult modelling.

These findings have been criticised by Volterra (1983) in an interesting study

Table 4.3. *Middle period of language development – those with deaf parents*

Researchers	No. of target children	Age (months)	Deafness Parents	Deafness Child	Data	Type of signing input	Comments
Volterra (1983)	1	24–30	Deaf	Deaf	Diary accounts and periodic video-recordings	Not specified	Showed both deaf and hearing have deictic *and* referential gestures. The main finding is that only the deaf child combined two referential gestures. When the hearing children reached the stage of combining two symbolic units they did so with words
Schlesinger and Meadow (1972)	1	31–65	Deaf	Deaf	Video-recordings monthly	Signs, finger-spelling and voice	A study of pivot words such as 'there x' showing the emergence of similar grammatical processes in sign, but questioning the pivot concept
Fischer (1973a)	2	24–48	Deaf	Deaf		Sign	Her claims are far in advance of Ellenberger and Steyaert (1978), such that the children were using location and direction at 42 months

Study	N	Age (months)	Mother	Child	Method	Language	Notes
Hoffmeister and Moores (1973)	1	25–28	Mother deaf	Deaf	Eight 30-minute video-recordings at a maximum of one month intervals	Sign	Study of pointing. Conclude that pointing glossed as THIS or THAT is different from hearing child's pointing gesture. Pointing is initial stage of ASL acquisition
Erting (1982)	3	43–49	4 deaf, 2 hearing	2 deaf, 1 hard-of-hearing	Video-recordings of food sharing and free play analysed	Varied, ASL, MCE	All parents college-trained and concerned that MCE (manually coded English) was available. Teacher recorded as well. Language results indicate complex varying interaction of child with different adults. Percentages of MCE and ASL varied with more ASL features in play
Ellenberger and Steyaert (1978)	1	43–71	Deaf	Deaf	Video-recordings of spontaneous conversation at home with mother	ASL	Important since it shows the role of pantomime in development; at 43 months it is pronounced, and modulation appears by 54 months, with the structuring of space at 61–71 months. Spatial modulation late in acquisition

Table 4.4. *Middle period of language development — those with hearing parents*

Researchers	No. of target children	Age (months)	Deafness		Data	Type of signing input	Comments
			Parents	Child			
Goldin-Meadow (1977)	6	17–54	Hearing	31–100dB	Video-recordings at varying intervals (½ month–11 months) and varying in number over children (2–11). 1–2 hour sessions	None; only oral method used	Two had older deaf siblings but it is claimed they did not know any signs
Mohay (1982)	2	18–38	Hearing	Deaf	30-minute video-recordings monthly, mainly of informal play activities with mother	None; oral method only	Identifiable gestural lexicon develops which is smaller than spoken lexicon. Comparable in semantic use to hearing children at same stage, but not at same age, i.e. significantly delayed

Study	N	Parent hearing status	Child hearing status	Data collection	Communication mode	Findings
Schlesinger (1978)	3	Hearing	Deaf	Video-recordings from 7–17 hours per child	Bimodal with speech	Children learn appropriate modulation by age 6
Schlesinger and Meadow (1972)	2	Hearing	Deaf	Video-recordings monthly	Signs, finger-spelling and voice. One used SEE	Clear indication of normal language growth reaching sophisticated levels. As sign production improves, so does speech
Collins-Ahlgren (1975)	2	1 deaf, 1 hearing	Profoundly deaf	Parents and author periodically recorded the girls' expressive language	Total Communication	Confirms natural stages of development as seen in Schlesinger and Meadow. Concludes from a case grammar analysis that deaf expressive language in sign equivalent to hearing in speech

of gesture development in both hearing children of hearing parents (children not exposed to an adult gesture model) and a deaf child of deaf parents (exposed to a sign language model). All children in her study developed referential gestures (gestures naming objects or actions, such as gestures for TELEPHONE, DRINK, etc.) and deictic gestures (pointing). All children also progressed to combining two deictic gestures (THERE THAT) and deictic and referential gestures (THAT DRINK), but only the child exposed to an adult model of sign language developed utterances consisting of two referential gestures (FISH EAT). Volterra analysed Goldin-Meadow's data according to this scheme (deictic, referential, deictic + deictic, deictic + referential, referential + referential) and claims that none of the children in Goldin-Meadow's study show combinations of two referential gestures. Only the child exposed to a sign language input takes this essential step towards development of language. Volterra concludes that since children both exposed and not exposed to adult models of sign can use symbolic gestures and combinations of gestures to communicate, then these do not depend on exposure to a linguistic model. What does depend on exposure to a linguistic model is the ability to combine symbols (referential gestures) with each other. This indicates that the symbolic capacity (meaning) and combination capacity (syntax) are separate, that both are necessary to the development of language, and that the ability to use both depends on adult input.

Other studies on the development of a sign language have looked for other stages parallel to those found in children learning a spoken language, drawing on research which examins errors in child language as revealing the process of construction of linguistic rules. Bellugi and Klima (1972) reported generalisation and over-generalisation of rules in children learning sign language (similar to errors such as *goed* or *feetses* in children learning English). In terms of the acquisition of 'phonological' features, children learning a sign language showed errors in handshape similar to pronunciation errors in hearing children learning a spoken language, with simplification of form and reduction of contrast. Fischer (1973a) and Ellenberger and Steyaert (1978) both examined the development of localisation and directionality in ASL (see chapter 7), although they differ about the age at which these structures are learnt.

Most studies have focused on the period from 2 to 5 years, the time when hearing children consolidate their spoken language acquisition and when the syntactic structures of a language are learned. Tables 4.3 and 4.4 provide a brief summary of some of the studies of this period.

The further studies in this area generally confirm the possibilities of English-based signing codes such as signed English, Paget-Gorman and others. Children could be seen to acquire English-based features such as '-ing' (Schlesinger and

Table 4.5. *Later period of language development – parents and school effects*

Researchers	No. of target children	Age (months)	Deafness Parents	Deafness Child	Data	Type of signing input	Comments
Tervoort (1961)	48	84–144	School	Deaf	Series of 10-minute films of pairs in conversation	None: oral only but peer communication in 'gesture'	Description of how gesture becomes formalised sign as it moves from situation-bound towards 'arbitrary'
Hoemann and Lucafo (1980)	1	84	Deaf	Deaf	One 25-minute studio interview	ASL	A detailed analysis of a child model of ASL. It illustrates the richness of content and sophistication of grammar of ASL
Sorensen and Hansen (1976)	44	72–180	Mixed	Deaf	Video-recordings of communication tasks	Signed Danish	Shows the effects of sign language features such as localisation as contributors to DSL grammar. Provides a notation system
Livingston (1983)	6	72–196	Hearing	Deaf	Video-recordings of spontaneous sign language over a period of 15 months	Signed English	Shows emergence of ASL in Signed English environment without adult model. Detailed analysis of proposed developmental levels of ASL acquisition

Meadow, 1972). The incorporation of English features into signing has been reported a number of times, and is taken as support for the view that Manually Coded English (MCE) does form a useful alternative, especially for hearing parents. It is a key question to be tackled in chapter 12, and it is only important to point out here that we are as yet unclear about how extensively the MCE features are retained in deaf–deaf interaction and how constructively they might be used cognitively.

Later studies of development are indicative of the range of grammatical processes found in young children: table 4.5 provides a summary. Hoemann and Lucafo's (1980) model of a 7-year-old boy's sophisticated ASL serves to highlight the effectiveness of ASL communication and its range. The boy exhibits features of modulation which are typical of adult discourse and the language development process can be seen to be just as effective in sign as in speech. Sorensen and Hansen (1976) describe sign order in Danish Sign Language and show the development of classifiers and simultaneity in a group of children. Even in the oral school situation, Tervoort (1961) was able to identify sign language features in deaf children's interaction.

It is rather difficult to provide a useful summary of the series of studies mentioned here, which in any case must be seen as only a beginning. We have not yet 'caught up' with child language research in the examination of discourse features and this may prove to be the most important future development.

Child language research has changed focus in the past ten years; from being primarily orientated towards syntactic development it now has a new orientation towards the importance of interaction and communication strategy. We discussed earlier in this chapter the psychological and linguistic approaches to language development. Here we would like to introduce an approach with a social and pragmatic basis. The importance of the social bases of meaning comes both from observations of the child's own utterances and those of his mother. Halliday (1975) has observed that the very earliest meaningful vocalisations of a child relate to the purposes and attitudes the child wishes to convey: in other words, they are concerned with the initiation and maintenance of social interaction. Griffiths (1979) notes that hearing children use gesture initially to indicate a desired or interesting object, and later use the names of objects for a similar function (see the discussion of Volterra's work earlier in this chapter). Little research has been undertaken, in studies of deaf children, on the topics introduced, their joint negotiation and development, and the adult and child contributions to such developments. Clearly, research into the development of linguistic interaction in deaf children, both those with hearing parents and those with deaf parents, is needed, particularly as researchers such as Gregory and

Mogford (1981) and Wood (1981) have observed abnormal conversational structure with deaf children.

Although a great deal of research on language development in deaf children remains to be done, a number of clear points have emerged so far which we can summarise:

1. The development of language can only occur where children are provided with input which they can perceive and where the adult and child are joint partners in creating communication.
2. The development of gesture and the development of sign language are discontinuous in the same way that gesture and spoken language development are.
3. In learning a language, whether spoken or signed, children must be regarded as active participants in generating the rules of the language. This can be seen in the types of errors they produce.
4. The development of articulatory skill and the development of a language are separate areas.

5. The building blocks of sign language

When we think about spoken language we see it as an 'auditory-vocal' system. Production and understanding take place using the articulators of the vocal organs to produce the language: tongue, teeth, lips, breath; and the ears and their perception structure to receive the language. When we think about sign language we have in the past seen it as a visual-manual system: production takes place using the hands, while the eyes receive the language. While both these observations are partly true, there is a great deal more to the use of both spoken and sign language than this. We will briefly discuss a linguist's view of the building blocks of spoken language, and then go on to look at the building blocks of sign language.

Spoken language elements

The aims of a linguist's description of a language are to establish the elements found in that language and the rules that affect the use of those elements. For spoken languages we have to look at the entire range of sounds which the human vocal apparatus can produce, and separate out coughs, whistles and so on, from potential speech sounds. Then for each language we must see which speech sounds are used and how they combine. If we compare English and German, for example, we find that some sounds in German do not occur in English, some sounds that occur in English do not occur in German, and that some combinations of sounds can only occur in one or the other language. In German, for example, we find the sound 'ch' (as in Scottish *loch*). This sound does not occur in English. On the other hand, the sound 'th' (as in *thing*) occurs in English but not in German. The sounds 'sh', 'l' and 'r' occur in both languages, but while we can have 'sh' and 'r' combined in English (*shriek, shred*) we cannot have 'sh' and 'l' combined. In German, however, 'sh' and 'l' are a permissible combination (*Schlüssel*). Two other observations can be made: firstly, two sounds which we think of as the same in a language (often because we look at the spelling rather than listen to the sound) can be very different. The sounds 'k' represented by the letters *k* and *c* in the English words *keel* and *cool* are actually different: the first is produced with the front of the tongue placed at the front of the palate, the second is produced with the front of the tongue at the back of the palate. The two are different because they precede different vowels, in other words their form is 'conditioned' by the context in which they appear. This is a concept we shall return to later when discussing the elements of sign language. The second observation we make is that just as the two sounds 'k' are different in *keel* and *cool*, so two sounds which appear the same may be articulated differently in different spoken languages. For example, the English sound 't' in *table* is produced by placing the area of the tongue just behind the tip against the bottom of the alveolar ridge, (the ridge behind the upper front teeth) while the 't' in the French word *table* is produced by placing the same area of the tongue against the backs of the upper front teeth, in front of the ridge. This difference, though slight, accounts for noticeable features of the French accent in English and *vice versa*.

When we look at languages less similar to English than French and German, we find more elements in use that are not found in English: for example, several African languages, such as Xhosa, make use of what are called 'clicks' as sound elements. The sound of one kind of click is best represented by *tsk*, *tsk*, used in English 'tut-tutting'. But there are no *words* in English which use that sound. Therefore clicks are not part of the English sound system but they are part of the Xhosa sound system. Another feature, found primarily in languages such as Chinese, are 'tones'. In a tonal language the pitch of voice on a single word changes the meaning of that word. While in English the pitch on a sentence may indicate a statement, question, or sarcastic comment, in tonal languages each word bears a fixed intonation. In Chinese, for example, the word *ma* has the following meanings:

high level tone	ma̅	mother
high rising tone	ma̗	hemp
low rising tone	m̃a̗	horse
low falling tone	m̃a̅	scold

It is very important to look at a number of different languages in order to get an idea of the range of structures which play a part. The same is true of sign languages. We must begin by examining the articulators used.

Sign language elements

To a first time observer of sign language, the most salient feature is the use of the hands and arms. Other articulators, however, also play a part in sign language structure, and these will be discussed in this and the following chapters.

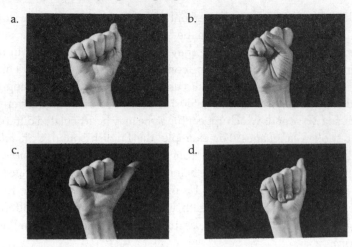

Fig. 5.1

Just as there are sounds we can make which are not part of any spoken language system, so too there are movements we can make which are not part of any sign language system. While all the words of a spoken language are composed of sounds we can make, not all sounds we can make are parts of words. While all signs are gestures, not all gestures are signs. Our aim, therefore is to specify which movements can be used in sign language. Just as tongue, teeth, lips, and so on are used in articulating spoken languages, the following articulators are used in sign language: left and right hands and arms, parts of the body and the face.

Hands

We have mentioned left and right hands, because signers show evidence of handedness: signs can be articulated with one hand or two, and this is relatively consistent for individual signers. The majority of signers are right-handed, but circumstances such as holding something in the right hand will result in a shift to the left hand, and there is no evidence that left-handedness causes problems of understanding. When we use the terms 'right' and 'left' in this and the following chapters, this should be understood as referring to dominant and non-dominant hand respectively; in a left- handed signer the left hand would be dominant and right hand non-dominant.

The hands are capable of assuming a large number of configurations, ranging from tightly closed fist to widely spread extended fingers. As we mentioned above, when referring to different versions of the sound 'k' which do not differ in meaning but appear in different contexts, hand configurations which are similar in appearance may actually differ slightly: fig 5.1 shows four different fist configurations.

Different sign languages use different hand configurations. For example, the hand configuration illustrated as fig 5.2a is not found in BSL, although it occurs in ASL. The hand configuration illustrated as fig 5.2b occurs in BSL but not in ASL.

Spoken languages have differing numbers of elements. Hawaiian, for example, has six consonants and six vowels, while English has at least 24 consonants and 17 vowels. Similarly, different sign languages have differing numbers of hand configurations. ASL has been described as having 19 different hand configurations; one count for BSL gives 23. These counts do not include, of course, contrasts such as those shown in fig 5.1.

Linguists researching spoken languages have also looked at similarities and differences between sounds, rather than just listing them individually. For example, the sounds 'g', 'p', 'b' have in common the feature of release of stopped-up breath; 'm', 'n' and 'ng' (the sound in *sing*) have in common the feature of nasality; the sounds 'p', 't', and 'k' have a common feature of voicelessness. We can therefore describe the sound 'b' as + stop, − nasal, + voice; and 'n' as − stop, + nasal, + voice. Linguists researching sign language have also explored the construction of these sorts of features for hand configurations, suggesting such features as ± compact (extension or non-extension of fingers), ± spread (spreading apart or closeness of fingers), ± concave (bending or straightening of the finger joints). The hand configuration in fig. 5.1a could be described as + compact, − spread, + concave. In the next chapter we will discuss sign formation and claims about the most basic hand configurations in different sign languages, based on this sort of feature analysis.

a.  b.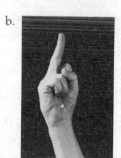

Fig. 5.2

Fig. 5.3   The signing space.

Parts of the body

As well as hands in particular configurations, sign languages use other parts of the body as articulators. The *location* of a hand configuration plays an important part; this can be thought of as a parallel to the location of the tongue in spoken language. Although gestures and mime can involve all parts of the body (for example, to indicate a shoelace one would presumably point directly to it; to mime tying a shoelace, one would bend down and enact the concept), sign languages use a far more limited space. Sign language is restricted to the space indicated in fig. 5.3: that is, a region bounded by the top of the head, the back, the space extending to elbow width on the sides, and to the hips.

Different points on the body may serve as locations for hand configurations: the brow, the abdomen, the shoulders etc. These points are not evenly distributed across the body, however. In the *Dictionary of American Sign Language* (Stokoe, Casterline and Croneberg, 1965), five points on the face are described but only two positions, neck and trunk, for the rest of the body (excluding the arms and hands). For BSL, nine locations on the face have been suggested and four on the neck and trunk (Brennan, Colville and Lawson, 1980). As the face is so much smaller an area than the trunk one must ask why so many points are used on the face and so few on the trunk. A number of researchers have addressed themselves to this question. Siple (1978) has observed that signers do not look at each others' hands but at each others' faces. Since visual acuity is greatest at the point of focus, one would expect that it would be easier to see contrasts in location in that area than in locations far from the point of focus. The actual space used (fig. 5.3) supports this claim, as signs are not located at a great distance from the face. So perceptual constraints affect the structure of sign language.

Other articulators

As well as hands in particular configurations and locations, other articulators are also found, although their role at the level of individual signs is less important than their role at the grammatical level. The head is involved as an articulator in some signs: that is, instead of serving as a static location for the hand it moves as part of the sign: SLEEP, for example, is articulated by bending the head towards the articulating hand. In signs such as HIKE and SCOTLAND the hands remain still while the shoulders and elbows move. In other signs the cheeks and mouth are active articulators: BALLOON requires puffed cheeks; SOUR uses drawn-in cheeks and puckered lips. Certain signs require specific mouth patterns or movements unrelated to English mouth patterns. It has been reported that some signs in ASL are articulated solely with the mouth, but no signs in BSL have yet been found of that type. Some signs however, such as SUCCESS, are obligatorily made with specific mouth patterns. The eyes and brows are also used to convey attitude and to refer to objects through size.

Building words and signs

It was mentioned earlier (p. 82) that to describe the structure of a spoken language we need to know not only which elements appear in the language but what rules govern their combination. In the example given we saw that although the sounds 'sh' and 'l' appear in English, they cannot be combined as 'shl'. In spoken languages the order of elements, as much as the elements themselves, determines the meaning of a word; although *bag* and *gab* contain the same sounds, their order is crucial in determining meaning. In contrast to this characteristic of spoken languages, sign language words (signs) are made up of simultaneously combined elements. We can see this contrast if we compare the English word (*to*) *live* with the BSL sign ('TO) LIVE (fig. 5.4). The English word is composed of three sounds: 'l' is formed by touching the back of the upper teeth with the tip of the tongue; 'i' is a vowel formed in the front of the mouth at mid-height; 'v' is formed by touching the upper teeth with the lower lip and allowing voiced breath to pass through. These three sounds occur one after the other, although the actual pronunciation of the word (*to*) *live* is continuous. The BSL sign (TO) LIVE, is, in contrast, articulated in the following way: the right hand, all fingers extended and spread apart except for the middle finger which is bent at the middle joint, is placed at the upper right chest, middle fingertip touching the chest, other fingers extended to the left, and the hand moves up and down about one inch, middle fingertip grazing the chest. In the sign, as opposed to the word, all elements occur in the same instant: the hand configuration, the location

87

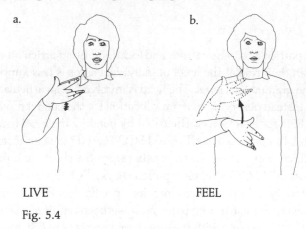

LIVE   FEEL

Fig. 5.4

of that configuration on the body, and the movement. The word *give* differs from (to) *live* because the first elements differ; *love* differs from (to) *live* because the second element is different. The BSL sign FEEL, on the other hand, differs from (TO) LIVE because the location of FEEL is in the centre of the chest rather than on the right side. So sign structure differs from word structure in how the elements are combined, as well as in the nature of the elements themselves.

Signs

William Stokoe was the first linguist to look at the structure of signs in the same way that linguists look at the structure of words. Before describing his analysis of sign structure, it will be useful to explain a few of the general concepts connected with sign and word structure. A 'word' in spoken language is the smallest *independent, meaningful* unit in a language; the sounds which comprise a word have no meaning in themselves. (There are some exceptions to this statement, which will be discussed below.) Other meaningful units may never occur independently. For example, if we compare the words *play* and *playing* we can see that *ing* never occurs as an independent unit in English, while *play* does. We therefore call meaningful units 'morphemes' whether or not they can occur independently, and reserve the term 'word' for independent forms only. English often strings morphemes together, as in *un-necess-ar-ily*, but there are words formed not by a linear addition of morphemes but by partial substitution, as in *ring : rang : rung, break : broke : broken*, or even by complete substitution *be : am : was*. As with words in spoken language, sign language has signs which may be composed of one or more morphemes, and these may undergo the same sorts of changes mentioned above. As with words, the elements which combine to form a sign are generally meaningless in themselves.

Stokoe (1960) noted that in describing an ASL sign three kinds of information were needed to identify the sign and to distinguish it from other signs. These three kinds of information were: firstly, the location of the sign in relation to the body, which he called the Tab (short for Latin *tabula*); secondly, the handshape – the configuration of the hand or hands involved in articulating the sign, which he called the Dez (short for *designator*); and thirdly, the movement executed by hand or hands, which he called the Sig (short for *signation*). Other linguists (Friedman 1977; Battison 1978) have claimed that a fourth parameter is obligatory – the Ori – the spatial orientation of the hands in relation to each other and the rest of the body. Thus, to describe a sign one would need to specify the location, handshape, movement and orientation of that sign, and to describe a given sign language, one would need to identify the range of configurations within each of those categories. Different authors have suggested different numbers of significant configurations. Battison (1978) suggests that there are approximately 45 different handshapes, 28 different locations, and a dozen movements in ASL. Klima (1975) claims that there are 40 significant handshapes, 12 locations, 16 to 18 orientations, and 12 movements in ASL, while Stokoe identifies 19 hand configurations, 12 locations, and 24 movements.

The method used for describing significantly different elements involves identifying minimal pairs. A minimal pair consists of two signs or words which differ by just one element. For example, the words *pin* and *hin* form a minimal pair in English; on the other hand, if we pronounced the 'k' in *keel* with the 'k' sound of *cool* the word would sound odd but would not mean something different. The difference in pronunciation between the 'k' in *keel* and *cool* is contextually determined. When we describe sign languages we follow the same criteria. Although more than 19 different handshapes appear in ASL, a number of these are contextually determined variants. The same occurs in BSL: for

B   B̊

Fig. 5.5

example, although the flat hand, fingers extended and together sometimes occurs with thumb extension and sometimes without (fig. 5.5), this difference never results in a difference of meaning; there are no pairs of signs for which the extension of the thumb in a flat hand changes the meaning of a sign. We can therefore say that we have two variants and only one distinct hand configuration.

A change in one of the significant elements of handshape, location, orientation and movement results in a change of meaning. In fig. 5.6 we show some examples of minimal pairs in BSL. Fig. 5.6a shows the examples mentioned previously: LIVE and FEEL differ in *location*. Fig. 5.6b shows a pair of signs differing in handshape: TALK and MAKE: TALK has the hands in a fist with index finger extended; MAKE has fists with no extension. Fig. 5.6c shows a pair of signs differing in movement: TROUBLE is signed by tapping the back of the left hand with the fingertips of the right hand while BLUE is signed by stroking the back of the left hand with the fingertips of the right. Fig. 5.6d shows a pair of signs differing only in orientation: SALT is formed with the left palm facing up and right palm facing down, FEW with the right palm facing up and left palm facing down. When we look at signs in this way we are able to see them not simply as unanalysable gestures, but as composed of linguistic building blocks.

Notation

Later in this chapter there are lists of the elements which appear in BSL in each of the four categories of handshape, location, movement and orientation. When we set out to write a description of the signs of a sign language there are a number of possible ways to indicate how a sign is formed. We follow Stokoe in the basic form of the notation system. Some seek to notate signs using variations of dance notation (Eshkol-Wachmann notation), pictorial representation (Sutton movement writing) and alphabetical notation (Teuber). Esam (1981) contains an excellent summary of these notations. The basic BSL variety of Stokoe notation was developed jointly by a number of BSL researchers in 1979 and 1980 (Kyle, Woll and Carter, 1979; Brennan, Colville and Lawson, 1980). Two slightly differing systems are now in use, but the notation can be easily translated from one system to the other. The notation system which we will describe here differs somewhat from Stokoe's in its approach to the problems involved in notating the relationship between hands and in the way we notate signs derived from the British manual alphabet. We have used the judgement of native signers to identify minimal pairs, but the intention has not been solely to develop a description of elements which contrast, but rather to use the insight of native

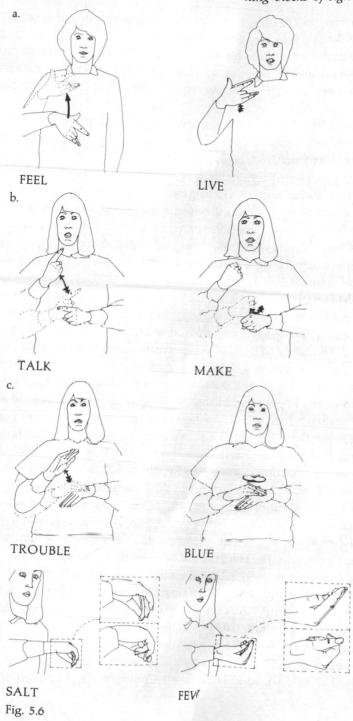

a.

FEEL   LIVE

b.

TALK   MAKE

c.

TROUBLE   BLUE

d.

SALT   FEW

Fig. 5.6

signers to develop a flexible, comprehensive notation system that can provide both very detailed and broader representation.

The elements of a sign are always notated in a particular order, and we can differentiate a number of types of signs (table 5.1). The convention that signs are glossed in upper-case letters is observed here and will be followed throughout the book.

Type 1 are those signs made with one hand only, articulated in free space without any body contact. Type 2 are one-handed signs which make contact with, or are in proximity to, a body part other than the left hand. Type 3 are two-handed signs with both hands in the same shape, active and performing identical or symmetrical action without touching each other or the body. Type 4 are signs where two hands with identical handshapes perform identical actions and contact each other. Type 5 are two-handed signs where both hands are active, in the same shape, perform identical actions and contact the body. Type 6 are two-handed signs where the right hand is active and left passive. They may have the same or different shapes.

The Tab (T) in the notation formulae in table 5.1 represents the location of the hand, either as a point or area on the body with which contact is made, or a point or area to which the hand is in proximity. The Dez (D) represents the shape of an active hand. The Sig (S) indicates the movement or movements which the hands undergo. Two orientation symbols are used for every active handshape. The first orientation (O_1) is the palm orientation. The second (O_2) gives the orientation of the fingers established by imagining the hand opened flat and notating the direction of the straightened fingers. A passive hand (in Type 6) is treated as a location (Tab) and receives a coding for palm orientation only.

One area that we have treated differently from Stokoe is the indication of point of contact in signs, more broadly, the question of how to show the relationship of hands in space. For ASL Stokoe used movement (Sig) symbols for both, placing the symbol after the two Dez symbols where the Sig symbol represented movement, and between the two Dez symbols where the Sig represented hand arrangement. An alternative, and the one which we have adopted, is to consider the relationship between the two hands in the same way as the relationship between a Dez and a body Tab. We have said that the Tab specifies the location of the sign either in neutral space (ø) in front of the body or in terms of the proximity of the Dez to a specific part of the body. But while Stokoe's notation specifies the part of the *body* involved, it does not treat the part of the *hand* involved. The solution devised (Carter 1980a) is to consider the distinctive parts of the hand which are in proximity to, or which contact, each other or the Tab as 'contacts'. The contact (Con) symbol is placed before the Tab

Table 5.1. *Sign types and notation*

Type 1. One hand only, articulated in neutral space, without any body contact.

FORMULA: T D o   o
                    1   2

(with superscript **s** above the second **o**)

EXAMPLE: WHICH

NOTATION: ØY ⌄ ⊥   (with superscript **z**)

T	=	∅	Must be Neutral Space
D	=	Y	Thumb and little finger extended
∩ 1	=	⌄	Palm faces down
o 2	=	⊥	Fingers point away from body (always coded as if fingers were extended)
ꜱ	=	z	Hand moves from side to side

Type 2. One hand only, articulated in contact with, or in proximity to, a body part other than the left hand.

FORMULA: T D o   o
                    1   2

(with superscript **c** above D and superscript **s** above the second **o**)

EXAMPLE: DEAF

NOTATION: ꜱ H ⟨ ∧   (with superscript symbols above H and ×)

T	=	ꜱ	Ear
c	=	✳	Fingertips
D	=	H	Index and middle fingers extended and together
o 1	=	⟨	Palm faces leftwards
o 2	=	∧	Fingers point up
ꜱ	=	×	Fingertips touch ear

The building blocks of sign language

Type 3. In neutral space, both hands active, identical and performing identical or symmetrical action without touching each other

FORMULA: T D o   o   D o   o ^{s}
            1 2   1 2

EXAMPLE: MILK

NOTATION: ⟨ N# ⟩ ∼ · [A]
           ØC › ⊥C ‹ ⊥

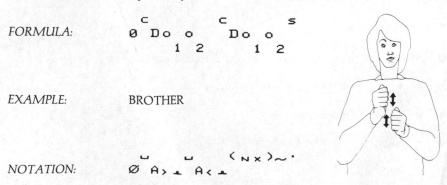

T = Ø		Must be neutral space
D = C		'C' shaped left hand
o/1 = ›		Left palm faces rightwards
o/2 = ⊥		Left-hand fingers point away from body
D = C		'C' shaped right hand
o/1 = ‹		Right palm faces leftwards
o/2 = ⊥		Righthand fingers point away from body
s =		Hands move up and down { N } simultaneously {⟨ ⟩}, closing
⟨ N# ⟩∼·[A]		{#}. They close to a fist [A] moving alternately { ∼ } and repeat {.}.

Type 4. In neutral space, both hands active, identical, and performing identical or symmetrical action in proximity to, or contact with each other.

FORMULA: ^{c} ^{c} ^{s}
          Ø D o o   D o o
             1 2   1 2

EXAMPLE: BROTHER

NOTATION: ⌣   ⌣ ⟨ N x ⟩∼·
          Ø A› ⊥ A‹ ⊥

94

T = ∅   Must be neutral space
c = ⊔   Left palm in contact
D = A   Left hand in fist
o₁ = >   Left palm faces rightwards

o₂ = ⊥   Left-hand fingers point away from body

c = ⊔   Right palm in contact
D = A   Right hand in fist
o₁ = <   Right palm faces leftwards

o₂ = ⊥   Right-hand fingers point away from body

s = ⟨ N × ⟩~ ·   Hands move up and down {N}, simultaneously {< >} touching {×}. They move alternately {~} and repeat {·}.

Type 5. Both hands active, identical and performing identical or symmetrical action in proximity to, or contact with, a part of the body.

FORMULA: T Do o   Do o   ᶜ ᶜ ˢ
              1 2   1 2

EXAMPLE: COW

NOTATION: ∩   Ɏ⊥∧   Ɏ⊥∧   ə× ə× ∅

T = ∩   Forehead
c = ə×   Left thumb in contact
D = Ɏ   Left thumb and little finger extended

o₁ = ⊥   Left palm faces away from the body

o₂ = ∧   Left-hand fingers point up

c = ə×   Right thumb in contact
D = Ɏ   Right thumb and little finger extended
o₁ = ⊥   Right palm faces away from body

o₂ = ∧   Right-hand fingers point up

s = ∅   No movement

Type 6. One hand active, one passive and serving as the location of the sign. Handshapes may or may not be the same.

FORMULA:

$$\begin{array}{ccc} c & c & s \\ T o & D o & o \\ 1 & 1 & 2 \end{array}$$

EXAMPLE: SHOE

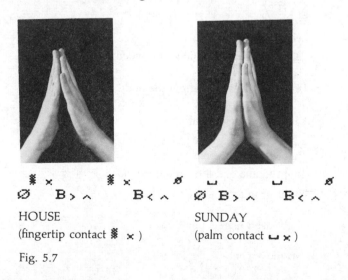

NOTATION:

c	=	⊔	Left palm in proximity
T	=	C	Passive left hand 'C' shaped
o₁	=	∧	Left palm faces up
c	=	⊔	Right palm in proximity
D	=	B	Right hand flat, fingers together
o₁	=	∨	Right palm faces down
o₂	=	<	Right-hand fingers point leftwards
s	=	(< ⊙)	Right hand moves left { < }, simultaneously { < > } entering { ⊙ } the curved space above the left palm

---

or Dez symbol depending on whether the hand is serving as the location of the sign or as the active articulator. We are in this way able to distinguish signs such as SUNDAY and HOUSE. (fig. 5.7).

HOUSE
(fingertip contact ⁑ ✕)

SUNDAY
(palm contact ⊔ ✕)

Fig. 5.7

Dez. The Dez symbols are derived from the American one-handed alphabet. These were suggested by Stokoe and we have followed his labels, although these handshapes are not found in the British two-handed alphabet. The Dez symbols used are shown in table 5.2.

Table 5.2. *Dez symbols as used in BSL notation*

A   Fist

A   Fist with thumb extended

A   Fist with 'hat'

B   Flat hand, fingers extended and together

B   Flat hand, thumb extended

B   Angled flat hand

97

B̈ Curved hand, thumb at side

B̂ Angled hand, thumb extended

C 'C' shaped hand

Ĉ Angled 'C' hand

E Fist with thumb alongside fingertips

Ë Clawed hand

F Thumb and index finger form circle, other fingers straight

F Thumb and index finger form circle, other fingers curved

G Index finger extended from fist

G Index finger extended and angled

H Index and middle fingers extended together

H Index and middle fingers extended and curved

H 'H' with thumb extended

I Little finger extended from fist

L Index and thumb extended at right angles

L Index finger extended and bent, thumb straight

O Circle with thumb and fingertips touching

O Angled 'O' hand

R Fist with index and middle fingers extended and crossed

'V' Fist with index and middle fingers extended and spread

V 'V' hand with index and middle fingers bent

W Index, middle and ring fingers extended and spread from fist

W 'W' hand with fingers bent

W 'W' hand with thumb extended

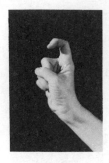

꘎ Fist with index finger extended
and bent

꘎ 'X' with thumb extended and bent
to form 'baby C'

꘎ 'X' with index finger and thumb
touching to form 'baby O'

꘎ Fist with index finger and thumb
extended and parallel

꘎ 'Baby O' but with thumb and
index finger straight, not bent

Ⴤ Fist with thumb and little finger
extended in opposite directions

Ⴤ Fist with index and little fingers
extended to form 'horns'

ᚽ Middle finger extended from fist

3̣ Thumb, index and middle fingers
extended from fist and spread

3̈ '3' hand with fingers bent

4 All fingers except thumb extended
and spread

5 All fingers extended and spread

5 All fingers extended, spread and loosely curved

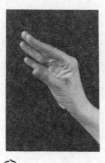

5 '5' hand with fingers angled

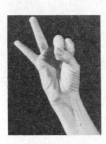

7 Fist with ring and little fingers extended and spread

8 Index, ring and little fingers extended and spread, thumb and middle finger form circle

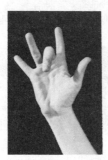

8 All fingers except middle extended and spread, middle finger bent towards palm

Tab. The symbols used for Tab have also been adopted from Stokoe, with some modifications. The symbols are based on a pictorial representation of the body part (table 5.3).

Table 5.3. *Tab symbols used in BSL notation*

▥	Back	ᗡ	Inside of wrist
[ ]	Area between shoulders and hips	ꐦ	Neutral space
> [ ]	Right hand on upper left trunk	○	Whole face
		̄∩	Top of head
> [ ]	Right hand on upper right trunk	∩	Forehead
[ ] < >	Hands on hips	⌂	Brow
[>]	Right hand on right side of chest	ʊ	Eyes
		⊔	Nose
[><]	Hands crossed on chest	⊃	Ear
⊔	Legs	⊐	Cheek
⌇	Shoulder and upper arm	∪	Lower face
♪	Elbow	⊽	Lips
✓	Forearm	⌣	Under chin
๙	Back of wrist	π	Neck

Table 5.4. *Ori symbols in BSL notation*

>	Right	⌣	Down
<	Left	⊤	To body
⌃	Up	⊥	Away from body

Ori. There are six Ori symbols used for both palm and finger orientation. These are designed to suggest the directions they represent (table 5.4).

Sig. These symbols are designed to suggest the movements they represent (table 5.5). Some of the same symbols as the Ori symbols are used. Where movements occur simultaneously they are bracketed together; where they occur sequentially they are simply listed. They appear as superscripts after the right-hand Dez.

Con. Con symbols are derived partly from the letter values of the British two-handed alphabet. They precede the Dez or hand Tab to which they refer (table 5.6).

The lexicon of a spoken or sign language may be thought of as consisting of all the words or signs and their variants which occur in that language. It must be remembered, of course, that the frequency of occurrence of an element in the lexicon, such as the handshape A, is not related to the frequency of occurrence of that element in use. For example, the sound found at the beginning of *the* only occurs at the beginning of a handful of English words, so in a count of its occurrence in the lexicon of English it would appear very infrequently. However, the words in which *th* appears in initial position, such as *the, these, this, that*, are very common words; the incidence of initial *th* in use is much higher than its frequency in the lexicon might suggest. Therefore, two sets of analyses must be done. Firstly the examination of the lexicon, and secondly, the description of a sample of text. Here we will restrict ourselves to the description of the lexicon.

Sign type frequency

Klima and Bellugi (1979) describe the percentage of signs in the ASL lexicon in which two active hands appear (Types 3,4 and 5), in which only one hand is used (Types 1 and 2) and in which one hand is actively used in conjunction with a

Table 5.5. *Sig symbols used in BSL notation*

✖ Touch	⊐ To and fro
· Repeat	Movement of wrists:
,, Prolong	⊲ Supinate
⁚ Rapid	▷ Pronate
	ω Twist
Movement of hands relative to body:	⌐ Flexion of wrist (nod)
⌃ Upwards	⌐ Extension of wrist
⌄ Downwards	⌐ Nodding involving flexion and extension
ᴎ Up and down	ᴆ Clockwise circle
⟨ Leftwards	ᴕ Anti-clockwise circle
⟩ Rightwards	Movement of fingers:
⤬ Side to side	⊐ Opening hand
⊤ Towards the body	⧘ Closing hand
⊥ Away from the body	⊰ Flicker
	⊘ No movement

ᵭ Crumbling with fingertips   ∼ Alternate

Movement of hands relative to each other: Other movement symbols:

ɔɕ Approach

[ ] Brackets enclose final handshape symbol where hand opens or closes

ɔɕ Interlock

⟨ ⟩ Brackets enclose simultaneous movements

⊙ Enter

╈ Hands cross each other or other body part

÷ Separate

ɕɔ Interchange

∷ Symbol separates components of two-part sign

---

passive hand (Type 6). We have classified the BSL lexicon in the same way; the two sets of figures are given in table 5.7.

We can see that the distribution of signs with two active hands, and of signs with one hand only, is rather different for BSL and ASL, although the proportion of signs with an active hand acting on a passive hand (Type 6) is the same for both sign languages. Why this may be so will be discussed below in the context of language change. If we examine the frequency of occurrence of particular handshapes (table 5.8) we can see that a relatively small number of handshapes dominate, four handshapes accounting for 50 per cent of all signs. These four are interesting for a number of reasons. They are mentioned in a number of papers as being the most basic and maximally contrasting handshapes. Battison (1978) describes them in terms of their geometrical properties: A as a maximally compact solid, B as a simple planar surface, 5 as the maximal extension and spreading of all projections, G as linear. They are among the first handshapes mastered by deaf children learning ASL (Boyes, 1973; McIntire, 1977) and BSL (Carter, 1980a). They are also found in all sign languages about which information is available.

These very common handshapes have also been described, in linguistic terms, as 'unmarked', that is, the most neutral handshapes. The concept of 'unmarked' handshape can also be seen by looking at the handshapes which occur in the left

Table 5.6. *Con symbols used in BSL notation*

Fingertips:	↳ Ring/little
ə Thumb	Groups of fingers:
℮ Index finger	⁂ Tips of fingers
i Middle finger	⁓ Lengths of fingers
o Ring finger	Edges of hand:
⊔ Little finger	L Thumb edge (from base of thumb to tip of index finger)
Base of fingers:	— Little finger edge
ə̲ Base of thumb	Surfaces of hand:
℮̲ Base of index finger	⊔ Palm
i̲ Base of middle finger	⌐ Back of hand
o̲ Base of ring finger	Wrist:
⊔̲ Base of little finger	⊣ Palm (inner) side
Between fingers:	⊢ Back of hand (outer) side
∣ Thumb/index	Elbow:
⁑ Index/middle	✢ Inner side of elbow
⊒ Middle/ring	✦ Outer side of elbow

Table 5.7. *Comparative proportions of sign types: ASL and BSL*

	ASL (Klima & Bellugi 1979) %	BSL %
Two active hands (Types 3, 4 and 5)	35	44
Only one hand in use (Types 1 and 2)	40	31
One active, one passive hand (Type 6)	25	25

Table 5.8. *Frequency of phonologically distinct handshapes in BSL*

Handshape as Dez	% of Lexicon
B	18
5	15
G	15
A	9
Ä	4
E , H , Â , B̂ , F , I	3
X , V , C , Ö	2
L , V , V̈ , L̈ , Ẍ	1
X , ö , Ë , Ḧ , W , ʌ , R	< 1

Table 5.9. *Handshape as Tab where Tab and Dez are different handshapes*

BSL	A	-	B	5	G	-	O	Å	B̈	I	V
ASL	A	S	B	5	G	C	O	-	-	-	-

hand in Type 6 signs. In just under half of the Type 6 signs active and passive hands have the same handshape (e.g. BLUE, MAKE); in the remaining Type 6 handshapes the passive and active hands differ in shape. However, not all possible handshapes which occur in active hands occur in these passive hands. In BSL only the following handshapes appear in a passive hand, where the shape differs from the active hand: A (fist), Å (fist with thumb extended), B (flat hand, fingers together), O (tips of all fingers touching), G (index extended), B̈ (curved with thumb alongside fingers), I (little finger extended), V (index and middle finger extended), and 5 (all fingers extended and spread). These nine handshapes occurring as Tabs where the active and passive hands differ are also among the most frequent handshapes generally. As table 5.8 indicated, five of the nine are the top five in frequency for the active hand as well. Table 5.9 lists these handshapes and those found in the left hand in ASL Type 6 signs.

If we compare the seven ASL handshapes with these nine, we see that C does not appear in the BSL list, but that Å, B̈, I and V do. Only seven passive handshapes (where they differ from the active handshape) appear in ASL: C (hand curved, thumb opposing) does not occur in BSL but B̈ (identical to C except that the thumb is alongside the fingers) is found. A and I, like C, are projections from a solid mass. Thus, although the specific handshapes found in a given sign language may differ from those found in another, the notion that there is a group of most basic handshapes is probably correct.

Constraint on sign form

We have seen that certain constraints appear on signs. For example, the restriction of signing to a small area, and the limitations on passive handshapes. Two other constraints have been proposed as universal restrictions on sign form. These limit the complexity of sign form and have been called the 'symmetry' and 'dominance' constraints. The dominance constraint has already been touched upon in the discussion of passive handshapes. It states:

The building blocks of sign language

If both hands in a two-handed sign do not share the same specification for handshape, then one hand must be passive, and the specification of the passive handshape is restricted to one of a small set of handshapes.

The symmetry constraint states:

If both hands of a sign move independently during its articulation, then both hands must be specified for the same location, the same handshape, the same movement (either simultaneous or alternating) and the specifications for orientation must be symmetrical or identical.

These two constraints clearly serve to limit the complexity of signs. Put very informally, if signs could have two completely different handshapes making two completely different movements in two different locations and with different orientations it would be much harder to understand a signer, and at the same time it would be much harder for a signer to articulate. In the next chapter we will discuss the relationship of sign form and meaning and will look at these constraints as they have operated over time.

6. The structure of signs

In this chapter we will be concerned with signs, their forms and their meanings. We will begin by discussing how signs are created and how they change, and then move on to mention the roles of fingerspelling and sign borrowing. The modifications which signs undergo will be discussed as a preamble to the chapters on morphology and grammar.

The creation of signs

New signs come into a sign language in a number of ways. Before discussing these ways, let us look at how new words are created in a spoken language. One source of words is onomatopoeia: the creation of words which suggest in their form the sound to which they refer. Words like *murmur, whisper, clang, jingle, fizzy, titter, crash* clearly resemble the sounds in the real world which they represent. Other words have resembled their referents in the past, but no longer do so today, for example *cow* (formerly *cu*); and words of onomatopoeic origin differ from language to language (English *whisper*, French *chuchoter*, German *flüstern*; or English *mumble*, Russian *myamlit*, Hewbrew *milmel*, French *marmotter*, German *mummeln*). Another source is sound symbolism. In sound symbolism, in contrast to onomatopoeia, words with related meanings share certain sounds but what is common to their meanings is not the sound of a referent but some other feature. Thus in English we have *blasted, blamed, bloody, blighted, blistering, blithering; glare, glow, glimmer, glitter, gleam*; or *bear, bairn, birth, bier, barrow, burden*. High front vowels like 'i' or 'ee' may stand for small size: *little, kid, thin, imp, pigmy, teeny-weeny*. This observation is important, because it is often thought that the words of spoken language have an arbitrary relationship with their referents, that the word *dog*, for instance, does not look, smell, or sound like a dog; but, as we can see, spoken languages use features such as onomatopoeia and sound symbolism a great deal. In sign languages, visual symbolism plays an important role in the creation of signs. Although this visual imagery is more immediately apparent and more widespread than in spoken language, the difference is likely to be of degree rather than kind.

113

BUTTERFLY   BIRD
Direct image   Metonymic image
Fig. 6.1

Visual symbolism occurs in signs as presentations and depictions. Signs often represent some feature of a referent, either in terms of visual properties or of an action. This can either be a 'picture' or 'icon' of the object or action itself (a 'direct' image) or of a part of, or something associated with, the referent (a 'metonymic' image). Fig. 6.1 shows two signs: one direct and one metonymic image.

Metonymic and direct images may be 'presented' or 'depicted'. In a presented image, the sign either enacts the referent or presents it. For example, the sign SMOKE (a cigarette) represents holding a cigarette in the fingers and moving it to and from the mouth. The sign HOT represents wiping a sweaty brow (fig. 6.2a). These two signs, therefore, present an action associated with the referent. Sometimes the action presented is not an overt action of the hands or body in real life, but is signed as an externalised action or state: for example, the sign LOOK presents an image by using two fingers to represent the path of the eye-gaze. Images can also be presented by pointing to, or grasping, the referent (NOSE, HAIR; see fig. 6.2b), or by indicating the general area of the referent (CLOTHES). To depict a referent, that is, to show the characteristic shape and/or movement of an object, the signer may either draw a picture of it (TABLE), or make the hand form a picture of the object itself (TREE; see fig. 6.2c).

Elements smaller than signs can also convey visual symbolism. Although in the previous chapter we suggested that the elements which combine to form signs generally carry no meanings in themselves, this is not strictly true. Just as the sounds 'gl' and 'br' suggest meanings in English, so too, elements in handshapes or locations may convey meanings. There are numerous signs in BSL which share some element and some meaning. For example, many signs which label 'emotional processes' are located on the trunk (FEEL, ANGRY, INTEREST) while many signs relating to cognitive processes are located on the temple (THINK, KNOW, UNDERSTAND). Another large group of signs share

114

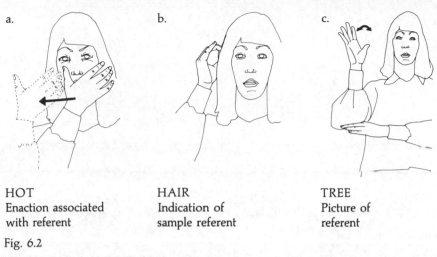

a.

HOT
Enaction associated
with referent

b.

HAIR
Indication of
sample referent

c.

TREE
Picture of
referent

Fig. 6.2

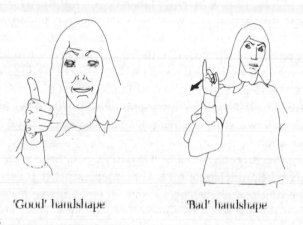

'Good' handshape

'Bad' handshape

Fig. 6.3

handshape and relate to attributes of 'goodness' or 'badness'. Pairs of signs such as GOOD:BAD, SUCCEED:FAIL, etc. differ only in handshape, the 'good' signs having Å, the 'bad' signs having I (fig. 6.3). Among the signs fitting into the group with Å handshape we have GOOD, BETTER, BEST, HEARING, SUCCEED, CORRECT, AGREE, APPROVE, FAVOUR, FRIEND, PROSPER, REAL, HEALTH, NICE, SWEET, VALUE, WISE. Among signs in the group with I there are, BAD, WORSE, WORST, FAIL, BLAME, WRONG, DIRTY, OBJECT, ARGUE, POISON, ILL, REJECT, TERRIBLE, TOO-LATE, UGLY, WICKED, SOUR, SORRY, ROTTEN. Clearly, the handshape element in these signs is conveying some generalised meaning.

Another group of signs with related meaning and the same handshape, are

115

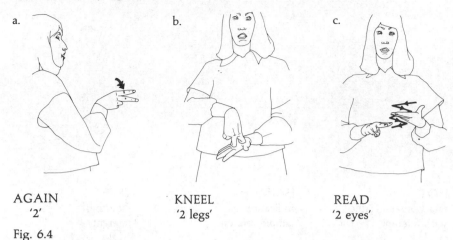

a. AGAIN
'2'

b. KNEEL
'2 legs'

c. READ
'2 eyes'

Fig. 6.4

those with the handshape V. Some examples are: BETWEEN, BLIND, DRUNK, EITHER, KNEEL, LOOK, READ, SUPERVISE, STAND, LIPREAD, VISION, WALK. While these may appear at first to have nothing in common, a closer look at the focus of these signs shows that in each sign some element of 'twoness' is being represented. In AGAIN, the right hand in a V handshape is shaken up and down (fig. 6.4a). In DRUNK, STAND, QUEUE, KNEEL, WALK, the V represents the two legs (Fig. 6.4b); in CARELESS, BLIND, LOOK, READ, SUPERVISE, LIPREAD, VISION, the V represents eye-gaze (fig. 6.4c). In a later section in this chapter we shall discuss how handshape can also convey grammatical information.

Metaphors in sign language can be viewed in two ways: either one can regard signs such as MAN as being metaphoric (i.e. a beard represents, or is a metaphor for, a man) or one can treat as metaphoric only those signs with meanings extended from their original scope to some other reference. There are many words in English whose original meaning has been extended. For example, we have a *head* of a state, a procession, a household, a river, or a cabbage. A person can *break down*, be *beside himself*, or be *all at sea*. While we can recognise some of these as metaphors, in other cases the original meaning has been lost and the extended meaning has become basic. For example, the word *ready* is derived from the verb *to ride*, and originally meant 'suitable for riding'. In sign languages similar processes occur. The sign PULL-THINGS-OFF-A-WALL has been extended to mean DECORATE-A-ROOM, even where this does not involve stripping wallpaper; the sign FULL has been extended to mean ENOUGH, and (with a specific facial expression) FED-UP (fig. 6.5).

New signs can be brought into the language through metaphor or visual symbolism. A sign which has appeared in recent years is TAPE-RECORDER.

FULL   ENOUGH   FED-UP

Fig. 6.5

The sign represents the moving reels of a recorder, but if we look carefully at the sign we can see that it is not a direct representation of the way tape reels move. Fig. 6.6a shows the form of the sign; fig. 6.6b shows an accurate representation of how reels move. The sign has a different movement from the mime of tape reels, the movements of left and right hands are mirror images of each other in the sign, while in the mime they move in a parallel way. The reason for this difference will be discussed in the next section. It is important, though, to remember two things. Firstly, that although the sign clearly involves visual symbolism it is not identical to a mime of the action. Secondly, the sign uses a feature of a tape-recorder to stand for the whole concept. The sign can be used to refer to cassette recorders, where the reels are not visible, and to video-recorders.

Sign change

In the last chapter we introduced the symmetry and dominance constraints. In this section we will introduce a third constraint and show how sign languages are continually changing. First, however, we will briefly introduce the notion of sign form. Most of the signs we introduced in the last section were simple in form, consisting of a handshape in a particular location. Some signs, which we will call complex signs, involve a change in handshape or location during their articulation. Handshape changes may involve opening or closing of the hand; location changes may involve changes, for example, from head to neutral space.

Compound signs are combinations of two signs (usually involving some modification in their articulation), often with a meaning different from either of the signs composing them. This occurs, of course, in spoken languages: we have examples of words such as *greenhouse, undertaker* and *blackboard* (note that it is

117

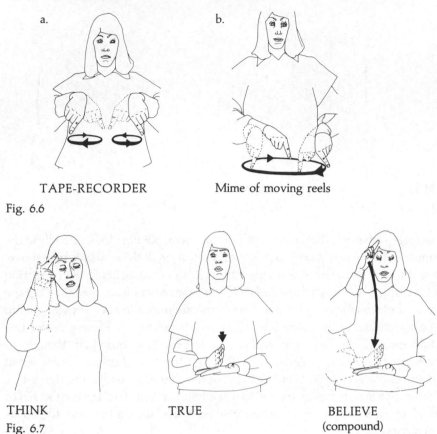

a.

b.

TAPE-RECORDER

Mime of moving reels

Fig. 6.6

THINK

TRUE

BELIEVE
(compound)

Fig. 6.7

perfectly acceptable to talk about a green blackboard). Sometimes compounding has resulted in such shortening and combining of the two elements that the result is no longer recognisable as a compound: as, for example, English *lord* from *hlaf-weard* (bread-keeper), or *barn* from *bere-aern* (barley place). In BSL we find compounds such as MOTHER/FATHER, (parents), and THINK/TRUE (believe). If we look at the form of these compounds compared with their forms as single signs we can see that certain changes have taken place, for example, there has been a loss of movement in THINK as part of the compound THINK/TRUE (fi.g 6.7). In MOTHER/FATHER the repeated movement is reduced to a single tap. The reason for these simplifications is the third constraint, the 'duality constraint'. This constraint states: signs with two of any element are more complex than signs with one, and two is the upper limit of complexity.

This constraint, in conjunction with the symmetry and dominance constraints, operates on new and existing signs to alter their form. If we look at the

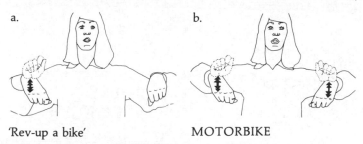

a.

b.

'Rev-up a bike'   MOTORBIKE

Fig. 6.8

sign TAPE-RECORDER again, we can see that the example in fig. 6.6b violates the symmetry constraint, although it is a more accurate representation of the movement of tape reels. The symmetry constraint states that hands should move symmetrically: only the version in fig. 6.6a meets this criterion. Another example may make this point clearer. Fig. 6.8a shows a representation of a motorbike. The left hand remains still, and the right hand extends at the wrist, in imitation of 'revving-up' a motorbike. Fig. 6.8b shows the sign for MOTORBIKE. In the sign, both hands move simultaneously, and they flex rather than extend at the wrist. Fig. 6.8a violates the dominance constraint because the left hand does not serve as a passive location for the right hand and yet it does not move. It violates the symmetry constraint because it does not perform the same movement as the right hand. In fig. 6.8b the gesture imitating a motorbike has been altered so that it looks less like a representation of revving-up a motorbike; instead it has been assimilated to the form of a BSL sign. Thus, as well as describing sign form, we can predict that where a sign violates these constraints by being too complex in form, it will change in the direction of a simpler form.

Historical change

We have historical records of British signs going back two hundred years. These records allow us to see what changes have taken place in the form of signs in that time.

The duality constraint states that two elements are more complex than one. We would thus expect to find reduction from two hands to one, two locations to one, two handshapes to one, two movements to one. Fig. 6.9 illustrates these reductions. Fig. 6.9a shows CENTRE as illustrated in 1880 and the modern sign CENTRE. In the older form there were two movements, a circular movement of the right hand followed by touching the left palm. In the modern form the circling movement is lost and only the touching remains. Fig. 6.9b illustrates loss of hand: FOREVER originally required two hands circling each other; the

119

a.

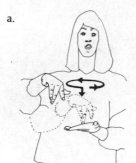 

CENTRE (1880)   CENTRE (modern)

b.

FOREVER (1880)   FOREVER (modern)

c.

BETTER (1880)   BETTER (modern)

Fig. 6.9

d.

GIVE (1915)   GIVE (modern)

Fig. 6.9 cont.

modern form uses only one hand. In very formal varieties of BSL the two-handed form is still occasionally seen, suggesting that it is in such variation between formal and informal style that changes originate. Fig. 6.9c illustrates the change from two handshapes to one: the 1880 version of BETTER has the passive left hand in a G handshape (index finger extended) and the active right hand in an Å handshape (thumb extended); in the modern form of the sign, both hands have Å handshape. Fig. 6.9d illustrates location loss: the 1915 version of GIVE involved touching the chest with the palm before moving it away from the body; in the modern form, there is no longer any contact with the chest.

A large number of signs have changed location. These location changes fall into several groups:

1. Signs located at the mouth move to the cheek or chin. The sign WOMAN (fig. 6.10a) illustrates this shift.
2. Signs located on the lower left arm change location to the left hand. Both TROUBLE (fig. 6.10b) and POLICE were formerly articulated on the left forearm; they are now articulated on the back of the left hand or wrist.
3. Signs located on the temple or upper face move away from the body. PERHAPS was at one time articulated at the forehead and is now articulated in neutral space without any body contact (fig. 6.10c). GIVE (fig. 6.9d) formerly involved chest contact, but is now articulated in front of the body.

These three groups of changes in location illustrate two tendencies: firstly, contrast between different locations lessens as signs move to more central areas (groups 2 and 3). Secondly, signs which cover the mouth move to areas around the mouth. These two tendencies are related. We said in the last chapter that the focus of vision is on the face and mouth of the signer, so it is perhaps not

121

The structure of signs

a. Shift from mouth to cheek

WOMAN (1880)   WOMAN (modern)

b. Shift from forearm to hand

TROUBLE (1880)   TROUBLE (modern)

c. Shift from forehead to neutral space

PERHAPS (1915)   PERHAPS (modern)

Fig. 6.10

122

surprising that signs covering the mouth move away from the mouth, and that signs articulated in the periphery of the visual field move towards its centre.

When we examine signs in this way we can see that, although they may have visual imagery underlying their adoption into the language, they still function as linguistic units rather than as simple pictures, much as onomatopoeic words in a spoken language are part of the language and obey phonological restrictions. A useful way to view onomatopoeia and other sorts of symbolism is to think of them as being on a continuum. At one end we have, for example, laughter. It is clearly not a part of any linguistic system. At the opposite end we have the word *laugh* which appears to be completely arbitrary. In the middle we have words like *ha-ha, tee-hee*, etc. There is no clear break between these categories; thus, a continuum of most linguistic—least linguistic is a useful concept.

Although many signs have their origins in visual symbolism, many other signs appear to be as arbitrary as many words of spoken languages. This is often caused by changes in sign form which have obscured the original symbolism. Signers (particularly hearing people) often attribute symbolism to a sign which, on historical examination, may be seen to be derived from an entirely different image. The sign WOMAN in BSL is a good example. The sign has been variously analysed as derived from 'curls on a woman's cheek', 'bonnet strings', 'soft cheek', etc., and the form of the sign as used now could support any of these interpretations. Historical records show, however, that the older form of the sign was located at the lips rather than cheek (fig. 6.10a); therefore, none of the supposed explanations involving the cheek can be true.

Often the search for the origin of a sign's symbolism can lead to changes in sign form. This is also found in spoken languages, where words change to match their supposed origins. *Primrose* is derived from French *primerole* 'first flower (of spring)', but has changed because of an association with *rose*. The *Jerusalem* in *Jerusalem artichoke* is a corruption of *girasole*. A *hangnail* is not a nail that hangs, but one that causes pain (*ang*). In BSL we find similar changes. The sign SUGAR (fig. 6.11a) has been interpreted as deriving from 'sugar dermatitis' (which causes itching). Signers (mostly hearing) who believe this interpretation articulate the sign with a different movement (fig. 6.11b) to represent scratching.

Fingerspelling

Throughout the world the manual, or fingerspelled, alphabet provides signers with another source for new sign formation. A manual alphabet represents the letters of a written language directly, and thus 'foreign' words may be spelled. There are a number of manual alphabets in existence throughout the world which are used to represent different alphabets or syllables. Most manual

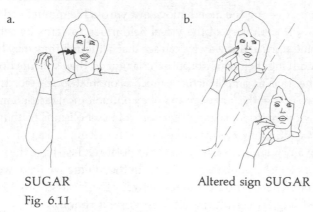

SUGAR   Altered sign SUGAR

Fig. 6.11

alphabets are one-handed (American, Swedish, Russian), but the alphabet in use throughout Britain is a two-handed alphabet whose origins go back to the 17th century. Examples of several alphabets are given in fig. 6.12. The finger positions in most manual alphabets suggest the form of the letters they represent.

Fingerspelling has in the past often been confused with signing, but fingerspelled words differ in form from signs. We have said that signs cannot consist of more than two parts, but a fingerspelled word may contain as many handshapes as letters in the written word. Fingerspelling is used in a variety of ways by signers. For signers in formal contexts, fingerspelled words may be used in place of signs. Signers from the north of England and Scotland often use a great proportion of fingerspelled words in all contexts. The names of places or individuals, and words for which there are no equivalent signs, may also be fingerspelled. Although fingerspelling represents the words of written language, it differs in some ways. Even an utterance articulated entirely in fingerspelling does not have upper-case letters, punctuation, indeed any breaks between words, but is articulated in a continuous string.

It was suggested, above, that fingerspelled words differ in form from signs. Fingerspelled words, however, can be borrowed in sign language and become subject to the same constraints on form as signs. Thus, just as visual imagery serves as a source of new signs, so do fingerspelled words. When fingerspelled words are borrowed into a sign language they begin to change form to accommodate to sign constraints. They may ultimately become unrecognisable as fingerspelled words because of the changes undergone. The sign ABOUT (fig. 6.13a), for example, is a compound sign (see chapter 5) which is derived from the fingerspelled word a·b·o·u·t· (fingerspelled words are conventionally represented in lower-case letters separated by dots). We can see that the movements and handshapes of the individual letters have been reduced to a

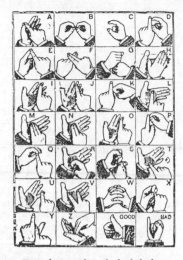

British two-handed alphabet

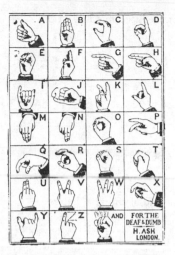

American one-handed alphabet

Irish one-handed alphabet

Fig. 6.12 Manual alphabets.

single handshape and movement, with only the beginning and end positions clearly remaining. Reductions in fingerspelled words fall into several groups: first and last letters, first letters of syllables, and first letters only; examples of these three groups are given in fig. 6.13. These signs can be considered as 'loan' signs from a foreign language – English.

125

The structure of signs

a. Reduced middle section

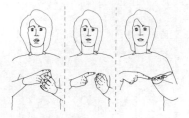

ABOUT (·a·b·t·)

b. Initial and final letters   c. Syllable-initial letters   d. Repeated initial letter

BIRMINGHAM (·b·m·)   NEWCASTLE (·n·c·)   KITCHEN (·k·k·)

Fig. 6.13

Just as these loans change to accommodate to the constraints of BSL, loan words borrowed from foreign languages into English change to match constraints in English. Loans in English such as *garage* and *chiffon* from French, and *hamburger* from German, are pronounced according to English phonology. Another parallel in spoken language is the use of acronyms, or words based on the initial letter or syllable of a phrase. Sometimes the letter names themselves are pronounced (e.g. Bee Bee Cee); sometimes a word is formed from the letters with inserted vowels (e.g. *Wrens* from WRNS); sometimes the letters themselves are pronounced as a word (MIRAS from Mortgage Interest Relief at Source).

The reduction of fingerspelled loans to single letters might be thought to pose a problem. If these loan signs continually simplify to a single letter we might expect a large number of loans to become homonymous. This does not occur, because simplified loan signs often become more complex through the addition of specialised movements. Loan signs such as QUARTER (from an

126

Specialised movements in loan signs

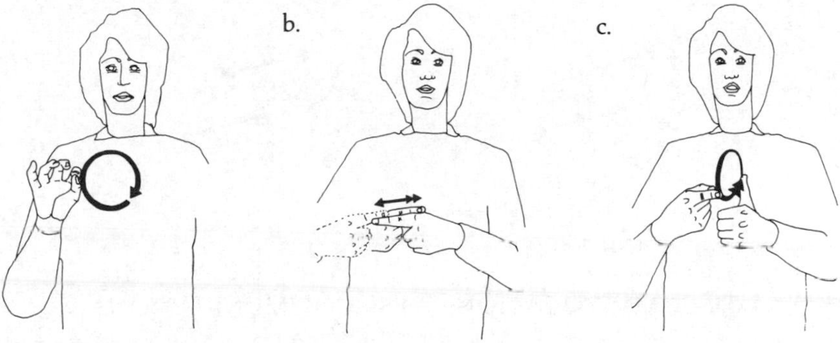

QUARTER (old·q·)   ENGLAND (·e·)   ANSWER (·a·)

Iconic movements in loan signs

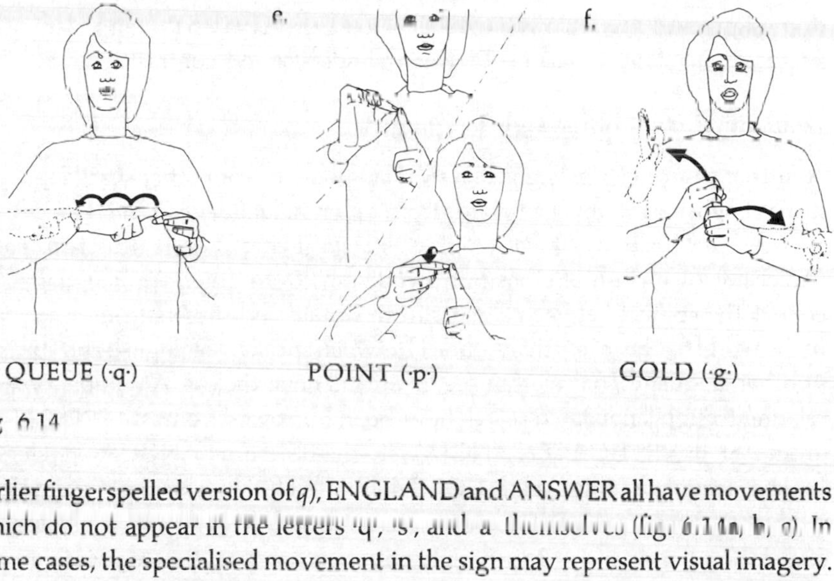

QUEUE (·q·)   POINT (·p·)   GOLD (·g·)

Fig 6.14

earlier fingerspelled version of *q*), ENGLAND and ANSWER all have movements which do not appear in the letters ·q·, ·s·, and ·a· themselves (fig. 6.14a, b, c). In some cases, the specialised movement in the sign may represent visual imagery. Loan signs with this kind of movement include QUEUE, POINT and GOLD (fig. 6.14d, e, f). We might suppose that these signs are the result of initialisation, a process well documented in ASL. In initialisation, a sign changes to the same handshape as in the fingerspelled initial letter of the word: for example, the American signs FAMILY, GROUP, SOCIETY, are identical except for handshape, with each sign having the handshape of the American fingerspelled ·f·, ·g· and ·s· respectively. This initialisation is a product of English influence on already existing signs, while signs like GOLD in BSL have developed from the

127

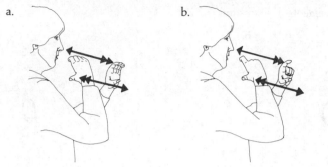

ASL COMMUNICATION   BSL COMMUNICATION

Fig. 6.15

opposite direction. The older form of the sign GOLD, for example, is a simple ·g·. The movement found in the modern sign GOLD (which is the same as in signs such as BRIGHT and SUN) is a later addition and serves to distinguish GOLD from signs such as GOVERNMENT (·g·g·) or AUGUST (·g·g·). Thus sign language maintains a balance between simplicity and contrast in form.

Loan signs from other sign languages

A further source of new signs in a sign language is from other sign languages. Just as English has borrowed words from different languages: *chair* (French), *law* (Norse), *tub* (Dutch), *alcohol* (Arabic), *magic* (Persian), *icon* (Russian), *potato* (Amerindian), etc., so BSL has borrowed signs from other sign languages. Of course, the contact between signers from Britain and signers from other parts of the world has been less than contact between speakers of English and speakers of other languages, but we can see its effects nevertheless. A number of signs relating to sign language research have been borrowed from ASL: RESEARCH (from ASL INVESTIGATE),LANGUAGE (the BSL sign LANGUAGE refers to spoken language only), and COMMUNICATION. This last example is interesting because the BSL loan sign has adopted the American initialisation convention but uses the British alphabet ·c· rather than the American ·c· (fig. 6.15a, b).

Other loans in BSL include foreign place and country names: AMERICA, SWEDEN, DENMARK, etc. These frequently replace indigenous place and country names. Other sign languages show even stronger evidence of the influence of foreign sign languages. Some researchers have described ASL as a creole of French Sign Language and some other sign language. Irish Sign Language also shows strong evidence of BSL and French Sign Language influences.

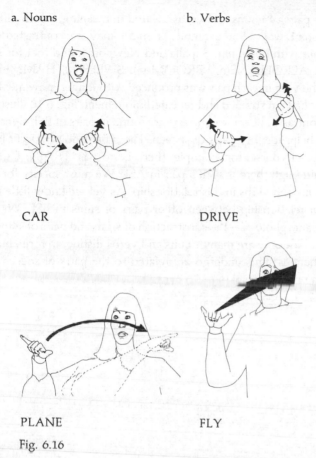

a. Nouns   b. Verbs

CAR   DRIVE

PLANE   FLY

Fig. 6.16

Parts of 'speech'

While in many languages parts of speech such as nouns, verbs, adjectives, etc. can be identified by form, in many other cases a part of speech can be identified through use only. The word *can* in English, for example, may be a verb referring to the action of canning (vegetables or meat), an auxiliary verb meaning possibility or ability, or a noun meaning a kind of container. Nothing in the form of the word suggests which meaning it has or which part of speech it is; only its usage conveys that information.

In the past, it was thought that there were no parts of speech in sign languages; for example, in BSL there are many signs such as those in fig. 6.16 which appear to be used both as nouns and verbs. Signs such as these in ASL were studied by Supalla and Newport (1978). They point out that subtle but consistent differences in movement separate nouns from verbs. In English, of course, there are pairs of nouns and verbs, related in meaning, which differ in small but consistent ways. For example, *'torment* may be contrasted with *tor'ment*; *'commune* with *comm'une*. Supalla and Newport found that for signs such as FLY(v.): AEROPLANE(n.), BROOM(v.): SWEEP(n.), HAMMER(v.): HAMMER(n.), the verb in each pair was produced with longer movement; the noun in each pair had a restrained and repeated movement. Fig. 6.16 illustrates the movement contrast. The same contrasts are found in pairs of BSL signs, and this information helps identify parts of speech. These pairs do not occur for all nouns and verbs, of course: for example, there is no pair TRAIN: GO-BY-TRAIN in BSL although there is such a pair in ASL. We must specify for each language the nouns and verbs in this relationship. As yet we know little more about the formal relationship between other pairs of signs in BSL. We will, however, discuss morphology – the construction of signs and pairs of signs – in the next chapter. Not only are many nouns and verbs distinct in form, but the processes and changes signs undergo are related to the parts of speech they represent and the role they take.

7. Sign morphology and syntax: the grammar of BSL

In this chapter we will present some of the research in the field of sign language grammar. We will discuss both morphology and syntax and draw upon research on ASL as well as BSL. We use the term 'morphology' to refer to the constructions and changes which affect single signs, and 'syntax' to refer to the way signs are combined in sentence structure. Of course, the description of sign language grammar is still in its early stages, so we can only concentrate on a small number of areas of the grammar. In the following chapter we will talk about some preliminary research in comparing the grammar of different sign languages, and many features described here will also be referred to there.

Morphology

The morphology of BSL is very complex. In contrast to a language such as English, BSL is relatively heavily inflected: to illustrate this let us look at two spoken languages, English and Biblical Hebrew. The sentence *You will praise him* in English can be translated by a single word in Hebrew, *tihalleluhu* We can analyse the English sentence in the following way:

You	*will*	*praise*	*him*
subject	aux verb	main verb	object
2nd person	indicating future		3rd person masculine singular, objective form

Apart from the word *him* there are no formal indications of subject, number or tense. The meaning is expressed by separate words arranged in a particular order. If we analyse the Hebrew sentence, we must describe it in the following way:

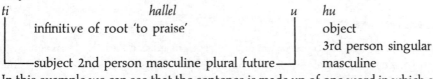

ti	*hallel*	*u*	*hu*
	infinitive of root 'to praise'		object
			3rd person singular masculine
subject 2nd person masculine plural future			

In this example we can see that the sentence is made up of one word in which a great deal of information is packed into single or discontinuous units. If we compare *ti . . . u* in Hebrew with *you* in English, we find that the English word *you* does not indicate number, or case of subject vs. object vs. indirect object (i.e. I told *you*; *you* told me; I gave *you* the book), while the comparable elements (not *words*) in Hebrew indicate time (future), case (subject), gender (masculine) and number (plural). We would therefore describe Biblical Hebrew as much more inflected than English. BSL is also a heavily inflected language in that very specific information about case, number, tense and aspect is found in the grammar. It also, like Biblical Hebrew, can contain a great deal of grammatical information in a single sign, and whole sentences often consist of a single, highly inflected sign. We will discuss five features as examples of BSL morphology: number, classifier, case, aspect, and quality.

Number

Number is a grammatical category found in most languages. In English we find number in plural vs. singular marking of nouns, and a remnant of number marking in 3rd person singular verbs (he paint*s*). In other languages, such as French, adjectives, nouns and verbs must all be marked for number (*Trois charmantes filles sont allées* 'Three charming girls went' vs. *Une charmante fille est allée* 'One charming girl went'). In both English and French, plurality in nouns is generally indicated by adding a suffix (-*s*). Other languages use reduplication to indicate plurality. BSL resembles this second group in that plurality is frequently indicated by the repetition of a sign rather than by suffixing some element. We thus find examples such as those in fig. 7.1a which contrast with the form of their English translation. (Reduplication is used for many other purposes in BSL, as we shall see later in this chapter.)

Nouns in BSL can be pluralised in other ways. The noun may remain unduplicated but be preceded by a sign indicating number: FIVE MAN, MANY MAN, etc. We can find a few comparable examples in those English words which do not have a plural form: *five fish, many fish*, where we understand *fish* to be plural by its association with *many* and *five* and by the fact that the verb form contrasts singular and plural nouns: *five fish are swimming* vs. *one fish is swimming*. Another type of reduplication signifying plurality is found, where two hands articulate the sign instead of one (fig. 7.1b).

Classifiers

Many sign language linguists have recognised similarities between sign languages and certain spoken languages which have a 'predicate classifier system'. The best known example of a spoken language with a predicate classifier system is Navaho, an American Indian language. McDonald (1983) shows close similarities between categories in Navaho and those in ASL. Verbs

a. Plurals with repetition of movement

BOOK   BOOKS

b. Plurals with double articulation

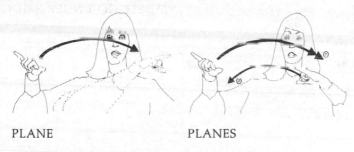

PLANE   PLANES

Fig. 7.1

in Navaho consist of a stem and prefix. The prefix indicates aspectual, adverbial and pronominal information, while the verb stems for movement and location are based on the shape of the object concerned. McDonald (1983: 34) cites several examples illustrating the type of information found in a Navaho verb:

-*lts'id	independent movement of a solid round object
-*ødéél	independent movement of a slender flexible object
*á	movement of a solid round object through continuing manual contact (e.g. carrying a ball)
-lné	movement initiated by an agent involving a solid round object (e.g. a ball bounces)

These verb stems are prefixed by adverbial particles indicating direction to produce a complex verb containing information on shape of object, type of involvement of object, direction of movement of object, actor on the object etc:

hà	ǹ'	aà	h	You take a round solid object out of an enclosed space
out	you	handle	a round solid object	

133

a. Class

b. Verb with classifier handshape insertion

Vehicle

CAR

VEHICLE-GO-UNDER-BRIDGE

LORRY

Person

MAN

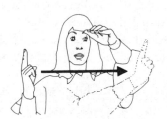

PERSON-GO-UNDER-BRIDGE

Dual

COUPLE

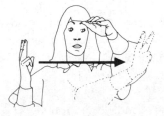

DUAL-GO-UNDER-BRIDGE

Fig. 7.2

a.   b.

Many

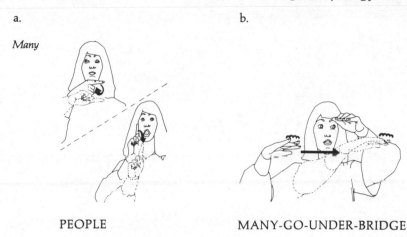

PEOPLE   MANY-GO-UNDER-BRIDGE

Fig. 7.2. cont.

The relationship of elements in the verb to classes of object is what defines Navaho as a predicate classifier language. BSL and ASL (and as we will see in the next chapter, other sign languages) also construct sentences in this manner, and can also, therefore, be labelled as predicate classifier languages. An example will illustrate this. There is a BSL verb stem meaning 'to go under a bridge', and it is represented by motion of the right hand under the left hand (fig. 7.2b). Information about whatever goes under the bridge is indicated by the shape of the right hand. The examples in fig. 7.2 illustrate different objects and the classifiers which exemplify their classes in GO-UNDER-BRIDGE.

As well as appearing in verb stems, classifiers also appear in a wide range of nouns, where the handshape of the noun indicates its class membership. For example, the hand, with fingers extended and together, is found in many signs referring to flat wide objects: FLOOR, DOOR, TABLE, WALL, BOX SIDES, CORRIDOR, SKY. Signs with index and middle fingers extended and spread refer to an object with two straight extensions: LEGS, SNAKE (its tongue), SCISSORS, GAZE (figurative extension based on rays extending from the eyes), OFFICER (stripes). New words are introduced into the language by drawing on this classifier system. One sign for cassette (fig. 7.3) derives from a handshape meaning to hold a thick flat object, and this means 'to push a thick flat object into something'.

Handshapes indicating number can be inserted into signs with temporal meaning. We find examples in BSL of the use of a handshape which is a number classifier (fig. 7.4). Thus classifiers serve as another means of indicating number in sign morphology.

CASSETTE

Fig. 7.3

Case and role

The notion of 'role' involves both inflections for case (the description of subject, object, indirect object etc.) and other devices by which the relationship between participants mentioned in a sentence is made explicit. BSL is a highly inflected language, with role relationships made explicit in a number of ways. In English, role relationships are generally indicated by position in the sentence, *Bill hit Tom* and *Tom hit Bill* being distinguished by order only. We know that *Bill* is the subject of the first sentence because of its position as the first noun; we know that *Tom* is the object of the first sentence because it occurs after the verb. The verb itself reflects nothing of the relationship between the two nouns except that the sentence is to be read as active rather than passive. Thus in English, the information about roles and cases is in the domain of syntax.

In BSL, information about role is conveyed in an entirely different way. To understand the way in which role is conveyed we must examine the use of space in signing generally. In English conversation speakers may point to locations to indicate a person or object. For example, two speakers may be discussing a third person who habitually occupies a certain chair; one speaker may point to that chair, or incline his head in that direction to indicate the person. In this sort of example a real location (i.e. the chair) is used. In BSL and other sign languages, however, a combination of conventionalised, relative and real locations is used. Use of real location is found in the same sort of circumstances as the English speakers' conversation just mentioned. Signers may point to, or otherwise indicate, locations, directions or objects. In relative locations a signer uses points in space to produce an image of some other location. For example, if a signer is

a. Age

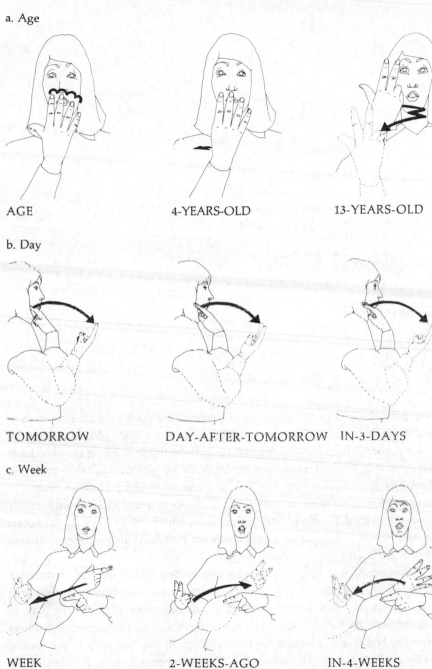

AGE   4-YEARS-OLD   13-YEARS-OLD

b. Day

TOMORROW   DAY-AFTER-TOMORROW   IN-3-DAYS

c. Week

WEEK   2-WEEKS-AGO   IN-4-WEEKS

Fig. 7.4   Temporal signs incorporating number.

137

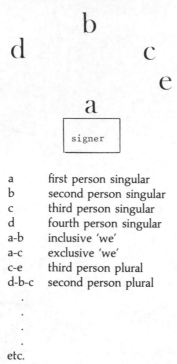

a   first person singular
b   second person singular
c   third person singular
d   fourth person singular
a-b   inclusive 'we'
a-c   exclusive 'we'
c-e   third person plural
d-b-c   second person plural

.
.
.
.

etc.

Fig. 7.5   Pronominal reference.

describing the interior of a house he will indicate the position and orientation of objects in the room by locating them on a minature 'floor plan' drawn in the space in front of him. This is done either by producing the sign for the object and then pointing to the location on the 'plan' or by articulating the sign in the appropriate location. While the first of these is used by hearing people in conversation, the second, of course, is not. The third use of space found in BSL is conventionalised location. This is found in the location of sign pronouns particularly. In conventionalised locations for pronouns the locations shown in fig. 7.5 are used.

Conventionalised locations can be overridden either by real or relative locations where available. Their most important role, apart from pronouns, is in verb inflections. Three verbs in sentences illustrate this role in BSL (fig. 7.6). In 7.6a the verb appears the same in both sentences. In 7.6b the second verb differs from the first in the direction the hand moves. In 7.6c the verb in the second sentence differs from the verb in the first sentence not only in terms of the direction in which it moves but also in the orientation of the hand: in I-ASK-YOU the palm faces outward; in YOU-ASK-ME the palm faces towards the

a. Invariant verb

I-ANSWER-YOU YOU-ANSWER-ME

b. Directional verb

I-GIVE-YOU YOU-GIVE-ME

c. Reversing verb

I-ASK-YOU YOU-ASK-ME

Fig. 7.6

d. Israeli Sign Language

ASK

e. Reversing vs. directional verb

YOU-LOOK-AT-ME   YOU-SUPERVISE-ME
(Reversing)   (Directional)

Fig. 7.6 cont.

signer. Many other verbs in BSL fall into one of these three types; we may call the first type 'invariant', the second type 'directional' and the third type 'reversing' (all reversing verbs are also directional). It might be thought that the categorisation of verbs into one or other of these types would depend either on form or meaning, but in fact neither of these accounts for the categorisation. Two examples will show this. The sign for ASK in Israeli Sign Language (fig. 7.6d) is very similar to the BSL sign ASK in fig. 7.6c; this Israeli sign, however, belongs to the directional class rather than to the reversing class; so, although it has the same meaning as BSL ASK, and very similar form, the categorisation is language-specific. Fig. 7.6e compares the BSL verb SUPERVISE with the BSL verb LOOK. Although the two verbs are similar in form and meaning, LOOK is

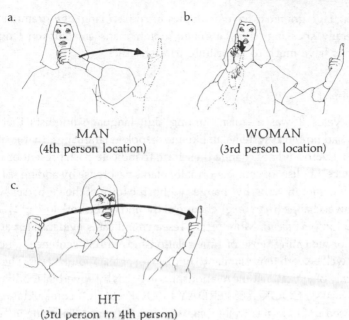

a.   MAN
(4th person location)

b.   WOMAN
(3rd person location)

c.   HIT
(3rd person to 4th person)

WOMAN-HIT-MAN

Fig. 7.7

reversing while SUPERVISE is directional. Thus role in BSL is conveyed by verb inflection for case, while in English it is almost entirely conveyed by word order.

Another way in which role is encoded in BSL relies on the availability of two articulators as well as on the use of location. In spoken languages, of course, such a construction is not possible. In this type of construction (a variant of the one illustrated above) a role is encoded on to each hand and then the hands act on each other. A sentence such as WOMAN-HIT-MAN may be signed in the following way (fig. 7.7a–c). First, MAN is signed with the left hand. Then the index finger of the left hand is held upright (person classifier) in fourth person location (fig. 7.7a). As the left hand is held stationary, the right hand signs WOMAN (fig. 7.7b). Then the right hand, in a fist, is brought towards the left hand (fig. 7.7c). The sentence can be schematised as follows:

			held		
Left hand: MAN	4th person singular				
Right hand:		WOMAN	3rd person singular	3rd person HIT	4th person

In the syntax section we shall see further evidence of simultaneity in sign language grammar. It is important, however, to bear in mind that most features

141

of sign language grammar have analogies in spoken language grammar, and that, generally speaking, sign language grammarians and spoken language grammarians have much to contribute to each other.

Time and aspect

For many years it was a truism among sign language linguists that sign languages had no tense systems, unlike most spoken languages: that is, it was believed that verbs did not change their form to indicate past, present or future time reference. English, of course, normally marks past tense by adding *-ed* or, in a number of common verbs, by changes within the form of the verb itself, either internal vowel change (*ring* : *rang*), change at the end of the verb (*bring* : *brought*), or substitution (*go* : *went*). More recent research indicates evidence for at least two ways of indicating tense or time relationships in BSL sentences, and that there may well be verb tense similar to English for at least some verbs. The most common way of indicating time relationships in BSL is by adverbial modification (TOMORROW I COOK, YESTERDAY I COOK etc.). Of course, this sort of device is used in English as well (*Tomorrow I go to London, I'm going to London tomorrow*, both of which are in present tense), and there are many spoken languages, such as Yoruba and Chinese, which are without tense in the sense that verbs do not specifically indicate time of an event's occurrence. Languages may, of course, use other devices, such as aspectual marking, to suggest time reference. This can be understood by looking at English, where in sentences such as *I have eaten*, although the tense is present the action is perceived as having taken place in the past because the aspect is perfective. Aspect in BSL will be discussed below, but here we will look at time marking itself.

Briefly, events can be placed in the past by adding an adverbial marker such as those mentioned above: YESTERDAY, TOMORROW, RECENTLY etc. Other signs such as FINISH and BEFORE can signify simply past time, as well as the completiveness implied in FINISH or the relativeness of BEFORE. The signs FUTURE and PAST are also used in this way, although their use is optional. Brennan's (1983) well illustrated paper includes many more examples of signs used in this way. She has also identified a number of signs which appear to inflect for tense in a way similar to English irregular verbs. These verbs include SEE : SAW, GO : WENT, WIN : WON (fig. 7.8). As yet, only these verbs have been identified as changing in this way, but others may remain to be discovered. Just as space is used to represent role relations, it can be used to represent time relations, with two main locations used. The first location is the space used to represent absolute time, particularly 'calendric' time (Brennan, 1983). The past is

a. Present

GO   WIN

b. Past

WENT   WON

Fig. 7.8

viewed as located over the right shoulder, with the cheek as the present, and the space in front of the right shoulder representing the future. Signs such as PAST and LONG-TIME-AGO are located over the shoulder; signs such as YESTER-DAY and TOMORROW at the cheek, and FUTURE in front of the shoulder (fig. 7.9a). This notion of past time as 'behind' and future time as 'in-front' finds parallels in most European spoken languages, where time and space are connected in the same way. For example, in English we can use the expression *in front of* or *before* both to indicate events in the future or location in space. Similarly *behind* or *past* can be used to refer to locations or to events (*I'm past that*). In other cultures, of course, time reference and space may have the opposite relationship. In Urubu Kaapor Sign Language, a sign language used

a. Time-line A

PAST   TOMORROW

b. Time-line B

BEFORE   CONTINUE

Fig. 7.9

among Brazilian Indians, the past is located in front of the signer, with the future behind. This reversal represents a world view of the past as something visible, and the future as unknowable (Ferreira Brito, 1983).

The second time-line found in BSL is located in front of the body. This line is used to represent succession and duration: BEFORE, AFTER, CONTINUE, NEXT (fig. 7.9b).

Relational time concepts such as BEFORE or CONTINUE lead us to the other means of expressing time: aspect. We can draw a distinction between tense and aspect by regarding tense as referring to relationships between events and real time, and aspect as referring to relationships between events in terms of each other. We can see the difference in English: *I had posted the letter* is not only in past

a. Base sign
  LOOK

b. Slow reduplication
  LOOK

c. Fast reduplication
  LOOK

LOOK

LOOK-AT-FOR-
A-LONG-TIME

LOOK-AT-OVER-
AND-OVER

Fig. 7.10

tense (*posted*) but implies that the letter was posted before another event in the past (*had*). We then have both past tense and perfective or completive aspect. In *I posted the letter* no such implication about other events is found, only that the action took place in the past. In *I am posting the letter* we have both a time reference to the present (*am*) and an indication of ongoing activity (*posting*) which we call continuous aspect. While in English we have only these two indications of aspect, continuous and perfective, in many other spoken languages we have other realisations of situation-internal time, such as durative (extending over a period of time) or iterative (occurring repeatedly). In English we express such meaning not by changes in verb forms but by adverbial modification of verbs, for example *keep on* or *always* to indicate durative, iterative or habitual aspect (*He kept on knocking at the door, She always reads*); reduplication of verbs can also indicate iteration or duration (*He waited and waited*). In most sign languages verbs undergo complex aspectual modification by changes in the form of the verbs themselves. These changes are often referred to in the literature as 'modulations'. We mentioned number and role modulations in verbs earlier. Just as verbs fall into classes of invariant, directional and reversing in space, they also fall into classes according to the types of aspectual modulation they undergo and the forms in which they appear. The changes include reduplication and modification. Bergman (1983) has identified three morphological processes that verbs undergo in respect of aspectual modulation: fast reduplication, slow reduplication, and initial stop. The categories of fast and slow reduplication were first discussed for ASL by Fischer (1973b). Although the terms 'slow' and 'fast' are thus well established, the two types of reduplication do

a. Base sign   b. Non-occurring   c. Reduplicated
                            simple reduplication   actual form

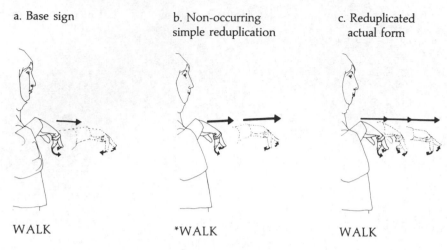

WALK   *WALK   WALK

Fig. 7.11

not differ so much in actual speed, but in the uneven, cycling nature of the slow reduplication, which appears as pauses between each repetition of the verb (fig. 7.10b). Fast reduplication is characterised by even movement, with less sense of cycles with intervening pauses (fig. 7.10c). The base sign is given in fig. 7.10a.

An important observation first made by Supalla and Newport (1978) in describing reduplication in ASL verbs, is that the modulations do not apply to the citation form, but to its underlying form. For example, the sign WALK in its citation form (as Bergman also points out for Swedish Sign Language) contains two movements (fig 7.11a). If this were simply reduplicated we would have four movements (fig 7.11b). Instead the movement occurs only three times in the reduplicated form (fig. 7.11c). This suggests that reduplication (two movements) is added to the single underlying movement rather than the repeated movement of the citation form.

The meaning associated with slow reduplication is either iterative or durative depending on the meaning of the verb modulated, that is, whether the verb is 'durative' or 'punctual'. A durative verb has the 'character' of an action which can continue over time (*walk, read, stand*) while a punctual verb has the character of an action which occurs as a single event (*jump, kill, drop*). A punctual verb which undergoes slow reduplication conveys the meaning of iteration, of the event happening over and over again (continual) (fig. 7.12b), while a durative verb which undergoes slow reduplication conveys the meaning of one action maintained over a period of time (continuous) (7.12a).

The meaning associated with fast reduplication also varies depending on whether the verb is punctual or durative. With a punctual verb fast reduplication

a. Durative verb
Base sign   Slow reduplication

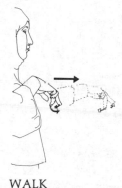

WALK   KEEP-ON-WALKING

b. Punctual verb
Base sign   Slow reduplication

JUMP   JUMP AGAIN-AND-AGAIN

Fig. 7.12

suggests regularity, repetition of the action or frequency (7.13b), with durative verbs, the meaning is habitual action (7.13a).

The category of modulation called by Bergman 'initial stop' appears in both durative and punctual verbs with the same meaning. In initial stop, the hand(s) start the movement of the sign (the base sign is given in fig. 7.14a) but then abruptly stop (fig. 7.14b). The meaning associated with this modulation is that the action did not occur, although it was about to. Bergman has coined the term 'inhibiting' modulation, as no spoken language exhibits this meaning morphologically.

A very important feature of verb modulation for aspect which we have not

a. Durative verbs
   Base sign   Fast reduplication

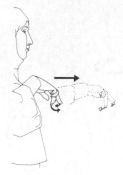 

WALK   WALK-OFTEN

b. Punctual verbs
   Base sign   Fast reduplication

JUMP   JUMP-A-LOT

Fig. 7.13

yet mentioned is the role of non-manual elements. We will also see in the next section the role of non-manual elements in other types of sign modification. In some of the aspectually modulated verbs discussed above, certain non-manual elements often appear. For example, the sign THINK can appear in two forms (fig. 7.15b,c), with the same meanings. Fig. 7.15b shows the slow reduplication discussed above. In fig. 7.15c the hand remains stationary while the head rocks in cycles. Fig. 7.15a, the citation form of THINK, has no movement, so it appears in examples such as this that the cycling movement can be imposed on the hand or on the head. Similarly the inhibitive aspect of the initial stop modulation in Swedish Sign Language sometimes occurs with open mouth and head and

a. Base sign   b. Inhibiting

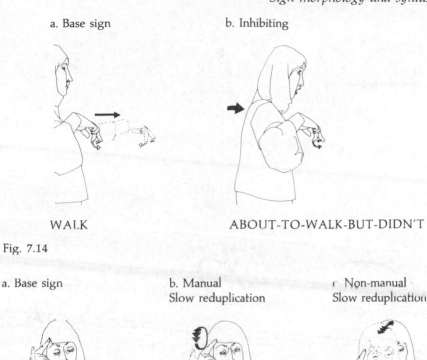

WALK   ABOUT-TO-WALK-BUT-DIDN'T

Fig. 7.14

a. Base sign   b. Manual   c. Non-manual
                      Slow reduplication   Slow reduplication

THINK   THINK-FOR-A-   THINK-FOR-A-
                      LONG-TIME   LONG-TIME

Fig. 7.15

eye-gaze sideways or down. The abruptness of the movement stop is matched by the abruptness of the mouth opening.

The last two types of aspectual modulation we will discuss are extensions discussed in Klima and Bellugi (1979). Distributive and reciprocal modulations occur in many verbs. Many signs with reciprocal meaning such as MEET (fig. 7.16a) are two-handed signs, but other signs without any intrinsic reciprocal meaning can be signed with both hands simultaneously. A sign such as LOOK (7.16b) when signed with two hands has the meaning LOOK-AT-EACH OTHER (7.16c). The distributional modulation involves movement of the sign

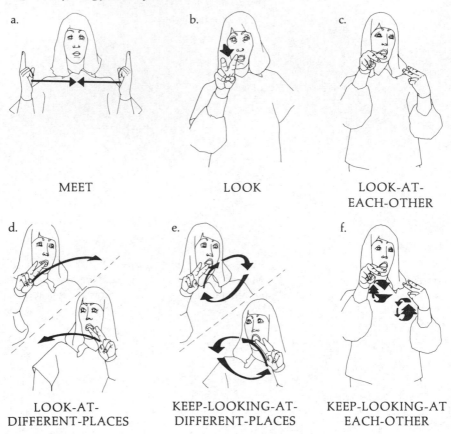

a.

MEET

b.

LOOK

c.

LOOK-AT-
EACH-OTHER

d.

LOOK-AT-
DIFFERENT-PLACES

e.

KEEP-LOOKING-AT-
DIFFERENT-PLACES

f.

KEEP-LOOKING-AT
EACH-OTHER

Fig. 7.16

across the space in front of the body. This modulation results in the meaning of repetition to more than one person or in more than one place. For example, the sign LOOK with distributional modulation means LOOK-AT-DIFFERENT-PLACES (fig. 7.16d). These modulations can be combined in many ways. For example, LOOK with both slow reduplication and distributional modulation means KEEP-LOOKING-AT-DIFFERENT-PLACES (7.16e). LOOK with reciprocal modulation and slow reduplication means KEEP-LOOKING-AT-EACH-OTHER (7.16f).

Quality

This section is concerned with those modifications of signs which alter the quality of the sign modified. We use the term 'quality' to refer to degree, manner or size of the referent. In English, words like *very*, *really* and *a little* can be added to

a.    b.

WALK-WITH-EASE   WALK-WITH-DIFFICULTY

Fig. 7.17

adjectives to alter quality: *very big, a little sad, really long* etc; or the tone of voice may indicate quality. In BSL a range of modifiers of quality is available, some involving alterations in the manual component, others requiring the addition of non-manual markers. Different types of modifiers of quality apply to different parts of speech; finding out which quality modification can be used is one way to test what category or part of speech a sign belongs to. We will start with quality modifiers for verbs, and go on to discuss quality modifiers for nouns and adjectives.

Verbs can be modified to indicate the qualities of (among others) effort, intensity, and speed. Bergman has noted a set of non-manual activities which accompany these quality modifications, and they appear to be similar in Swedish Sign Language and BSL. A verb can be modified for ease or effort by adding a specific mouth and eyebrow movement to manual movements. The neutral form of the verb can be considered as having no special marking, with the qualified form having one of two opposing sets of markers. For example, the quality modifiers 'ease' and 'effort' may be considered as opposites. A feature found with 'ease' should have its opposite found with 'effort', while the neutral form should have no marking at all. The unmarked verb WALK was shown in an earlier example. WALK marked with 'ease' quality is illustrated in fig. 7.17a. WALK with 'effort' quality in fig. 7.17b. In the 'ease' modification the mouth is closed, with slightly protruding and rounded lips. The mouth may open in rhythm with the movements of the hand, and eyes are slightly widened with eyebrows slightly raised. The head may tilt from side to side, also in rhythm with the hand's movements. This sign can be translated as WALK-EASILY or WALK COMFORTABLY. In the 'effort' modification the mouth is open, tense and spread, and the lips may be drawn back. This modification can be translated as WALK-WITH-EFFORT. Note that the features in these modifications are opposed: closed, relaxed mouth vs. tense, spread mouth; tilting head vs. rigid

a.   b.

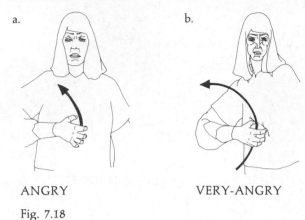

ANGRY   VERY-ANGRY

Fig. 7.18

head; raised brows vs. lowered brows. We therefore can describe these changes as part of one modification, and describe the features as + or −. In other words, the + 'effort' modification is :   + tense mouth
                                    + head rigid
                                    + brows lowered
The − 'effort' (or 'ease') modification is: − tense mouth
                                    − head rigid
                                    − brows lowered
The neutral form is: ø tense mouth (free to move)
                        ø head rigid (free to move)
                        ø brows lowered (free to move)

Intensity (e.g. English *very tired, really angry*) is indicated in BSL by a combination of manual and non-manual features. This modification has been termed by Bergman 'initial hold'. In the 'initial hold' modification, the movement is held momentarily before being completed. Along with the movement modification, the head may turn away from the initial hand position. Fig. 7.18 shows the neutral and modified versions of ANGRY. The meaning of ANGRY modified by initial hold would be VERY-ANGRY, and this modification appears with verbs referring to a state of being, rather than an action. Such verbs include HAPPY, SORRY, ANGRY, COLD, DEAF (note that although these words are adjectives in English, we are treating them as verbs or predicates in BSL).

There is also a modification for verbs of motion in BSL which conveys the meaning of 'great speed'. This modification contrasts with the 'effort' modification, but can be combined with it to mean, for example, 'He drove really hard down the motorway'. In the 'speed' modification, the movement of the hand(s) is reduced and repeated rapidly so that they may just appear to oscillate, the body

THE
NORTHERN COLLEGE
LIBRARY
BARNSLEY

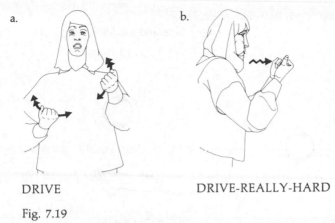

a.

b.

DRIVE   DRIVE-REALLY-HARD

Fig. 7.19

leans forward, and the mouth is closed with cheeks puffed out. Air may be expelled steadily from the mouth throughout the articulation of the sign (fig. 7.19b). The base sign is given in fig. 7.19a.

As well as verb modifications of quality, nouns and adjectives may also undergo changes related to quality. These changes also involve non-manual as well as manual components. The form of signs is directly related to their ability to undergo different types of modifications. In the last chapter we discussed different types of iconicity in sign form; the derivation of a sign from one of these types of image controls the modifications it can undergo. This can be seen clearly when modifications for size are examined. Modifiers for size can be incorporated into the sign itself, can be added as a modifier element, or can require substitution of the base sign. Fig. 7.20 illustrates these three types.

The sign TRAIN in fig. 7.20a cannot be altered in form to show length because the sign is formed by 'substitutive depiction' using the hand to form the referent. Other signs formed by substitutive depiction are PLANT, TREE and TELEPHONE. To indicate the quality of size a modifier such as LONG, TALL, SHORT, is added.

The sign TABLE in fig. 7.20b is formed by 'outline depiction': the hands are used to trace an outline of the shape of the referent. Other signs of this type include BOX, HOUSE, TICKET, BALL. To modify this type of sign for size requires incorporation of the modifier into the articulation of the sign, by altering the space used in the movement of the hands.

The sign HAIR (fig. 7.20c) is deictic, that is, an example of the referent is indicated by pointing, grasping or otherwise indicating. Signs of this type include most parts of the body. Signs formed in this way are modified by substituting a deictic gesture indicative of the modified meaning. In the example, HAIR

153

a. Invariant signs (substitutive depiction)

Sign   Sign and modifier

TRAIN   LONG-TRAIN

b. Incorporating signs (outline depiction)

Sign   Sign and modifier

 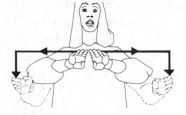

TABLE   LONG-TABLE

c. Substituting signs (deictic)

Sign   Sign and modifier

HAIR   LONG-HAIR

Fig. 7.20

Intensifiers

a.

b.

VERY-SMALL-TABLE   VERY-LONG-HAIR

Fig. 7.21

involves grasping the hair; in the modified version the hands are used to indicate both the hair and its length simultaneously.

Size can also be indicated through the addition of non-manual elements. These convey an intensification of the size modification (fig. 7.21a,b); we can see the non-manual modifier indicating VERY-SMALL-TABLE and VERY-LONG-HAIR.

Syntax

So far in this chapter we have seen the sorts of modification, both manual and non-manual, which individual signs undergo; in the remainder we will be concerned with the syntax of BSL. As with morphology, the analysis of BSL syntax is at an early stage, so we will discuss here a few selected topics in syntax as examples of the sort of analyses now being carried out. The two major areas we will discuss are sign order and sentence type. In the section on sign order we will describe attempts to define rules for the order of elements in a sign language sentence; in the section on sentence type we will look at how different types of sentences, such as interrogatives, are formed.

Sign order

Linguists often define languages according to the predominant order of elements in sentences. This study of word order typology has sought to class languages according to whether their predominant order is subject–verb–object, verb–subject–object, topic–comment, or a number of other possibilities.

English, of course, is an SVO language according to this classification; the predominant order of elements in a sentence is subject–verb–object. There are passive sentences, where the order is object–verb–subject, but these sentences are marked as more complex than SVO sentences. Welsh is a VSO language. Other spoken languages, such as Chinese, are described as topic–comment languages. An example from Chinese (quoted in Li and Thompson, 1976) is *Those trees tree-trunk big* (those trees (topic) the trunks are big). This type of sentence occurs in English, but as a rather unusual form: *Ice-cream – I love it*. Li and Thompson have suggested a two-way division among languages: topic-prominent (topic–comment) and subject-prominent (any permutation of S, V and O). The issue for sign language linguists is whether sign languages can be analysed according to the same criteria, and thus defined as topic-prominent or subject-prominent. An early paper by Fischer (1975: 5) claims that 'The basic word order in ASL is subject–verb–object (SVO).' Friedman (1976) presents a well argued criticism of this position, claiming that ASL is a topic–comment language, and that evidence of SVO order is due to contact between ASL and English and is not centrally important. Deuchar (1983) draws on both these studies in an analysis of sign order in BSL. She agrees with Friedman that topic-prominence is the characteristic feature of BSL as well as ASL. The sort of data she uses to support this claim are the following types:

VO	CLEAN ALL	(I cleaned everything)	(T)C
OV	TEN·p·PUT-IN	(I put in 10p)	T C
SV	FATHER FALL	(Father fell)	T C

If we analyse these sentences according to subject–verb–object order, we have three different orders for three different sentences. Deuchar instead analyses them as topic–comment. Because topics may have a scope larger than one sentence (unlike subjects), the topic may not appear before every verb, although it must appear where there is a change of topic. Topics need not be nouns; they can be adverbs (*There* we two go). Deuchar also points out that non-manual marking may accompany topics. An example she cites is:

Eyebrows:	....	pause	raised	....	||
Hands:	·k·i·l·b·y BEFORE GOOD		NOW GOOD		

She argues that the topic is ·k·i·l·b·y BEFORE GOOD, as the non-manual element indicating a question does not appear until NOW. This example could be translated into English as:

Kilby, who was good before,   is he good now?

topic   comment

Another way to emphasise the contrast between topic and comment relies on the availability of two hands as articulators. Deuchar's example, TEN·p·PUT-IN, had the form:

Right hand: TEN·p·................... | |
Left hand: PUT-IN | |

with the right hand remaining in the position for ·p·, while the left hand signs PUT-IN. Here the topic is signed first and held while the comment is signed.

Deuchar goes on to ask how it is that some researchers (Woodward, 1973; Hansen, 1975) have identified topic–comment as the basic structure of sign language sentences, while others (Fischer, 1975; Liddell, 1980) have found SVO structure as basic. In fact, the researchers finding topic–comment structure have generally used recordings of spontaneous signing, while the researchers finding SVO structure have used elicited sentences. She suggests that the communication situation may have an important effect on sentence type. This effect relates to other areas of sign language (and spoken language) research. One would not want to draw conclusions about English generally by listening to, for example, a sermon. Researchers must always evaluate the effect of situation on the data they record.

We mentioned the simultaneous use of both hands in topic–comment constructions. There are other constructions in which use is made of either linear or simultaneous structures. Earlier in this chapter we discussed size modifiers and how they could be added to signs, incorporated in signs, or substituted for signs. Here we will discuss modifying phrases and their internal structure. There are four options available for phrases such as SMALL BOY. The first and second involve addition of the modifier SMALL either before or after the sign BOY. The choice between pre- and post- modifiers is, as far as we know, optional: that is, there appear to be no rules governing the use of one or the other. Some researchers have suggested that the basic order is base sign + modifier, and that modifier + base sign phrases occur because of the influence of English. We do not yet have enough evidence to support this theory. The third type of phrasal modification is simultaneous modification. In simultaneous modification the base sign is articulated with one hand and the modifier with the other. An example of this type of construction is:

Left hand: BOY................ | |
Right hand: SMALL | |

In all examples of this type that we have recorded, the left hand is used for the base sign and the right hand for the modifier. Note that in the examples quoted above from Deuchar (1983), she found that topics were articulated with the right hand and comments with the left. The contrast between the use of left and right hands is one way in which we can tell that BOY SMALL quoted above is a phrase translatable as 'small boy' rather than a sentence translatable as 'boy (is) small'.

The fourth type of modification is called 'bracketing'. In bracketing the

modifier occurs both before and after the base sign it modifies: WHITE/SHIRT/
WHITE. Just as holding still the hand which articulates the topic while the other
hand articulates the comment, or holding the base sign still while the modifier is
signed, indicates the scope of one relative to the other, so too bracketing reveals
the scope of the modifier. Everything occurring between the bracketing is
affected by the modifier. While in WHITE/SHIRT/WHITE this is a single sign, in
other examples, an entire clause or phrase is contained within the bracketing. So
both the repetition of signs or the holding of one sign during the articulation of
another can be used to indicate the scope of the sign.

Sentence types

Most languages in the world contrast declarative (statement) and interrogative
(question) sentence types. Interrogative sentences are generally differentiated
from declarative sentences by word order, special interrogative particles or
intonation. In English, for example, we use word order contrasting *He can drive*
with *Can he drive?* by inversion of subject and verb, as well as by intonation.
Within the category of interrogatives, polar interrogatives (questions to which
the answer is *Yes* or *No*, e.g. *Can he drive?*) are distinguished from wh-
interrogatives (so-called in English because they involve using question words
which begin with *wh-*, e.g. *who, where, why, when, which* and *how*). Rather than
requiring an answer *Yes* or *No* these require additional information of an
explanatory nature. There is also a category of interrogative which in English
can be interpreted as requiring either *Yes–No* or a choice of options depending
on intonation (e.g. *Do you advocate the overthrow of the government by force or
violence?* can be answered either with *No* or *Force, but not violence*, depending on
whether the question is seen as presenting alternatives which can be considered
separately). Lyons (1977: 760) has claimed that 'The distinction between yes–no
questions and wh- questions is a logical, or semantic, distinction that is universal,
in the sense that it can be drawn independently of the grammatical and lexical
structure of particular languages.' We therefore expect to find these distinctions
in BSL: firstly, that declaratives are distinguished from interrogatives; and
secondly, that yes–no questions are distinguished from wh- questions.

In our discussion of basic sentence structure earlier in this chapter we said that
order in a sentence depends on which elements are perceived as topic, and which
as comment. We would therefore not expect to find change in sign order as a
feature of questions, since such a change would indicate a basic alteration in
meaning rather than an interrogative. We would therefore look at either
interrogative particles or intonation as possible sources of contrast between
declaratives and interrogatives. We have not identified any interrogative
particles, so we must turn to intonation.

Intonation in spoken languages is concerned with pitch variation extending across sentences. Just as intonation occurs simultaneously with articulated words, so we might expect whatever marks questions in BSL to occur simultaneously with articulated signs and to extend over stretches as long as a sentence. What we find taking the role of intonation in BSL is facial expression. In other words, specific facial expressions, occurring simultaneously with signs, differentiate declarative sentences from interrogatives. Furthermore, yes–no questions and wh- questions are differentiated by contrasting facial expressions. Baker-Shenk (1983b) includes a detailed discussion of the role of facial expression in this and other areas.

Wh- questions

Just as with English wh- question words, there are a set of signs which appear in wh- questions. Several of the wh- question signs resemble each other; instead of beginning with *wh-* they share a common handshape and movement. The same handshape and movement (five fingers extended, separate and wiggling) occurs in WHEN, HOW-MANY, and HOW-OLD (these latter two are single signs in BSL).

The appearance of these signs in a sentence does not, of course, suffice to form an interrogative any more than the use of *when* or *who* in the sentences *She'll go there when she has time* or *I don't know who's paying* does in English. Signs such as WHEN and WHO are sometimes used as relative pronouns just as the English words are. Signers clearly interpret utterances as wh- questions only when particular non-manual features occur.

Bracketing of utterances with 'wh- signs' frequently occurs: WHY YOU GO AMERICA WHY; WHAT WORK WHAT etc. As in the example cited earlier, where bracketing occurs it emphasises the scope of the question. Thus in a complex utterance such as:

WHEN HER SISTER BROTHER TRAVEL (by) CAR-THERE p·a·t· STAY ONE WEEK COME SELF *HOW-LONG* HER SISTER STAY THERE *HOW-LONG*

(When her sister and brother travel there by car (with) Pat, (who's) staying
one week and coming back herself, how long will her sister stay there?)
the bracketing with HOW-LONG emphasises that the scope of HOW-LONG does not include the part of the sentence referring to Pat's brother and sister, travelling time, or to Pat's coming back, but only to the length of time Pat's sister is staying.

As we mentioned earlier, the presence of signs such as HOW-LONG and WHERE does not simply identify an utterance as a question. It is in the combination of certain facial movements that unequivocal information is given that distinguishes questions from statements. Also we should expect there to be some way of distinguishing yes–no questions from wh- questions if this is truly a semantic universal, as Lyons claims.

Yes–no questions, unlike functionally similar questions in English, are not distinguished formally, in terms of manual sign order, from other sentence types: that is, one cannot tell from a gloss of the signs in a sentence that the utterance is a question. A number of optional manual markers may appear in conjunction with facial expressions to distinguish questions from statements, but these are also found where no question is implied. In examples where these optional manual markers are not found with questions they serve as 'turn-relinquishing' devices, occurring at the end of an utterance. As questions also relinquish the turn of speech to the other person, these markers may just serve as additional emphasis that a question is being asked. They include:

(1) holding hand or hands out, fingers pointing away, palm up, heel of hand higher than fingertips

(2) pointing to the addressee

(3) prolonging the duration of the last sign or facial expression

(4) index finger raised, palm away from body, held still or wiggled side to side (as in BSL WHAT)

An example of an utterance using one of these devices is:

THINK p·o·p·e· COME TO IRELAND THINK YOU (data from Worswick, 1982) where YOU falls into category (2) above (also note the bracketing with THINK). Worswick found that 82 per cent of the yes–no questions she investigated showed prolongation of facial expression and/or final sign: these markers can be quite common as a feature of questions.

The facial expression found in yes–no questions consists of head and shoulders forward, chin forward enough to keep the face vertical, and eyebrows raised. All the yes–no questions described by Woll (1981) use these facial expressions; all but one of Worswick's 65 examples did.

The facial expression found in wh- questions is different. Here the eyebrows are lowered and together (as in a frown) and shoulders are hunched as well as forward. This marking appeared in all the Woll and Worswick data, although in one example only the eyebrows were lowered. For both wh- and yes–no questions the facial expression extends over the entire clause which is being questioned. In the lengthy example HOW-LONG HER SISTER STAY HOW-LONG, the question facial expression begins at the first HOW-LONG and continues until the end of the utterance. A detailed micro-analysis of the role of facial expression has recently been reported by Baker-Shenk (1983a). She discovered that non-manual features appear before the onset of the manual activity in questions in ASL. Baker-Shenk (1983b) contains an expansion of this and provides an elaboration of how non-manual features function in ASL. Much of the analysis seems likely to apply to BSL, but research will require to confirm this.

One must not assume, of course, that other utterances occur with absolutely no facial expression. Rather, question facial expressions are marked as *distinct* from other facial expressions. Other utterances may incorporate facial expression as an essential part of their meanings: for example, sentences with negatives, where the manual component is the same in negative and positive statements but with specific facial expression and head movement distinguishing them.

In this chapter we have been able to give only a 'taste' of current research on sign language linguistics. We have tried to show the areas of interest for students of language, and the new understanding of sign language structure we have gained. Linguistic research on sign languages is still in its infancy, yet despite the difference of channels used for communication and the very different traditions of sign and spoken language use, we continually find points of similarity. The 'design features' of language are common across superficially differing languages, and the search for universals of language structure can only be enhanced by attention to sign language.

8. Comparing sign languages

The subjects of this chapter are comparative and international aspects of sign language. These topics have been touched upon briefly in earlier chapters; they will now be brought together and discussed in greater depth, along with new material from current research.

As Battison and Jordan (1976) point out, writers in the past, by using expressions such as *the* sign language, have tended to present sign language as universal and easily understood. They cite Long's (1918) *The sign language*, and Michaels' (1923) *A handbook of the sign language of the deaf*, and we can add to their list Nevins' (1895) *The sign language of the deaf and dumb*, and *Guide to the silent language of the deaf and dumb* (anonymous and undated). The clear implication is that there is one universal sign language. An author who studied the American Indian sign system used for ritual story-telling reported that the sign language of Indians, of deaf people, and of everyone else 'constitute one language – the gesture speech of mankind, of which each system is a dialect' (Mallery, 1881).

A writer, Berthier, who was deaf himself, stated 'For centuries scholars from every country have sought after a universal language and failed. Well, it exists all around, it is sign language' (quoted in Battison and Jordan, 1976: 54). Other writers answered the question of the universality of sign language with less certainty: 'though all nations do not use the same mode of signs, one having a knowledge of the signs herein delineated will experience little, if any difficulty in understanding other modes, and of being understood by those who use a different mode' (Michaels, quoted in Battison and Jordan, 1976: 54).

Two more detailed and better considered responses to this question were those of Wundt and Tylor. Wundt, a 19th-century psychologist, researched the signing of German deaf children with the aim of discovering the universal properties underlying all languages. Wundt thought that the universality he perceived in sign language was related to the concreteness of its concepts:

Systems of signs that have arisen in spatially separate environments and under doubtlessly independent circumstances are, for the most part, very similar or indeed closely related; this, then, enables communication without great difficulty between persons making use of gestures. Such is the much-lauded universality of gestural communication. Further, it is self-evident that this universality extends only to those concepts of a generally objective nature: for example, you and I, this and that, here and there, or earth, heaven, cloud, sun, house, tree, flower, walking, standing, lying, hitting, and many other such objects and actions perceived according to their basic features. (quoted in Mayberry, 1978: 351)

As Mayberry points out, if sign language only has concrete concepts then the signs are iconic and universally understood. Conversely, if sign language is universally understood, then it must be limited to concrete and picturable concepts.

Tylor, a 19th-century anthropologist, also studied sign language in an attempt to understand the nature of human communication and its origins:

the celebrated sign-languages of the American prairies, in which conversation is carried on between hunting parties of whites and natives, and even between Indians of different tribes, are only dialects (so to speak) of the gesture-language.
. . . there is a great deal of variety in the signs among particular tribes, but such a way of communication is so natural all the world over, that when outlandish people, such as Laplanders, have been brought to be exhibited in our great cities, they have been comforted in their loneliness by meeting with deaf-and-dumb children, with whom they at once fall to conversing with delight in this universal language of signs . . . This 'gesture-language' is universal not only because signs are 'self-expressive' (their meaning is self-evident) but because the grammar is international. What is done is to call up a picture in the minds of the spectators by first setting up something to be thought about, and then adding to or acting on it till the whole story is told. If the signs do not follow in such order as to carry meaning as they go, the looker-on will be perplexed. (Tylor, 1895: 118-19)

With the advent of linguistic research on sign language from the 1960s onwards, attitudes towards universality of sign language changed considerably, often to the point where mutual unintelligibility between sign languages was reported, with researchers at pains to identify sign languages as completely different from each other. Very frequently in the literature earlier discussions about sign language universality are described as myths or misconceptions. As Mayberry (1978: 33) points out: 'Today it is common practice to begin papers by setting the record straight, so to speak, sometimes with what strikes the reader as being an unusually strong position regarding inter-sign language comprehension given the current state of knowledge.' There are a great number of references, for example, (very often American) to the mutual unintelligibility of ASL and BSL (Mayberry cites Stokoe, 1972; Fischer, 1974; Lane, 1977 among others).

One by-product of regarding sign languages as mutually unintelligible has been the attempt to create an international, artificial sign language, similar in aim to Esperanto. Gestuno, as it is known, was developed by the World Federation of the Deaf for use at international conferences of deaf people. The attitudes of deaf people to its use is that it is no easier, and possibly more difficult, to understand than a foreign sign language.

The reasons for the shift from regarding sign language as one universal form of communication to seeing sign languages as highly different from each other are easy to understand, but the result has been confusion over what questions remain to be asked about the differences between sign languages. Battison and Jordan (1976) asked five questions; although posed so long ago, the answers are not clear. In this chapter we will discuss these questions and the preliminary answers we have, suggesting possible ways of answering them in the future:

(1)   Do deaf people around the world use the same signs?
(2)   Can signers understand each others' sign languages?
(3)   Can signers from different countries communicate with each other even if they don't know each others' sign languages?
(4)   Do signers have a clear idea of the separateness of different sign languages, or do they feel and act as if they are all basically the same thing?
(5)   What attitudes do people have about their own sign language and about foreign sign languages?

A sixth question should also be added: Do deaf people around the world use the same grammar? This question is needed because even if signs were the same around the world, the grammar of sign languages in different countries might be different.

Battison and Jordan report several types of study to determine if signers from different countries understand each others' signing. The first (Battison and Jordan, 1976) reports the results of an attitude survey among deaf people from different countries attending an international conference. While they acknowledge that the data on their first two questions, as to whether sign languages are understood by foreigners, were mostly self-reports, they conclude that signs used in foreign countries, or even in different parts of the same country, are largely unintelligible in connected discourse. This conclusion is based on comments such as:

A young woman from Lyons reported that she refuses to visit Paris without her friend who has been to Paris more often and understands the Parisians' sign language better.

A standard story, repeated by travellers and natives alike, holds that if you travel 50 miles in Britain you will encounter a different sign language that cannot be understood in the region you have just left. (Battison and Jordan, 1976: 59)

Clearly, people's reports of communication difficulties and the actual difficulties encountered are different, as research on sign language in Britain has found one sign language, called BSL, albeit with dialectal differences.

Apart from anecdotal and self-report data, two other kinds of study have been reported. In the first of these, lists of signs in dictionaries are compared (e.g. Woodward, 1978); in the second, referential communication experiments between signers of different countries are performed (e.g. Jordan and Battison, 1976; Mayberry, 1978). It should be noted that the referential communication experiments of the type conducted by Jordan and Battison and by Mayberry are designed to answer question (2) rather than question (3). In other words, signers are not asked to try to communicate information to a foreign signer, but are instructed to use their own sign languages when addressing a same- or different-language partner. Even in this strict condition, signers performed better than would be expected for two unrelated spoken languages.

Of course, possible historical relationships between different sign languages should not be excluded as a reason for similarities between two sign languages. There have been attempts to explore similarities in terms of historical links. Most of the comparative work has been concerned with ASL and French Sign Language. It is generally assumed that ASL is historically linked to the French Sign Language of the early 19th century, researchers seeing evidence of cognate signs in French Sign Language and ASL (fig. 8.1). (Cognates are pairs of words or signs which are historically linked, as opposed to being coincidentally similar or borrowed.) The most comprehensive sign language comparison is Woodward's (1978) glottochronological study. Glottochronology is a technique developed for spoken languages which has a basic assumption that languages change at a relatively steady rate. Thus, by comparing the percentage of cognate words in two related spoken languages it is possible to estimate fairly accurately the date at which they separated. For example, we would expect to find a very high proportion of cognate words in British and American English but a much lower percentage if we compare English and German and still lower if we compare English and Russian. When applying glottochronological analyses it is crucial that only cognate words are compared, and not words which are coincidentally similar, or which may have been borrowed from one language into another: to include these would give a false high rating of similarity. In Woodward's study, signs from French Sign Language and ASL were compared. Historical evidence would suggest that American and French sign languages began to go their separate ways in 1816, when French Sign Language was imported with the French deaf teacher Clerc; one would therefore expect a very high degree of similarity, as 1816 is very recent in glottochronological terms, and the percentage of cognate signs should be over 90 per cent. Instead, Woodward obtained a cognate figure of 60 per cent. This low figure he attributed to ASL being a creole, or combination of French Sign Language and at least one other sign language. This is reasonable, as one would expect deaf people in the USA to have been

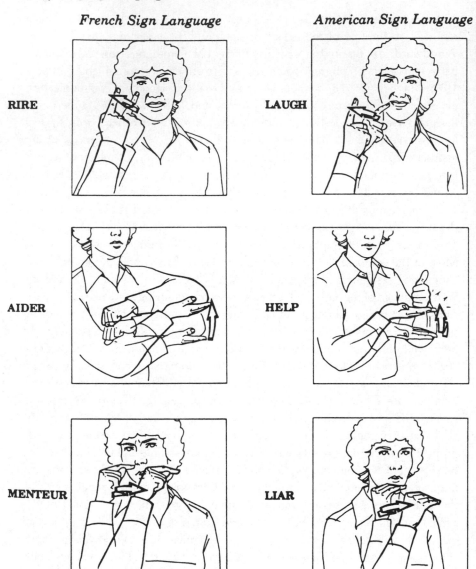

Fig. 8.1   'Cognates' (from Baker and Cokely, 1980).

using some sign language before the imported use of FSL. What is not explained satisfactorily in Woodward's paper is why the 60 per cent of similar signs were regarded as cognate, rather than coincidentally similar or loan signs.

An extreme version of the historical relationship approach is Anderson (1979) where large 'pre-historic' families of sign languages are postulated on

A	G
French	British
Italian	Swedish
Danish	Finnish

Fig. 8.2

such evidence as whether the sign for ONE is formed with the extended thumb (Å) or index finger (G) (fig. 8.2).

It is clear that the choice of signs for comparison will affect the results of such an exercise; a balance must be sought between too small a number and too great. Generally, for spoken language glottochronology two lists have been used, a 100-word list and a 200-word list (which includes the 100-word list), both developed by Swadesh (in Samarin, 1967). Woodward (1978) used Swadesh's 200-word list with some modifications; Stokoe and Kuschel (1979) have developed another 200-word list for sign language data collection. None of these lists, however, is wholly useful for the study of urban deaf populations, as all three have been designed for anthropological study of one sort or another, and include words such as *spear* and *dung*. The spoken language lists also include items not relevant to deaf populations. The Stokoe and Kuschel list was developed for use by anthropologists on field work, and also does not include items relevant to deaf culture. The list developed for the study reported here (Woll, 1983) contains in its full form 257 items, many of which do appear in the other lists. The words which do not appear in other lists fall into several important groups: signs relevant to deaf culture, signs which might be subject to borrowing by languages in contact, signs where compounding is likely to occur, number and colour terms.

As with other dictionary comparisons, however, a number of 'warnings' must be given. The first is that where dictionaries are used as a data source often little is known about, for example, how formal the sign is, whether there are other social or regional variants, how well the translation represents the meaning of the sign. With the technique adopted in Woll (1983) of recording signers translating a word list into signs, the data include only one signer from each sign language. Therefore, when the term 'British Sign Language' is used, it can only mean signs *used* by a British signer. Secondly, any subset of a lexicon, whether from a dictionary or word list, can only give a partial, and perhaps unrepresentative, view of language. Thirdly, as mentioned above, because we know little about historical relationships between sign languages it is difficult to disentangle historical influences and similarities between signs arising from other causes. This problem also appears in glottochronological studies of spoken languages, of course, as the example below illustrates. The following are words meaning 'mother' in several spoken languages:

English: mother
Latin: mater
Russian: maht
Hebrew: imah
Chinese: ma

We already know that English, Latin and Russian are related languages, so we would see these data as revealing the common origin of these languages. Hebrew is thought by some linguists to be very distantly related to the first three languages, and by other linguists not to be related, so the reason for the similarity cannot be definitely given. It is fairly universally accepted that Chinese is not related to any of the four other languages, so the similarity cannot be because these words are cognate. The Chinese word *ma* might be a loan word, it might be coincidentally the same, or the similarity might arise from another factor. In fact, the widespread finding that the word for 'mother' in unrelated languages often includes the sound 'ma' might lead us to look for sound symbolism as the underlying common factor.

The last observation about dictionaries or word lists is that they may underrepresent similarities between different sign languages: for example, the American and British signs for WALK are quite different, but British signers would certainly use a sign resembling the American sign in certain contexts. In other cases the particular translation of a sign may fail to show similarity: the Danish and British signs for WOMAN are different, but the British sign LADY resembles the Danish sign WOMAN; such information is not picked up by this method of data collection.

Word list translations have been obtained and analysed in 15 different sign languages. The most striking finding from this comparison (Woll, 1983) is that the average percentage of similar signs in two different sign languages is 35–40. This figure, of course, is much higher than one expects for two unrelated spoken languages. Languages with a known close historical relationship show far higher percentages of similar signs: 80 per cent for British and Australian Sign

Languages. Among other interesting observations from the study is the similarity of the Flemish and Walloon Sign Languages, the sign languages which are used by deaf people who belong to different spoken language communities in Belgium. This finding suggests close interaction between deaf people belonging to these different groups. In contrast, Flemish and Dutch Sign Languages, although found in adjacent countries with the same spoken language, are very dissimilar. In terms of findings, Woodward's 60 per cent cognate score for American and French Sign Languages represents quite a low degree of similarity over what one would expect from any two unrelated sign languages, and this suggests that ASL and French Sign Language are *not* very closely related. Another interesting finding relates to the signs illustrated in fig. 8.1. In the 15 sign languages analysed, the following signs were found for LAUGH, HELP and (tell a) LIE. In all 15 sign languages, the sign for LAUGH was located at the mouth or lower cheek; the hand was either held with index finger extended, or index and thumb extended and moved from side to side. In all 15 sign languages HELP was signed with the right hand lifting and moving forward the left hand, forearm or elbow. In all the sign languages except Chinese Sign Language, (tell a) LIE was located at the lower face, with the hand moving sideways. Clearly, the similarity between the French and American signs is not in itself indicative of an historical relationship. What the data show is that the issue of sign universality cannot be easily described as confirmed or disproved. Further attention must be devoted to sign forms and their derivation. This can be seen in the context of new sign formation.

Apart from the word list, the comparative study reported above also included the signing of a text based on a picture book story *The snowman*. In the recounting of this story, several objects are referred to for which most sign languages do not have already existing signs. These include a skateboard and a punchball. Eleven of the 15 signers signed 'skateboard' in terms of its shape (oval with pairs of wheels), its movement (forward and side to side) and how a person interacts with it (standing on the board, balancing with arms and body). (The other four signers referred to only two out of three of these features.) Similarly for 'punchball', the predominant way of signing it was threefold: shape (ball on a stick), movement (springs to and fro on a pivot) and how a person interacts with it (hands punching alternately); these three are salient features. Signs in use for many referents reflect one or two of these properties, and thus we should not be surprised that comparisons of sign lists result in such a high degree of similarity, as the appearance, movement, and use of an object can be expected to be similar across different cultures. Other similarities can be explained in different ways. Nine of the sign languages studied used similar signs for AMERICA. This form, which is also found in ASL, is likely to have been borrowed by other sign

Table 8.1. *Common grammatical features in different sign languages*

(1) Aspect marked on verbs by movement alteration:

Language	Slow reduplication		Fast reduplication		Slow movement
	(+ punctual)	(− punctual)	(+ punctual)	(− punctual)	
BSL	iterative	durative	——— habitual ———		
ASL	iterative	durative	——— habitual ———		
FSL	——— iterative ———				durative
RSL	——— iterative ———				

(2) Modality marked by auxiliaries preceding, following, or bracketing verb:

BSL	WILL, MUST, etc.	
	WILL ASK	'I will ask'
	AGREE WILL YOUNG	'The young will agree'
ASL	MUST, CAN, etc.	
	ME CANNOT a·f·f·o·r·d CANNOT	'I can't afford it'
FSL	WILL (VA-VA), CAN, etc.	
	MOI S'OCCUPER-DE VA-VA	'I'll take care of it'

(3) No copula:

BSL	HE NO—GOOD	'He is no good'
ASL	LYNN SINGLE	'Lynn was single'
FSL	LOUP LUI	'He is a wolf'

(4) Facial expression distinguishes questions and statements:

BSL	GO THERE eyebrows raised, head forward, eyes widened, eye gaze at addressee	'Are you going there?'
ASL	FATHER BECOME-ANGRY eyebrows raised, widened eyes, head forward, eye gaze at addressee	'Did Dad get angry?'

(Examples 1–3 taken from Deuchar, 1984; example 4 ASL from Baker-Shenk 1983b) languages from ASL. This is the case for two reasons: many signers report another sign for AMERICA which is disappearing; the sign itself is not 'transparent', and there is no known link between the sign and any visual image. In other cases, similar signs are found only among sign languages with known historical links. The sign for BAD in BSL is formed with the little finger extended from the fist, and the same sign occurs in New Zealand, Australian and South African Sign Languages. The similarity between signs can thus be accounted for by historical links, borrowing of signs through contact between signers, or cultural universal propensities to label concepts in particular ways. Sign languages reflect all these processes.

Less is known of sign language grammar universals than of lexical similarities. Throughout this book, however, we have drawn on examples from research in other sign languages and found parallel or identical structures. Table 8.1 summarises some research on grammatical features in different sign languages which are also found in BSL and which have been discussed in this book.

Many of the features common to different sign languages are also found in spoken languages. We can therefore attribute some similarities of grammar to universal properties of language, whether spoken or signed.

In a study of communication among signers from different countries at an international workshop, Moody (1979) noted that three features were found: grammar, mime and 'international' gestures.

Les règles syntaxiques de toutes les langues de signes que nous avons pu observer semblent recourir à l'espace, au mouvement et à l'orientation des signes d'une façon proche.

Les gestes internationaux sont constitués par du mime, tout en recourant à une utilisation de l'espace, du mouvement et de l'orientation extrêmement proche de celle observée dans les différentes langues des signes. Les 'gestes internationaux' recourent aussi à un ensemble de gestes généralement reconnus comme étant des 'vocables internationaux'. Ils comprennent aussi des termes empruntés à une langue des signes, des gestes inventés qui ont un sens précis (seulement dans le contexte de la situation), des expressions faciales ou des postures).

(The syntactic rules of all the sign languages we were able to observe appear to have recourse to space, movement and orientation of signs in a similar manner.

'International gestures' are composed of mime, using space, movement and orientation very similarly to the way they are used in different sign languages. 'International gestures' are also composed of a collection of gestures generally understood as international. They also include terms borrowed from a given sign language (these terms may be understood by reference to context, or by explanation) invented gestures which have a precise meaning (only in the situational context), facial expression, or body movements.)

171

Comparing sign languages

The vocabulary required is rapidly and easily established through interaction between signers, clearly with a shared grammar, recourse to mime and a percentage of shared vocabulary. The process of communication is greatly facilitated. But perhaps the most important feature which makes communication possible across different sign languages is the shared culture of deaf people. The deaf of all countries face similar educational experiences and suppression of their sign language. This has helped to unite deaf people and provides a common experience as well as common linguistic structure on which to draw.

9. Learning and using BSL

While the study of the language is critical to the development of BSL and its acceptance, it is also true to say that there is a more pressing problem in relation to BSL, at least in the eyes of deaf people, and that is how to learn and use it. Deaf people in the community appear to learn BSL easily, even if they have to wait until they have left school. However, the learning of the language is not simply a matter of being deaf, since those who become deaf later in life very seldom achieve a fluency in BSL which allows them to be accepted within the community. In one sense this is a hopeful sign, at least for hearing people, since BSL learning is not determined solely by the inability to hear but more probably by motivation and the identification of the learner with the community of users (see chapter 1). From all the discussion so far, one would predict that BSL as a language should be no more difficult to learn than a foreign language, except, that is, for the fact that BSL is not a high status language and its users are often treated as failures. Our discussion here will consider the variables normally found important in second language learning, and consider how they might be used to predict BSL learning. In a final section, Krashen's (1981) theory of second language learning will be explored and its implications for BSL learners considered.

There has been very little research into BSL learning, and certainly no systematic analysis of the skills needed. There has always been a lingering suspicion that BSL is a very difficult language to learn once beyond a few preliminary signs. Indeed, the principal argument against its use in education has often been the claim that hearing people find it almost impossible to use effectively. This is at least untrue in the USA, where there is a comprehensive system of further education for deaf people in which the medium is an accepted form of ASL which hearing instructors use. Hansen (1980) maintains that hearing people can learn sign language to a satisfactory extent and can be successful in passive learning, i.e. understanding deaf people's signing, within a short time. However, it is certainly the perception of people working in the field that the level of sign language skill exhibited by hearing people, even those who function as interpreters for deaf people, is much lower than it should be. If deaf people's link to the hearing world and to the information distributed by the hearing world is faulty, then unless they have recourse to a second hearing person who can act as a check they will be unaware of the faults of the first hearing signer. Even if the faults are apparent, a deaf person would be very wary of criticising for fear that the interpreter would no longer co-operate and that even the slim link to what is being discussed in hearing company will be taken away. Therefore, the analysis of hearing people's skills in BSL is not simply a matter of eliciting deaf people's views on hearing BSL users, but must take into account a societal element not apparent in the evaluation of skills in, say, French.

There are, nevertheless, many features of foreign language learning which will be familiar to those who are learning sign language. In introducing the principles of language learning, Brown maintains:

Becoming bilingual is a way of life. Every bone and fibre of your being is affected in some way, as you struggle to reach beyond the confines of your first language and into a new language, a new culture, a new way of thinking, feeling and acting. Total commitment, total involvement, a total physical, intellectual and emotional response is necessary to successfully send and receive messages in a second language. (1980: 1)

In fact, according to Brown it is virtually impossible to *teach* a language; what one can hope to do is to provide a situation where the complex variables which contribute are maximised. These views simply emphasise what is often forgotten; that learning any language is a difficult task. As a result, a great deal of the research on foreign language learning focuses on the problems involved, and usually on the errors made by the students of the second language. BSL learning usually begins beyond what is normally considered an optimal age and should therefore be compared with the learning of foreign languages later in life. There are usually problems. The case of Zoila highlighted by Shapira (1978) is almost certainly a typical case.

Despite Zoila's everyday contact with English speakers in the USA, her use of English after three years of learning was very poor. Shapira's explanation is that Zoila had reached what was for her a satisfactory level of interaction and was not motivated to progress. Her initial negative view of English and the tolerance of her poor English by others meant she could 'get by' with her deviant grammar and limited vocabulary and articulation. Shapira's view is that she still used English through a translating frame from Spanish and had not fully embraced the language form. This may be compared with the apparent slowness of hearing people's learning of BSL. Schumann's (1977) model of 'social and psychological distance' seems particularly applicable to Zoila's case. The closer one is to a second language group, either socially or psychologically, the greater the probability of adequate learning. Social distance can be expressed as a series of questions constituting a rating scale. In sign language terms these would include:

Do hearing people control the fortunes of deaf people politically and economically?

Do hearing people tend to occupy more influential positions in technology than do deaf people?

Do hearing people have a significant role in raising the level of deaf people's lives to help them fit into society better?

Is the hearing community much larger than the deaf community?

Is the contact of the learner with the target language group likely to be intermittent rather than extensive?

Positive answers to most of these questions (which is what would be typical) indicate a poor language learning situation according to the model of social distance. We should go through the questions again, substituting 'English' for 'hearing' and 'French' for 'deaf'. We can see that the social distance between French and English is much less. Hearing people are members of the dominant culture, who usually wish to preseve their hearing status and whose length of stay among deaf people is often no more than a few hours at a time. Sign language is therefore less accessible than French, for example. According to Schumann, the greater the distance the more likely is the pidginisation of the target language. This happens with Latin American workers in the USA and it also happens with ASL users (Fischer, 1978). In order to overcome such a learning situation, Schumann suggests that psychological distance must be minimised. This is done by high motivation and especially by immersing one's own identity in that of the culture of the target language group. In learning sign language the opportunities for doing this are relatively few, and so sign language learning takes place in a less than ideal environment. Nevertheless, it is of some importance to try to establish what the effect of this learning environment is on the actual communication between deaf and hearing people.

Kyle, Woll and Llewollyn-Jones (1981) have described the opportunities available to BSL learners, and it is quite clear that these are less than adequate in relation to decreasing social distance. Even though one would probably not question the desire to minimise psychological distance, since most students are highly motivated and continue to attend courses for very long periods, it is clear that there is little loss of personal identity and very little contact with deaf people. Courses primarily of the one-hour-a-week variety and based on vocabulary with English–sign equivalents can do no more than serve as an introduction. Unfortunately they may also prove a hindrance if BSL is presented only as manual English, through the tutor's adherence to English or through the other necessity of providing English syntax for deaf people one is in contact with, since 'it will help their English'. In this instance, the caring role of the learner may well interfere with the task of adequately learning the language. The extent of the problem will be discussed later in this section, but clearly there are other factors in language learning and some hearing people do learn to use BSL and achieve communication fluency with deaf people. Our framework for under-standing this is, as with social distance, based firmly within the literature of second language learning. Virtually all the settings in which sign language is learned can also be found in second language learning. Languages can be learned because the student has a specific purpose for his own development (such as improving his career prospects), or because he has an interest in the culture or the language itself. Languages can be learned 'at home', where there are few opportunities for mixing with the native users of the language (such as evening class French) or they can be learned in a second language situation, either in the country in which that language is native or in one's own country where the language is used for a specific purpose (such as learning English in parts of Africa where it is used as the commercial language). Each of these situations exists in sign language learning, although the total immersion options are usually reserved for those people with deaf relatives. It is possible, then, to systematically examine these factors which are often proposed in describing spoken language learning and to indicate how they might apply in the sign language situation.

Strategies for language learning

Given that an individual has a purpose in seeking training in a second language, there is a whole range of in-built techniques for learning which the student can bring to the learning environment. Most of these techniques have been described in psychological terms and are particularly useful in explaining the errors a new student makes in using the language. Most of the functioning of an individual is now considered by cognitive psychologists to be controlled by strategies of one sort or another. The learning process consists of the acquisition of adaptive knowledge in the form of new facts or new strategies. The knowledge is adaptive when it can be fitted into an already existing framework within the individual but allows an extension of his capabilities. Learning occurs not because the person is somehow 'ready' for the next stage but because he is able to organise the incoming information in a satisfactory way. The human system is geared to this acquisition, and even when what is learned appears to be maladaptive or produces negative traits, it derives from a natural process. Errors made in the learning of a language, whether it is a first or a second one, are often indicative of the range and type of strategies used. One useful strategy in language learning is generalisation, but it is most noticeable when it exists as over-generalisation. The child who uses *goed* or *comed* is guilty of over-generalisation, while in sign the use of repetition to convey occurrence over a long time would be appropriate in WAIT-WAIT-WAIT, meaning 'wait for ages' but not in KEEP-KEEP-KEEP, where it would probably mean to 'keep three' things rather than to 'keep over time'. However, most of the time generalisation works appropriately and it is absolutely essential since the student will never experience all occurrences of the words or signs of the language. It has to be possible to produce spontaneously original sentences which are based on implicit rules which allow generalisation. The learner's ability to do this quickly and effectively from an early stage is obviously an important feature of language growth. However, not all strategies, though natural, are productive.

Interference from the native language is probably one of the most noticeable aspects of the early stages in second language learning. It is often apparent in sophisticated users of the language, and shows up as recurrent mistakes, usually of syntax, one school of thought, however, to be discussed later, considers this another strategy and not interference). In sign language learning, because of the greater status of the learner over the native user, the first language intrusion may frequently go uncorrected, as occurred in the case of Zoila.

The importation of English grammar into BSL is a particular feature of low status languages, where the learner's language interference may continue unchecked until there is a communication breakdown and where it is usually the lower status person who accepts the responsibility for the breakdown. A further complicating factor is that English interference in BSL occurs at times under the guise of improving the English skills of deaf people, so that the interlanguage (a variable form of signed English) may be given a higher status than the original language. The hearing learner then seeks only to master the interlanguage, which has no cultural base, and which therefore lacks the social depth of either language.

Avoidance is a negative strategy seen in language learning. It is most likely in communication settings where topics about which the learner is unhappy are avoided or ignored. As a strategy in the general learning situation it can be particularly damaging, and this is also true of language learning. In sign, it can be seen in the learner's apparent acknowledgement of comprehension of a statement by the deaf person which the hearing learner in fact has not understood, or it involves an immediate switch of topic by the hearing learner to something in which he feels more competent, without answering the deaf person's query. This latter tactic often succeeds because of the unwillingness of the deaf person to try to force the point or to contradict the hearing person.

As is becoming apparent, sign language is a language at risk; a language

177

which may be dominated by the learner to the extent that a distorted view of discourse with a native signer will be obtained. This is even more of a problem: it will not only damage the perspective of the learner but it will also effectively bar him from experience of the full language, since the native users will be unwilling to use it in his presence. This of course takes us into the domain of attitudes and feelings of the learners, and is an area more influenced by emotion.

Affective factors

If we consider the commitment required for the task of learning a language then it is not surprising that there is a large affective or emotive component in the eventual success of the learner. It is a factor recognised for a very long time in relation to language learning. There may be a number of reasons for this, but a very likely one relates to the whole question of our treatment of people within the community who are different. As was pointed out by Kyle (1981b), the field of special education engenders an isolation whereby children are viewed as totally unique, and their development is a personal co-operation with the adults around. The teacher's relation with a child is much more intense and long-lasting than for a teacher of a normal child, since they will be together in close contact during a longer period of growth. This is no bad thing at all, but it tends to produce a conflict of knowledge and practice. The resulting adult–child interaction is clouded by this conflict.

The conflict arises in two major ways: firstly, the most basic need of all, to understand the functioning of the child, is confounded by a need to hide this functioning, since it is this which makes the child most different from the community. So the teacher of a blind child, while allowing all along in the child's education for the difficulties he encounters, still prefers to emphasise to everyone the sameness of the child (his skills and achievements). The teacher of the deaf also alters the child's educational environment but still proclaims his hearing ability (i.e. the 'residual' hearing). Neither of these situations is in itself damaging, except that it may produce a denial of the actual preferred functioning of the child. Sign language is a particularly obvious stigmatising feature for the young deaf child, and so produces very negative feelings in the teacher (as exemplified in appendix 1), and thereby in those, such as parents, influenced by the education process. Any difficulty of sign language learning arises because of this negative feeling and not *vice versa*.

Secondly, and perhaps inevitably arising out of the first situation, the young adult who joins the sub-culture of deafness and uses sign language has, in the community's eyes, given up the search for sameness and therefore society's help comes in a 'care for the disabled' package. This has traditionally given lower role status to those who work in the field, but has also made their language learning goal an educational and care one. The task of interpreting has been seen in the UK only in terms of social service, often voluntary, but never in an enabling framework. So while interpreters working from spoken English to sign language are called upon to work for nothing as a service to these normal, intelligent 'disabled' people, those in the foreign spoken language interpretive role, where language users are equal, may rise to occupy one of the highest status roles in diplomacy, and correspondingly command high financial rewards. The point of all this is that the personality of the individual who chooses to learn sign language must therefore be one which can resolve these tensions or pressures from the community and invoke sufficient motivation to ensure success.

The motivation issue is not an easy one to discuss, since it is an item which is seldom adequately defined. Gardner and Lambert (1972) examined two kinds of motivation – 'instrumental' motivation and 'integrative' motivation. The former is one based on the career needs of the individual, and refers to the need to achieve a particular level (passing an exam or reading technical material in that language), and the latter occurs when the learner seeks to identify with the culture and become part of it. They claim that better language proficiency occurs when integrative motivation is prominent. Language teachers may tend to present the view that it is the *only* way to learn the language. However, research on Indian students learning English suggests that to learn the language for commercial purposes it may also be effective to have instrumental motivation. Brown (1980) takes this as evidence that there is a range of language contexts and that these may be influenced rather differently by these aspects of motivation. Therefore it would also seem possible to learn a functional sign language without a positive desire to become deaf on the part of the hearing learner; nevertheless, it has been the case in the past that those who have learned sign language have often been cast in the integrative mould and have had their views devalued by the hearing community because of it. They are seen as deaf 'camp-followers'.

The self-esteem of the individual learner of sign language must therefore be particularly strong and will be apparent in his convictions as well as in the ability to exhibit empathy in relation to the other users of the language. Each of these features appears and re-appears in the literature on the effectiveness of language learning, and they are equally potent factors for sign language learning.

Socio-cultural factors

Much of this area has been introduced by the analysis of social distance; there are, however, other social factors which are of some importance. The acquisition of a stereotype by a subgroup of the population usually works to its detriment, and although perhaps preserving a grain of truth in relation to the subgroup's activities, it is also misleading for members of the whole population who use the stereotype. It may conflict with views discovered by the language learner in his environment and so produce a culture shock which has to be resolved. The discovery of deaf tutors in a sign language class causes a review of the concept of 'the deaf' as disabled, since for the first time the student may be in a learning situation where the person whom he feels he should be helping is actually shown to be more competent than he is. Particularly noticeable is the discovery that the supposedly communication-handicapped deaf people communicate more effectively than hearing people.

Attitudes can then be shown to be important in the learning of a language, whether signed or spoken. The fact that deafness is an emotive area of practice anyway tends to heighten these factors and can determine the eventual success of the learner. How we seek to describe these attitudinal variables has always been a problem, and how they can be easily harnessed to the task of language learning has still to be adequately determined.

Equally difficult to quantify are the variables of age and experience, although they are expected to play an important role in language learning.

Age factors

Intuitively, one feels that older learners are at a disadvantage in relation to learning a language, but research shows the situation to be rather more complex.

Age effects were discovered by Oyama (1976) in studying Italian learners of English, at least in terms of their acquisition of the phonetic aspects of the language. It has been suggested, however, that there are different strategies at work for adults and children, the former requiring more formal language learning situations and perhaps benefitting more from a grammatical approach (Krashen and Seliger, 1975). It has also been found that age effects can be explained in terms of speed of learning of the language, which is much faster the younger the learner. Snow and Hofnagel-Höhle (1978) showed the advantage of adolescent learners over adults for learners of Dutch, but add that older learners have an advantage over the very young in learning rule-governed aspects of the language, though their teenage group were superior to the adults. Like Oyama, they found little difference in the acquisition of the phonetic systems of Dutch. Fathman (1975) also uses speed of learning as the explanatory variable for younger people learning more effectively, but she points out that the order of acquisition in second language learning does not change with age.

We have, therefore, some agreement on the existence of effects which seem linked to age of the learner; however, there may be a number of confounding factors. Krashen (1981) suggested length of residence (LOR) in the second language environment and 'reported use' of the second language as key variables. It seems that younger people are likely to have more contact with the community (to go on exchanges, visits etc.) and have more use of the language (at school, with peers of the second language community). The main effects reported, however, are on children. Walberg, Hose and Raster (1978) showed the significant relationship between LOR and proficiency in English with Japanese children in the USA, but also point out that the rate of learning slows down very quickly over time, so that in the first two months the child learns as much as he will in the next five months, the next year and so on. However, Krashen (1981) maintains that LOR 'works' to the extent that it also indicates greater interaction with the community.

Attempts to measure interaction level are usually based on self-report studies, which do have methodological problems. Nevertheless, Schumann (1977) found a relation between proficiency in English and subjects' report of the amount of contact with English in work time. For BSL and its community we can see that both of these opportunities may be less available to hearing learners.

Bearing these two variables in mind, the argument for age effects becomes less clear and Krashen (1981) maintains that age itself may not be an effective predictor of attainment or even rate of attainment. In a review of the field, Krashen, Long and Scarcella (1979) can conclude: (1) adults are faster than children through the early stages of second language development (if time and exposure are controlled); (2) older children are faster than younger children; and (3) those who have natural exposure to the second language in childhood reach a higher level of proficiency than those who begin as adults.

There are great difficulties in measurement of proficiency but adults probably acquire more, faster because of their already developed knowledge and because the level of their communication is higher and more complex. In BSL these points are equally applicable and levels of skill and prediction of skill can be discussed in these terms.

Kyle *et al.* (1981) report a national study in the UK on the levels of performance of those using BSL. The results indicate problems for hearing people in using sign language effectively which might be traced directly to the problems of the language learning situation. Using a series of specially devised tests of production and comprehension it was possible to identify a pattern of sign language learning among social workers for the deaf in the UK which is different from that for second language learning. Not only does BSL learning apparently take much longer ('beginners' were people with up to three years' experience) but only the beginner group showed the normal pattern of understanding being better than production. Even when age of acquisition and age at time of test are controlled there is a consistent gap in favour of production over comprehension of BSL for groups of signers with average six, 12 and 20 years' experience (Kyle, Woll and Llewellyn-Jones, 1981). In fact there is little change in understanding of BSL across these groups. More experienced people do not seem to understand more of BSL.

Measuring language performance in this way, of course, misses much of the qualitative essence of language use. The appropriateness of grammatical construct and the use of idiom are not adequately illustrated. In reality, from the study of the videotapes made of the language performance of most of the 150 people who took part, the language level actually being achieved did not bear a great similarity to the BSL as used by deaf people. Even where the signers had deaf parents there was still a very strong influence of English on the syntax of the signing. Use of idiom was almost totally lacking in the samples of signing collected, partly because these were fixed tasks of description of pictures rather than conversational (though even in conversations which we recorded with interpreters the signing was dominated by English), and partly because there is a feeling that BSL in its deaf form is somehow inappropriate for the formality of a test situation. The question of whether those taking part actually had sufficient command of BSL to make a conscious decision to withhold that form of signing is rather debatable, since virtually all those involved had difficulty with the deaf people's signing which they had to translate. We therefore have a situation where language acquisition seems to be geared towards an interlanguage rather than deaf people's BSL.

The degree to which this has occurred can be seen from the analysis of different signers presented in Kyle, Woll and Llewellyn-Jones (1981). Transcripts of hearing people and deaf people signing a sequence of three cartoon pictures were compared in a number of ways. Three signers were presented as illustrations: a deaf man (signer 1), a hearing man with eight years' experience (signer 2) and a hearing man whose parents were deaf and who learned BSL as a first language (signer 3). The first possibility in relation to BSL–English mixtures is to use speech in conjunction with sign. It appeared that signer 2 very clearly used speech throughout, one presumes to make lip-reading easier for a deaf audience. However, the penalty was that English grammar dominated his description and there were, therefore, long sequences where signing stopped and only English was produced, since there were no direct sign-for-word translations. Signers 1 and 3 also used lip-patterns in conjunction with English, but these supported the signing and never appeared on their own.

The use of English forms was also clear in a notable example where the English expression *to dress-up* forced signer 2 to make the sign DRESS with an *upward* movement (which means to UNDRESS in BSL) when the BSL sign properly carries a downward movement. In practice, these features were repeated frequently throughout our samples.

Two further indicators of BSL use are simultaneity and mime, or direct visual representation. Again, signer 2 differed notably from the others in his inability to use two lexical items simultaneously. In miming aspects of the events, signer 2 also used inappropriate mime which only partly visually represented the actual event. If comparisons are made by deaf people of these signers, they comprehend and value the signers in the order 1, 3 and 2. It appears that deaf people using BSL, sign in a more recognisably BSL way than do hearing people who have acquired BSL as children; for those who have to learn BSL as adults (like signer 2) their target seems to be a form of BSL greatly influenced by English. The grammar of English is carried over into the signing and presumably evaluation of the adequacy of BSL is based on the ease with which it can be fitted to this English format.

It is commonly accepted that educated deaf people prefer hearing people to use English-based sign and Woodward (1973) has suggested that the normal form of communication between deaf and hearing people is Pidgin Sign English. The truth of the first point needs to be examined in terms of the degree to which comprehension takes place, and the inevitability of the second needs to be questioned. The learning of English-based sign places severe limitations on the learner's understanding of BSL as used by deaf people and forms a barrier to understanding of the deaf community and its culture.

Kyle, Woll and Llewellyn-Jones (1981) attribute most of these difficulties to the problem of courses in BSL which are currently provided in the UK, as tending to strengthen the Englishness of sign use among hearing people. Schumann's (1977) social distance model does fit the data reported very well, where hearing people's strong motivation to 'learn in order to help' low status deaf people makes the acceptance of BSL as a language more difficult. To what extent the level of knowledge of BSL is acceptable, given the needs of deaf people for interpreters and social workers, cannot really be estimated from the data, which is relative to the types of measurement used. Certainly it would appear that foreign language learners who would have six years' experience at school followed by three years' university training plus a year in the country of that language, are treating the learning task much more seriously than sign language learners. Not surprisingly, therefore, they appear to be reaching a higher level of competence. We have tried out these tasks with users of French and do find much greater levels of competence. If one is prepared to act on this view of the need for more extensive training and greater access to deaf people, there are still other series of factors concerning language learning to be accounted for. Kyle *et*

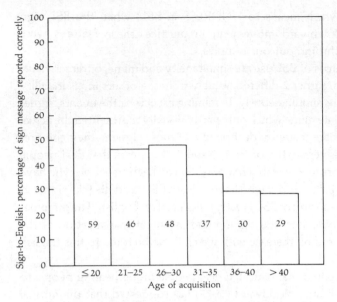

Fig. 9.1   Early age of acquisition significantly helps performance in sign-to-English
test for those with 4–15 years' experience.

al. (1981) describe a further series of measures which relate to the factors
presented above but which allow us to consider some basis for the prediction of
sign language skills.

Predicting skills in BSL

Age of first contact with BSL

In the total sample of those working with deaf people described in Kyle, Woll
and Llewellyn-Jones (1981) only 23 per cent were native users of sign language
(i.e. had deaf parents). For all the others there had to be a process of acquiring
sign after the age of 15 years, with the average being somewhere in the mid-20s.
In fact this seems to be the critical variable, and statistical analysis of sign
measures proves significant. Fig. 9.1 illustrates the nature of the relationship.

Those people who learned before the age of 20 years, the majority of whom
had deaf parents (some had deaf siblings), are able to translate effectively just
under 60 per cent of the information on average. Unfortunately there is a
confounding factor of experience in this: the earlier sign has been learned the
more experience one is likely to have had in using it by the time the sign
language testing occurs. When these were matched and pairs of hearing signers

184

were established, only eight pairs were found in our data where people acquiring sign before the age of 25 years had similar experience to those who had acquired it after the age of 30 years. Nevertheless, the difference between these proved to be significant in favour of better translation skills in those learning before the age of 25 years.

Needless to say, the results must be interpreted with care. Although there is evidence that those who choose to learn sign language after the age of 30 years will not reach the level of understanding of those who begin earlier; and although there is a declining performance as the age of sign language learning increases, it does not mean that *all* those over the age of 30 years cannot learn BSL, nor that they will be unable to communicate. Each of the factors of length of residence or contact, and amount of use of the second language, must be taken into account. The effect can also be interpreted as evidence that training courses in sign language for those over the age of 30 must be structured very differently, and there is no doubt that we need to consider the learning requirements of this group much more carefully.

We can see that age of acquisition may be taken as a predictive factor for current sign language training but that it is not a pure, uncontaminated variable. Experience tends to improve performance but has a lessening effect as the age of acquisition increases. However, the second language literature has been able to go beyond this simple finding and attributes the age effect to the various underlying variables of motivation, as well as degree of contact. The problem with adult learners is that they already have strategies for grammatical analysis and can efficiently use context in communication. This makes their speed of acquisition initially faster, but with the lack of knowledge of BSL grammar and rules the only strategy available is to impose English rules. It is this aspect which then makes them more likely to produce the interlanguage of signs in English order. There is, therefore, a need to re-examine training methods for those who come into contact with deaf people later in their careers, since it would appear that the methods currently available underestimate the complexity of this second language learning situation.

Cognitive factors

There is a general acceptance among educators that intellectual ability is a critical factor in learning in virtually all educational settings. More recently, intelligence as a predictor has been replaced by the variety of cognitive processes available to an individual. These processes turn out to be as widely varying as the tasks upon which they are to be used, and we are therefore only in the very beginning stages of understanding how they combine to predict emerging skills.

In second language learning situations factors such as reasoning ability are often semi-controlled by having those with lower levels of ability 'streamed out'. So lower ability children in British schools may be given less language training. More recently, however, a move towards providing language experience (rather than language instruction) for poorer ability groups has indicated that levels of proficiency in language use may be reached by a wide range of people.

It is relevant here to ask the simple question of how processes commonly related to intelligence are predictors of sign language learning. A measure of perceptual reasoning was used in the battery of measures given to the hearing signers in the study (Kyle *et al.* 1981). This consisted of two sub-tests of Cattell's Culture Fair Test (Cattell, 1973), which is highly loaded on 'g', the core factor of intelligence. They are non-verbal tests, though there are verbal instructions which had to be translated into sign for deaf participants. The test is very brief and the scores are additive.

One also expects direct perceptual skills to be a feature of sign learning. Mills and Jordan (1980) examined timing sensitivity as a predictor of ASL learning, and discovered positive correlations between ability to discriminate patterns differing only in timing of onset of components of the pattern, and grade scores for sign language proficiency. Although significant, their correlations were low, and the relationships accounted for a small proportion of the variance in the sign language performance scores. For our purposes a new measure was developed, based on the principles of the ACER Speed and Accuracy Test (Australian Council for Educational Research, 1962) designed to predict office skills and visual awareness. Items consisted of two pairs of hands which were either similarly or differently orientated, and pairs of faces which had either the same expression or a different one. Participants under time pressure had to designate as many pairs as they could as either the same or different.

Two measures of language sensitivity were also used in the battery of tests. These consisted of measures of language knowledge elicited in limited time. They were developed by Gerver (personal communication) and his tests were slightly adapted for our purposes, but consisted of a tape-recorded message which had errors inserted in the story (error detection) or had whole words omitted (cloze). The errors were either semantic, where a similar part of speech had been inserted; or grammatical, where the wrong verb tense was used; or vocabulary, where a nonsense word had been inserted. Participants listened to the story read at an even pace of around 120 words per minute and had to write down all the errors they could detect as they heard them or insert the missing word. In cloze they were scored for the grammatical accuracy as well as the semantic correctness of their suggestions. Gerver (1980, personal communication) had reported a high correlation between these measures and foreign language interpreting abilities, and it appeared to make little difference which language the text was presented in. Our passages were audio-recordings in English.

A final measure dealt with the area of cognitive style. The concept of field dependence was first discussed by Witkin (1950) and has since been discovered to be a relatively stable trait of the individual. Field independence allows the individual to separate the parts of an item or a situation from the whole, and implies an analytic approach to problems; however, field dependence emphasises the whole object and allows one to deal efficiently with material which does not require decomposition. There are, therefore, both positive and negative aspects to the concept, and it is not simply another way of describing intelligence. There is a wide-ranging literature on the subject.

There is a relation to age, with younger and very old people being more field-dependent but with those over 24 being in a period of relative stability, having reached greater field independence. Field independence also relates to one's sense of separate identity, or developed sense of one's own feelings and needs. Less developed field dependence often goes with greater need to rely on other people for evaluation of one's own attitudes. More field-dependent people are literally more attentive to people's faces and remember them better (Crutchfield, Woodworth and Albrecht, 1958). More field-dependent people are likely to be open to influence from those in a position of authority (Bell, 1955). The embedded figures test, which highlights these factors, has been used in a wide range of cross-cultural situations to support research work, and broadly differentiates types of perception arising within different cultures. It consists of outlining hidden geometric shapes in larger complex figures.

In summary, those who are primarily field-independent tend to be more self-confident and are associated with a freer, more independent democratic culture. Field dependence tends to arise in those who are more socialised and group-orientated in a society which emphasises order; these people tend to have stronger perceptions and feelings for others. The prediction in relation to language learning is to some extent confusing. Brown (1980) suggests that field dependence should correlate highly with natural language experience approaches to language instruction, while context independence should relate to more rigorous classroom-orientated learning. Naiman, Frohlich and Stern (1975) support this conclusion in showing significant positive correlations between field independence and school children's French learning. Also field independence increases with age, so that one would tend to predict better learning with grammatical approaches with older people. Krashen's (1978) 'monitor' model of language learning tends to reinforce this.

Learning and using BSL

In examining the results of these cognitive tests there are few systematic differences emerging. Deaf people perform rather less well in nearly all of these measures. This is particularly the case for reasoning, where the group of deaf people performs much less well than hearing groups. Although the test is claimed to be culture-fair and the instructions were presented in BSL, performance was lower, giving weight to the view of Kyle, Woll and Llewellyn-Jones (1981) that deaf people are subject to a test effect which generally depresses scores. In addition, and perhaps against the prediction, deaf people tend to be much more field-dependent. One might interpret this in relation to stronger group orientation, as expected of those who are field-dependent, nevertheless the task might be expected to be easier for those who are more used to visual processing. This did not appear to be the case.

The cognitive factors which are significantly related to sign performance in hearing signers are reasoning, cloze and embedded figures, with the last one being most highly related to sign-to-English translation. The more one's reasoning abilities are developed the better one's anticipation of the syntax and vocabulary of English, and the greater the field independence then the better the performance in sign language tasks. This latter effect is the more strikingly consistent when age effects are taken out. Nevertheless, when combined analysis is carried out it is age of acquisition which has the larger effect than any of the cognitive variables.

In summary, there is positive predictive value in tests of cognitive abilities in relation to sign language proficiency, but the effects are not as consistent as one might hope and they are outweighed in magnitude by the age at which sign language is learned.

Attitude variables

In view of the lengthy discussions on the nature of the deaf community, one might expect language attitude effects in learning sign language. Burstall (1975) reports that primary and secondary school attitudes towards learning French are strongly related to success in the language. However, McDonough (1981) points out that it is quite possible to consider the favourable attitude to the language simply as a result of success in its use. Oller, Baca and Vigil (1977) support the view that positive attitude towards the target language group is a predictor of language learning. However, there are specific problems in measuring language attitudes, particularly with rating scales.

Attitudes towards deafness are notoriously difficult to deal with. Schroedel and Schiff (1972) claim that deaf respondents were significantly more negative in attitude towards deafness than hearing respondents. Deaf people also imagined hearing people to hold more negative attitudes than they actually did.

This is mirrored in a survey by Bunting (1981) in the UK, where it appears that the general public hold some realistic and generally favourable views of deaf people even though there is no understanding of the language needs of pre-lingually deaf people. Kyle *et al.* (1981) were unable to show any consistent pattern of attitude to the deaf community as related to sign proficiency. Generally speaking, more positive attitudes to rated concepts of the deaf community tend to go with better skills, but these relations would not meet statistical criteria. In effect it implies a very complex situation in relation to attitudes and one which cannot be resolved here. Whether attitudes towards BSL can be altered or not, those who come into work with deaf people will have to approach the task of learning BSL and it may be that the weight of sign learning must rely on motivation to the task and the cognitive and age factors.

Learning BSL: some theoretical considerations

The more the study of BSL has progressed, the more it has been seen to fit general language principles. The more exploration of BSL learning that has taken place, the more relevant second language learning research becomes. The major difference which appears from the beginning is that sign language does not require voice and therefore allows the possibility of a mixing of two language codes, something which rarely occurs in the spoken situation. (Certain aspects of borrowing in spoken languages imply a mixing of codes.) The language form which becomes the target for many acquirers of BSL is therefore not BSL itself but rather some pidgin sign form incorporating a great deal of English syntax. We believe this arises out of a lack of knowledge of the nature of BSL, together with the factors described as social and psychological distance which, when producing significant effects, predict the creation of some pidgin form. The pidgin form used (and it can exist with or without fixed English syntactic markers) has naturally given way in the USA and Scandinavia to a greater interest and access to the sign language as used by deaf people. In effect, in the classroom teachers find their signing intelligible to the deaf children but they cannot understand the sign language used by those same children among themselves. Our interest in exploring BSL learning is justified by this trend, which is beginning to be apparent in the UK also. In any case, the task of learning any form of the language seems to be governed by the same variables as demonstrated in the preceding section.

Krashen (1981) has offered a set of postulates concerning second language acquisition which forms a coherent model of this language task and it is useful to consider how BSL satisfies the series of five hypotheses which Krashen sets out:

The acquisition–learning distinction This point concerns the difference between language acquisition (the process whereby children learn their first language, which is usually subconscious and constitutes 'picking-up' the language naturally) and language learning (conscious knowledge of the rules of the language). The hypothesis is that adults have available both ways of developing competence in a second language.

An earlier view of second language knowledge was that only children could *acquire* while adults *learned*, but Krashen maintains that adults do not lose their language acquisition device and make considerable use of natural learning of the second language. For BSL, evidence on the distinction has been difficult to acquire. In the studies described earlier, those who were most proficient in BSL were those learning it as a first language (albeit with English as another first language). Of those who have developed BSL skills later in life, few will have had the opportunity of language exposure which would be available for, say, English people learning French in France. Relatively few have had the chance to 'acquire' the language simply through contact with deaf people in their culture and community.

That it must be language acquisition therefore which is taking place is clear, not only because of these simple observations but because of the fact that the rules of BSL have never been researched sufficiently until now for there to be a language learning situation. Hearing BSL learners cannot use the traditional language learning approaches of dealing with grammar in the written language or phonology in the language laboratory, since there has simply not been enough information available.

One can see, therefore, that the first part of Krashen's hypothesis is supported in BSL learning. Adults are at least able to acquire, even though this may not be at a sufficiently high level of competence. The fact that the language acquired in this way often has English grammatical rules added to it, may be indicative of the adult's need to learn as well as acquire. It is clear that BSL learners need to have more access to both options if BSL competence is to be achieved.

Natural order in acquisition This hypothesis states that the discovered natural order of development of first language competence also applies to second language learning. One would expect this to occur in natural acquisition situations, such that adults' and children's interaction with others can be compared. The hypothesis primarily deals with errors in syntactic rule formation rather than vocabulary and is illustrated in such comparisons as:

How he can be a doctor? (Kilma and Bellugi, 1966; learning first
language)

and

What she is doing?   (Ravem, 1974; child learning second language)

Unfortunately there is no evidence to offer from BSL since the natural order of emergence of BSL has not been studied at all. Preliminary work on ASL has begun (Bonvillian, Orlansky and Norvak, 1983; Scroggs, 1983) but these still mainly deal with the surprising findings of earlier development of signed versus spoken language (see chapter 4). If natural order is an important feature of second language acquisition, then it is a pressing problem for those interested in BSL.

The monitor hypothesis This is a development of the first hypothesis and suggests that acquisition processes create the utterances in a second language (producing fluency), but learning monitors this production. The 'monitor' corrects or edits the output of the second language user. In order to use the monitor however, the speaker must have sufficient time to mentally prepare the utterance (usually this means it cannot be used in conversation), must be concentrating on the form of the message itself and must have complete knowledge of the rule, or rules, which have to be brought into use. Evidence for the distinction comes from the differences in error pattern between situations where these conditions are met (e.g. written grammar tests) and those where they are not. Krashen maintains that in practice it is difficult to encourage monitor use, but that it has the advantage of being able to draw consciously on language competence to produce utterances at levels which have not yet been acquired.

This is a very interesting proposal for BSL, not because we can see the conscious efforts of BSL learners to match their signing to BSL grammar but rather because there is a matching to English grammar. What this means is that the rule-based competence which the monitor offers to the BSL learner is the already established grammatical knowledge of English. The learner is taking BSL signs, acquired through contact with users, and monitoring the output to English syntax. This is most noticeably the case when we examine education (chapter 12), and it is probably this situation which comes closest to a monitor situation. The teacher with a prepared lesson and a captive audience which may not interrupt has a much greater opportunity to actively edit the signing she is producing. In addition, of course, the goal of deaf education is the production of English literacy and communication, so that the teacher can legitimately impose rules of English on the form of signing. It is therefore very close to a situation where the learned competence is that of a first language (in the absence of rule-based knowledge of the second language) monitoring the creation of a message in the second language from signs which have been acquired. It is rather difficult to know whether this is support for Krashen's proposal or not, but it certainly implies the separation of the process of meaning construction from the determination of final output form. This certainly occurs in a great deal of BSL use.

The input hypothesis This is probably the core of the whole theory. The hypothesis suggests that if natural order is valid, then in order to move from one stage to the next highest stage the acquirer must understand input from this next highest stage, where understanding is concerned with meaning and the form of the message.

This is a particularly powerful idea and one which has not really been considered in BSL, though it has begun to be practised in BSL teaching (see appendix 2). The input hypothesis is fairly revolutionary in second language terms generally. Normally one expects the individual to acquire a structure then practise it until he achieves competence in it in communication; but the input hypothesis says the opposite is true: in order to acquire structure, we first need to deal with meaning.

Krashen adds a further two parts to the hypothesis. Firstly, input at the next highest level need not only contain information at that level, since if the user understands the message then automatically the next stage is provided. The implication for teaching is that texts or situations should not be devised where only the next level of 'difficulty' is provided, since these are not necessary. Secondly, production of the language does not need to be taught: it emerges itself in time, through the understanding.

Krashen presents a range of evidence supporting this hypothesis from first and second language acquisition work. In child language understanding always precedes production and, what is most important, the adult dealing with the child constantly modifies her output to be ahead of the structures which the child is producing (Wells, 1981). In the second language situation the speaker often modifies his output to the perceived competence of the acquirer, as the hypothesis predicts would be effective. In addition, second language acquisition is characterised by a 'silent period' where little production is offered by the acquirer despite the obvious development of comprehension. The existence of this silent period is to be expected in virtually all natural acquisition settings, but in a formal classroom setting the individual may not be allowed to have a silent period. The adult being taught is asked to produce very early in his development. Newmark (1966) claims that this causes the learners to fall back on first language rules, i.e. they use the syntax of the first to speak the second. This seems to be exactly what has happened in most BSL situations – the form of instruction has been formal and production-based, and we have a very strong concentration of skills on the interlanguage of English syntax coupled to BSL signs. As was pointed out earlier, hearing users of BSL are not progressing to full competence in the language and are very likely to use English syntax for sign-based messages. Krashen explains why:

use of L1 (first language) rules is hypothesised to be the result of the first language knowledge when a second language rule is needed in production but is not available. It may temporarily enhance production but may not be real progress in the second language. The real cure for 'interference' according to Newmark is not drill at the points of contrast between the two languages (Newmark and Riebel, 1968). Drill will, at best, produce learning and as we have seen, this is only a short term cure. The real cure 'is simply the cure for ignorance' (Newmark, 1966): real language acquisition. This can happen only when the acquirer obtains comprehensible input. (1981: 29)

The affective filter hypothesis. This concerns the factors of affect and attitude already described in some detail, and we have explored how negative affect will tend to produce less contact with users of the language. However, Dulay and Burt's (1977) concept of the filter goes further. Those whose attitudes are negative and who consequently will have a powerful filter, even when they understand a message in the second language, will not allow it to reach that part of the brain responsible for language acquisition. In Krashen's terms, the filter exists outside the acquisition process so that even those with a great deal of contact with users and a considerable amount of comprehensible input may never reach competence or fluency. Selniker (1972) describes the individual as 'fossilizing'. Kyle, Woll and Llewellyn-Jones (1981) describe BSL users with over 20 years' experience of work with deaf people who still describe BSL as a 'secret language' among the deaf, or 'their language', or 'low verbal language'. It is also clear from the results that the lack of acquisition arises from this over-protective filter emerging in negative attitudes towards deaf people.

Krashen's (1981) views are particularly relevant to the study of BSL, not only because they lay the base for a fundamental re-examination of teaching methods (see appendix 2) but because they allow us to understand more clearly the language learning problems of BSL acquirers. These problems are by no means unique to language in a signed mode and, as before, what appears to be true of spoken languages also can be shown to occur in BSL.

Conclusions

From this very brief review of second language learning it can be seen that BSL acquirers have a great deal in common with those struggling with any spoken language. What makes BSL different are the emotional and social factors attached to deafness and the more obvious opportunity to mix both English and BSL in production since they, superficially at least, occupy different media.

While age has emerged as a predictor of the current linguistic achievement in BSL, it need not always be the case if BSL teachers are able to learn from the second language literature. A greater awareness of the possibilities for adults in both acquiring and learning should allow a better exploitation of their obvious motivation to achieve fluency in BSL.

The question of which form of BSL is to be attained, whether it is an English-based form or a deaf form, remains to be established. It seems likely that any hearing user must understand both and certainly needs BSL in order to adequately construct visually appropriate sequences in a signed English form. But there may be a major question as to which form is suitable on which occasion. Chapter 13 looks at the requirements of educators in using signed messages and argues that even in a teaching environment where English has to be reinforced the teacher requires access to both BSL and signed English. On this basis we may stress the need to revise language teaching methods to come more in line with second language acquisition.

Krashen's views on language acquisition are very helpful in characterising BSL and its users but, conversely, BSL is an appropriate test case for the input hypothesis and the monitor. Both seem to apply, but not quite in the way envisaged by the theory. Even this preliminary comparison, therefore, allows us to predict a fruitful interchange of ideas among those interested in second language acquisition and those involved in the training in BSL skills.

10. The psychology of sign

Much of our previous discussion has concerned the outward features of BSL, its linguistic structure as seen in communication and the measurement of skill in the language. This has proved to be a very proper framework for the analysis of communication. Nevertheless, the internal processes which underlie the way we perceive and think must be of relevance to an understanding of the way sign language works for deaf people. In this type of study the psychologist has tended to identify difference in a way which has implied deviance. Deaf people may be seen as handicapped and failing and our studies can easily be presented in this way. However, the study of difference has acquired a newer meaning and can now be seen in the light of a test of our theories of development and language, and in a way which does not isolate a particular group under study.

Social perspectives on cognition have come to accept cultural differences not as deficits but as important variation. In the past a deficit approach has been used to construct developmental theories where the missing parts in the subgroup's culture can be added. The stages of development were identified:

so that modifications could be introduced in the physical, social or educational environments of these children which would help them achieve at the same level of conceptual development as is found in children from western societies. (de Lemos, 1974: 380)

The fact that this approach to cultural differences is now largely discounted is a powerful aid to the acceptance of deaf people. Curran (1980) maintains that experimenters in the West have an implicit ethnography which allows them to share processes and experiences with their subjects. When this is not the case, as with non-Western cultures (and as it might be with deaf people), then the theories produced may be of limited value. The evaluation of processes in sign which are presented in this chapter arise in this context, such that results are available to inform our theories of perceiving and remembering as they apply to spoken language.

We have examined these processes in three different areas: perception as far as it can be determined from neurophysiological and laterality studies, remembering in a short-term memory context, and organisation in recall as it occurs in story-telling.

Perceptual processes

Evidence from studies on auditory deprivation

By most reckoning, the study of neurological differences arising from sensory deprivation at birth is a difficult one. While we have accepted that visual deprivation from birth produces considerable neurological change in animals (e.g. Borges and Berry, 1976, for cats) there is little information on similar studies with auditory deprivation. It is also true that studies of this kind tend only to highlight differences without revealing the qualitative nature of the differences. So, although we can show that deprivation produces loss of function on certain tasks, these studies do not indicate how the loss may be combatted, if at all and, from a psychological point of view, they do not give any idea of how this changed processing affects other aspects of function.

As one would predict, the few experiments on auditory deprivation confirm that there may be extensive loss of functioning. Kyle (1978, 1980a) reviews some of the evidence from the study of animals deprived of sound at birth. Batkin *et al.* (1970) show that for rats there are problems of perception of sound at a later stage if temporary deprivation occurs at birth. Stein and Shuckman (1973), in a study of direct cortical stimulation after deprivation, demonstrate poorer response in the auditory cortex after deprivation of sound. Ruben and Rapin (1980), in a thorough review of the literature, show that development of auditory perception is crucially dependent on early stimulation. They draw implications in the world of a deaf child's hearing through the early fitting of a hearing aid and point out that even under these advantageous circumstances a deaf child's functional hearing may not be comparable to that of hearing children at the same sound levels.

Loss of auditory stimulation at birth or shortly after is therefore not simply a loss of some hearing experience, but may create a loss of potential auditory processing at a later stage. The language choices of deaf children may be limited (Conrad, 1980) and this limitation may make the acquisition of spoken language extremely difficult. Even after the appropriate hearing experience is restored at the periphery, even though sound stimulation can be heard through the aid, the higher processes for dealing with sound may no longer be available. It is a tempting leap to suggest that sign language may be the natural alternative development when auditory deprivation occurs at birth, but it is clear that objective evidence on this is not easily obtained.

Evidence from hemispheric studies

Since the development of neurophysiology, the search for localisation of function within the brain has been intense. The fact that the cortex consists of two hemispheres which may be doing different things has particularly excited writers in recent years. Split-brain studies have science fiction overtones which have led to their widespread publicity in more recent times. However, the interest of neuophysiologists has a considerably longer history. The idea that language might be localised came from the studies of Broca (1861), who was the first to observe that aphasia arises as a result of unilateral left hemisphere lesion while no similar effect occurred with right hemisphere lesions. Wernicke (1874) confirmed this and showed that auditory comprehension was linked to the left hemisphere. Although there has been intermittent interest in this area since that time, it is only more recently that there have been suitable techniques for more effective study. Direct cortical stimulation (Penfield and Roberts, 1959) and intra-carotid injection of sodium amytal (Milner, Branch and Rasmussen, 1964) confirmed that for right-handed people language function was primarily controlled by the left hemisphere.

There are difficulties in these techniques and it has proved more effective most of the time to use techniques which involve perception rather than direct interference with brain processes. In this way normal healthy people may be tested without inducing any damage in their brain. The principal techniques are dichotic listening tasks and visual hemifield identification tasks. The latter technique allows the presentation of signed stimuli since it involves brief visual presentations of material. Because of the nature of connections between eye and brain, information falling on one side of the retina is transmitted firstly to one hemisphere. If the position in space of an object is varied, its image will fall on a predetermined part of the retina which transmits to right or left hemisphere. Information in the right visual field (RVF) goes firstly to the left hemisphere. However there are a number of important controlling factors: firstly, the subject fixates centrally (usually he has to report a digit which is presented in order to confirm this central fixation); secondly, the stimulus is exposed for less than 200 milliseconds to avoid eye movement; thirdly, the visual angle of the stimuli from the fixation point should be between 2.5° and 5° (otherwise, confounding effects occur). The use of these parameters in this type of study confirms the left hemisphere or right visual field advantage (RVFA) for verbal materials and the right hemisphere or left visual field advantage (LVFA) for visual materials (Cohen, 1977).

Cohen also suggests that the reason for this dominance is that the left

197

hemisphere is specially suited to serial processing while the right controls spatial processing. Sasanuma *et al.* (1977) confirm this idea in a study of perception of the two scripts of Japanese: *Kana* perception (this script is phonetic) shows a left hemisphere advantage (LHA) while *Kanji* (non-phonetic) has a right hemisphere advantage (RHA). This makes, therefore, for the very tempting prediction that sign language perception should show a RHA, since it appears to be spatially organised. Results have not always been clear.

It is normally found that although hearing people report more words presented to the RVF rather than to the LVF, deaf people show minimal asymmetry for both English words and drawings of signs (Phippard, 1977). Kelly and Tomlinson-Keasey (1977), Scholes and Fischler (1979) and Ross, Pergament and Anisfeld (1979) all showed slight LVF advantage for English words among deaf subjects, but these results did not reach significance (although they were significant for hearing people as a RVFA). Other studies indicate a RVFA for both deaf and hearing people for English words but with hearing people showing a stronger effect (McKeever *et al.*, 1976; Manning *et al.*, 1977; Poizner, Battison and Lane, 1979). Unfortunately, there were differences among these studies in measurement and in the subjects chosen, so direct evaluation is difficult.

Studies involving the perception of statically presented signs, however, tend to produce greater agreement and a general LVFA. Processing signs has clear right hemisphere involvement (Lubert, 1975; McKeever *et al.*, 1976; Manning *et al.*, 1977; Poizner and Lane, 1978; Poizner, Battison and Lane, 1979). Discussing these, Poizner (1979) infers that spatial processing dominates in sign perception even though these lexical items may normally be experienced in temporal sequences, just as in spoken language. This view may not, however, be generalisable to the more common experience of perceiving moving signs where temporally salient cues are present as well as spatially salient cues.

Poizner, Battison and Lane (1979) included moving signs in their study by simulating movement from combined still frames of strategic points in the moving sign. This gives an impression of fluent, though probably 'speeded', motion since the 'sign' must be executed in a stimulus duration less than eye movement latency. The study has no fixed hypothesis since analysis of the motor sequence of the sign might lead to a LHA while spatial analysis would produce a RHA. The result showed a slight, statistically insignificant, RHA, which was taken to suggest that sign language processing was more bilateral than spoken language processing. There is, however, some difficulty in the study in relation to the choice of stimuli and in the fact that only neutral facial expression was used – while it is clear that facial characteristics are important to the holistic perception of the sign.

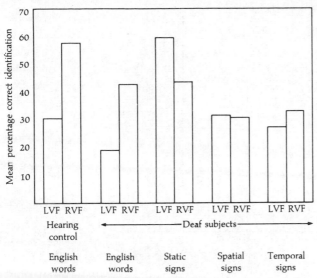

Fig. 10.1   Mean percentage correct identification for left and right visual fields for words and signs (Evans, 1981).

In relation to the choice of stimuli there are two critical parameters: movement and position. Moving signs, while using some form of sequence information, can either be temporally redundant (i.e. have position features which are similar at the start and finish of the sign) or be temporally salient (i.e. have position features which are different at the start and the finish of the sign). These two types are labelled 'spatial' and 'temporal' signs, respectively, in fig. 10.1. In each case, Tab and Dez remain constant (though secondary Tabs may change) and the movement is simple; but in the one case the movement produces no additional spatial information while in the other the spatial information changes at the end of the sign.

This aspect of moving signs was studied by Evans (1981) in an unpublished short study in Bristol. Using the normal constraints for visual hemifield studies, four conditions were administered to a small group of eight severely/profoundly deaf native signers (i.e. with deaf parents):

(1) English high frequency three-letter words printed vertically to prevent scanning, presented 3° from the visual fixation point

(2) Statically recognisable signs in BSL which were bilaterally symmetric about the midline of the body, presented 4.4° from the central fixation point: these BSL signs included LOVE, READY, FRIEND

(3) Moving signs where orientation and position were similar at the start and finish of the sign, and again the symmetric principles were observed: examples include PLAY, BICYCLE, CHANGE

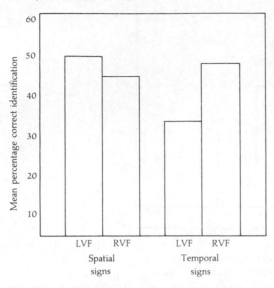

Fig. 10.2 Mean percentage correct identification for moving signs, excluding handshape accuracy.

(4) Moving signs where orientation or position changed between start and finish: examples include TICKET, BOOK, TABLE

The stimuli were constructed as in Poizner, Battison and Lane (1979) by combining four still frames to produce a stimulus duration of 160 milliseconds. Stimuli were presented either to the right or left of a fixation point which had a digit presentation for the same duration as the sign or word stimuli. Only trials where the digit was correctly reported were used in analysis, to ensure that the stimulus was presented to the appropriate hemisphere.

Figure 10.1 shows the percentage difference in correct identification of stimuli between visual fields for each condition. There are significant differences between visual fields for condition (1) for both deaf and hearing controls and for condition (2), but not for conditions (3) and (4). Examining responses in these last two conditions and accepting responses where, apart from the Dez parameter, the sign was reported correctly, produces the results as shown in fig. 10.2. Since reports were in sign the lexical identification of individual items often derived from the other parameters. In this case, condition (4) shows a significant effect, but not condition (3). Repeating these measurements with laterality coefficients (Marshall, Caplan and Holmes, 1975) to take into account error rates, simply confirms these findings.

The results are in line with the simple prediction that moving signs which have temporal (i.e. locational) salience will be more easily perceived in the RVF.

Deaf people show LHA for words and temporally salient signs, and RHA for statically presented signs. No asymmetry is present for moving but temporally redundant signs.

These results have to be treated with some caution because of the small numbers of subjects involved (though most studies have this limitation) and the weaker effects for conditions (3) and (4). However, they are indicative of a feature of sign use which is critical to studies of this sort. One might claim that the signer is simply being flexible. Where there is temporal, sequential information of importance, then this will be most effectively dealt with in the left hemisphere, while if the information is static and only spatial then right hemisphere processing may be sufficient. When both types of information are available and the temporal cues are redundant, then there may be little advantage.

The findings cannot be neatly tied up and one or two loose threads are left, but the likelihood is that general processing of signed sequences proceeds through left hemispheric involvement in a similar way to spoken language. There are circumstances, however, where the visual–spatial characteristics of signs may work to advantage in the perception and processing of BSL. This implies a situation similar to that of the perception of *Kana* and *Kanji* script in Japanese subjects, and also to that of the perception of English words and pictures. In both cases hemispheric processing is differentially invoked by the system.

In summary, studies of perception from a neurophysiological base are not conclusive. Auditory deprivation studies suggest that deaf people will have problems in speech and auditory processing even though auditory experience is reinstated by the use of hearing aids. This does not mean, however, a corresponding lack of left hemispheric processing (where speech is apparently localised). Deaf people in some conditions of sign presentation provide evidence of LHA when temporally salient cues are available, but at the same time show the superficially confusing effect of RHA for statically perceived signs. It is clear that sign language perception will involve both hemispheres.

Short-term memory

Just as the study of perception of the language used by deaf people starts from the discovery of difference, so does the study of memory. Conrad and Rush (1965) showed that deaf children do not exhibit the same type of coding in memory tasks as do hearing children. Since that time, researchers have struggled to try to establish just what the form of representation is that is used by deaf children.

Despite the early view that deaf children are poorer in short-term memory tasks than hearing children, Conrad (1979) has shown that if proper controls are exerted deaf children's memory capacity is no different from that of hearing children. Memory tasks, when they involve serial recall, produce well documented effects in hearing people according to the nature of the stimulus material. Words presented visually or auditorily are less well recalled when they are similar sounding than when they are different sounding. Coupled with a series of similar findings in different paradigms, it is taken to mean that hearing people, when processing potentially verbal material, use a code based on speech to represent and retain the items over short periods of time. Conrad (1971) has shown that this has a developmental pattern and Baddeley (1979) has linked it to the development of reading. The fact that deaf children do not spontaneously use anything like this speech code and also read poorly reinforces this link. Since psychologists see this short-term memory code as critical to general thought and functioning, the obvious question arises as to what deaf people do to mediate learning if they do not use a speech code.

A number of studies have suggested that a visual–spatial code might be available (O'Connor and Hermelin, 1973), or that dactylic coding (fingerspelling) may be used (Locke and Locke, 1971; Hoemann, 1978), or that both may occur (Dornic, Hagdahl and Hanson, 1973). The most obvious candidate for the mode of representation is, however, sign coding, and evidence has been presented by Bellugi, Klima and Siple (1975). In serial recall for signs they demonstrated primacy and recency effects in the recall curves and indicated that substitution errors made by deaf subjects coincided with sign-confusable items. The study involved the writing down of English glosses for the signs, and the fact that deaf people had poorer recall overall may result from this cross-modal task. Klima and Bellugi (1979) maintain, however, that similar results are obtained when subjects make their responses in sign.

Kyle (1980b) describes a series of experiments which examine the nature of serial recall in sign. The results agree with Bellugi's interpretations, though certain striking differences between speech and sign coding begin to emerge. While serial position effects are found and there is evidence of the use of a visual store in the final items of the list, there is no evidence of 'articulatory' enhancement of recall in sign that one gets from overt rehearsal of spoken items. Hearing people have significantly better recall for items which they vocally repeat at presentation, while deaf people find it more difficult to recall items when they have to overtly repeat the sign when it is presented. There is no obvious effect of 'signing aloud'. Since the effect is confined in hearing people to the final items in recall, it suggests a different form of coding in sign. At the same time, recall suppression was discovered when deaf subjects were instructed to hold blocks of wood while watching the presentation of items, in a way similar

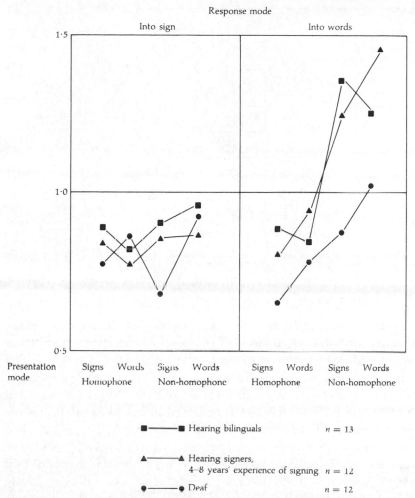

Fig. 10.3   Relative recall of words and signs in silent conditions.

to suppression experienced by hearing people in tasks where they have a redundant phrase to say aloud at presentation. These results are therefore not unequivocal in their support for sign coding.

Kyle (1981b) has compared deaf and hearing-bilinguals (i.e. people equally fluent in spoken English and sign) in serial recall tasks, offering presentation in sign or in words, and response in sign or words. The bilinguals behaved usually as English speakers, and clearly showed all the normal effects of speech coding (homophone/non-homophone differences and overt rehearsal better than silent rehearsal). Deaf people too tended to prefer recall of words, but showed no effects of overt rehearsal of words. Fig. 10.3 shows the direct comparison of recall efficiency for two bilingual groups and a deaf group. Silent serial recall of

203

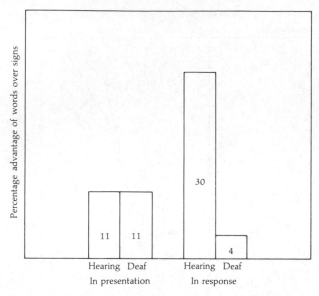

Fig. 10.4   Marked hearing advantage of words over signs in response condition.

similar-sounding words (homophones) or signs sharing the same handshape (non-homophones in English) was used as a base for considering the effects of overt rehearsal either in sign (into sign), or in words (into words).

The study is more fully reported in Kyle *et al.* (1981) but fig. 10.3 emphasises the lack of effect of sign coding in deaf people. In the first half of the figure deaf recall effects are no more different from their baseline silent recall than are hearing-bilinguals'. In the second part, however, hearing people's recall is different. They have a huge facilitation effect of words overtly rehearsed, although this applies only when the words are not confusable in sound. Deaf people, too, seem sensitive to the same patterns but do not recall as effectively with overt speech rehearsal. The results probably show that all subjects are relatively unfamiliar with a serial recall task involving signs and that deaf people tend to be sensitive to the language base of speech coding though they do not have a significant facilitation in overt rehearsal. This can be seen most easily in fig. 10.4. It seems that there is the possibility of using a sign code, but it does not express itself among deaf people in this sort of task as clearly as speech coding does in hearing people.

Shand (1982) gives further evidence for an interpretation of short-term memory effects in keeping with sign coding. Predictably the study is a small-scale one with no indication of whether recall is serial or not. It also uses English recall, as does Klima and Bellugi's (1979) work, and this must affect the output code, which is seen to be most important in the work outlined above.

Further work on the short-term memory paradigm by Poizner, Bellugi and Tweney (1981) produced confirming results that deaf people do use serial processes in a way similar to hearing people. They appear to be insensitive to semantic and iconic similarity but differ on decrement in performance with signs which are similar in their physical components (i.e. handshape, movement etc.). In addition, work on inflected signs (Klima and Bellugi, 1979) suggests effects similar to the abstraction of meaning arising in spoken words. In this case, however, the results could be interpreted in keeping with an 'English gloss' mediation and with the effects of additional length of lists. Siple, Brewer and Caccamise (1980) present results which point in the same direction. Deaf signers exhibit effects of language knowledge on the form of coding inferred from results of short-term memory experiments.

In an important study, Shand and Klima (1981) found suffix effects which could be explained in sign coding terms. These effects occur when sets of items are followed by an item which does not have to be recalled. This final item reduces the amount of recall because it occupies coding capacity which is normally occupied by the list of items. The discovery of sign suffix effects is a further part of the jigsaw of sign processing effects.

In trying to summarise these findings, it may be said that linguistic knowledge does appear to be the important variable. Both deaf and hearing people do interpret stimuli presented for memory in terms of linguistic knowledge of both the task and the stimuli themselves. This capability never excludes either a sign or a speech coding and with increasing attention results are pointing to a great division in the effects, with deaf people showing greater use of sign-based coding when responses are made in sign.

Thinking and remembering

In this area of interest one normally looks at the classic work of Bartlett (1932) as providing the first base for the complex analysis of how people's thought and language come together in their recall of complex materials. Bartlett's work was a reaction to the strict controlled experimenting of Ebbinghaus, using nonsense materials, and he set out to establish that the process of learning involved a restructuring on the part of the individual towards a better organisation from his own point of view. Bartlett was particularly concerned with stories, and in his method of serial reproduction people re-told the same story at varying intervals up to several months after it was presented. The results supported his view that in recall people make an 'effort after meaning' and in so doing they make characteristic changes to their recall. Characteristically stories became shorter over time, and the individual relies on particular detail around which to structure

205

the recall. A 'schema' for the story is established and the recall is tailored to this, producing particular transformations of detail and of order in the story. The individual sees the story in one way, which becomes rationalised over time, and the language used to re-tell the story should reflect the power of the whole process.

Despite the length of time since Bartlett published his work, much of his approach remains unchallenged as a view of the inference process at work in recall. Bransford and McCarrell (1975) show clearly that without inference comprehension may not take place effectively in textual material, and that particular contexts produce different structures of organisation and comprehension. In effect, knowledge and thinking about events are determined by the degree to which the events can be organised to fit our personal knowledge and meaning system. The way in which the process of understanding works can be seen only in the way we produce a response or description of some kind. Language provides the vehicle for this, and the syntax and content of the recall or response tell us much about the way the individual thinks and remembers. In saying this, of course, we are simply restating the fundamental question of psycholinguistics and it is not to be expected that there is some answer to the problem of explanation or even a commonly agreed way of investigating the issues involved.

The problem in relation to deaf people is nevertheless a challenging one since not only is their language different in vocabulary and grammar from spoken languages but it is also largely carried out in a different medium. Accepting even a weak Whorfian view that language used influences thought and representation to some degree, then one might expect great differences in the way that deaf people structure information.

There has been a traditional tendency to expect just that. Deaf people even after they began to be educated, were thought only to deal with concrete information, to understand only the here-and-now. BSL was discouraged because people felt that it would chain the deaf person to a concrete, visual mode of thinking. Even though we should now have reached beyond this view there is still lingering uncertainty as to what the world of experience and thought is when perceived through a language such as BSL. Myklebust (1964) claimed there was an 'organismic shift', at least producing a different experience of events but probably producing different thought. If blind people's drawings of objects (more or less as they would be touched) reflected their thoughts, then deaf people's writings obviously showed a difference. Unfortunately, both circumstances particularly highlighted skills which were difficult to acquire or monitor and could hardly act as evidence on the nature of thought. The fact that blind people can talk makes their world more accessible; the fact that we can now begin to describe BSL makes it much more likely that we can get an effective picture of how sign language reflects the internal organisation of deaf people.

Evidence on cognition in deaf children has never been clear-cut. Green and Shepherd (1975) used the Semantic Differential (a technique to examine how meaning is assigned to concepts) to show that deaf children share major dimensions of meaning with hearing children but lack a factor concerning abstract meaning and have an additional one of sensory judgements based on vision and touch. Furth's (1966) view is that there is an experiential deficit which appears repeatedly in test situations, but this does not coincide with a cognitive deficit. Meadow's (1980) review is more positive in separating the linguistic academic achievement from cognitive achievement; in the latter, deaf children appear to be very similar to their hearing peers.

In more specific terms of the language, Newport and Bellugi (1978) were able to show that deaf people are not deficient in category structure in ASL because there appear to be no signs for category names such as 'tool' or 'furniture'. ASL compensates by using compound signs such as TABLE/CHAIR etc. for the concept of furniture. This can also be shown to be true in BSL, indicating that surface features of languages may be used in different ways to express conceptual material but that these differences should not be seen as deficits.

Siple, Fischer and Bellugi (1977) were able to demonstrate that semantic aspects of ASL signs are stored (for recognition purposes) similarly to lexical items in the English language. This simply means that meaning shared by words or signs allows them to be located close together in the system which allows them to be identified internally.

It is possible to see from these studies that differences between deaf people and hearing people are small when the language differences are taken into account. However, nearly all the studies deal with the structure of the system of storing meaning or of the language itself and not with the dynamic processes of thinking and remembering.

Story material is unfortunately very difficult to deal with, and recent work tackles only simple linear structures in the story. Mandler and Johnson (1977) maintain that such a linear sequence (i.e. 'he did this, then he went there, then this happened' etc.) is an *ideal* structure and the more a story conforms to this the better will be the recall. They also make a specific suggestion that causally connected episodes will be better recalled than temporally connected episodes. Both of these are major considerations in comparing deaf and hearing recall; unfortunately they are not so easily realised when stimulus material is non-verbal.

Chafe (1977) too has examined the problem of explaining people's understanding and subsequent recall of stories or events. His stimulus material was a film and he particularly noted the expression of parenthetic information (asides, or personal expression of feeling) in the recall of such events (something which does not appear in recall of verbally presented stories). In describing his principles for applying schema to the understanding of events he makes a number of points of relevance here. Firstly, that in dealing with experience the individual breaks it into parts, or chunks and sub-chunks. These are still only ideas and it is at a later stage that they become language. However, the language units which do arise are 'propositions', and central to each of these is a verb, attached to which is an agent and object.

Secondly, in determining the language units to be used some form of categorisation takes place so that we decide whether to call the agent 'Fred', or 'the fat boy', or 'Paul's son' or 'he'. Chafe (1977) maintains that the categorisation arises as a result of the experience itself, the needs of the discourse, and especially the centrality of the word to be used as indicative of the category. This last part corresponds to Rosch's (1973) idea of prototypes in concepts, where certain words are more typical of the concept. However, the major point here for us is that if the chosen word is central to the category meaning which is to be conveyed then it will be produced without modification. Where the needs of discourse or the story require more specific information then a modifier is used: 'the boy' becomes 'the small fat boy' or 'he obtains the ticket' becomes 'he secretly obtains the ticket'. While English tends to modify by use of adjectives or adverbs, BSL tends to use inflection especially in relation to the verb and it is this which makes its story formation rather different.

Thirdly, in re-telling a story there is an element of personal feeling to be injected, a re-living of the original experience. This is mental imagery, though not only visual, and it leads to and encourages a reconstruction of events and a process of creativity. There are very large individual differences in this and it can affect each of the stages so far mentioned. This brings Chafe's view of the processing closer to that of Bartlett, where recall is based on the production of particularly salient features of the original and the reconstruction of other features around these. This comes clearly into focus with a realisation that the differences in recall at different times by the same person are to be understood through this creativity process. Chafe (1977:244) criticises the typical psycholinguistic tree structures which assign agents and roles to the words used in the recall as being 'able to capture only certain decisions that were made during certain particular verbalisations. They show not what was known about the event, but only some aspects of how it was talked about'. Chafe's view is that the event is held in some abstract form which allows the recreation of sub-chunks and propositions on the basis of the needs of the story situation at that time.

We do, therefore, have a framework for beginning to examine the recall by deaf people in BSL and for making meaningful comparisons with English recall. While story grammars seem ideal for working with simple English written stories they have problems where the surface structure (particularly verb tenses) do not correspond to the ideal structure as set out in Mandler and Johnson's (1977) approach, or where in fact there is no verbal structure (as in the silent film, to be discussed). Nevertheless, there is a specific prediction to be examined and that is whether causally connected episodes are better recalled than temporally connected episodes. Chafe's (1977) approach offers potentially more for the study of recall. He understands events as wholes broken into chunks for recall and created as propositions by identification of central aspects, most closely corresponding to the verb in an utterance. Critical is the view that the event is stored and that the particular realisation of it in linguistic form is variable and does not depend on stored information of agent, recipient and so on.

Kyle (1982, 1983) has reported a study of recall in BSL and English by deaf, hearing and bilingual subjects. The stimulus material was a short silent comedy film made by Mack Sennet around 1925. The story concerns the misdemeanours of a husband when he goes dancing with another woman when he is supposed to be at a boxing match. Transcriptions 1 and 2, in BSL glosses and English, indicate the story content.

Transcript 1: *Deaf person's story recall in sign*
PICTURE ABOUT MAN WIFE WITH MOTHER IN LAW. KNOCKED. CAME. WHAT. POSTMAN GAVE WIFE. OPENED. TWO TICKETS FOR DANCE ROYAL – BAD NAME SO MAN – NO BAD NAME WON'T GO – BAD NAME SENT BACK. SAMETIME FOOL WIFE. GAVE. KEEP ME. PAY MONEY. RECEIVED THEN GONE. TOLD WIFE NIGHT ALWAYS OUT BOXING. WIFE ALRIGHT. WENT TO DANCE ENJOYED HIMSELF DANCE. SURPRISED WON CUP. HOLD. THEN MICROPHONE ON WIRELESS HIS NAME WON IT. HE NO NO, WIFE FIND OUT. WIFE HEARD IT LOOKED MOTHER NOD HEAD. GET IT WHEN HE COMES HOME. WHEN HE CAME HOME WIFE HUG. WIFE GOOD WATCH BOXING. SAW ENJOYED. GOOD BEAUTIFUL FIGHT.

Transcript 2: *Hearing person's story recall in speech*
About an hour ago I watched a silent film which was a comedy film Mack Sennett film in fact in which the hero and his wife were unfortunate enough to be lumbered with the hero's mother-in-law who according to the film stayed on after the wedding and had forgotten her return ticket. She is not a very pleasant lady as far as the husband is concerned, particularly when she starts playing the piano in a loud objectionable manner he clears off – and he decides rather that he would like to clear off and arranges for a ticket to the Café Royale to be delivered to the house. Unfortunately when the ticket to the Café Royale is delivered his wife comes to the door and sees these tickets have arrived which means that her husband has to pretend he knew nothing about them and it must be a mistake and pretends to send the boy away with the tickets. However he does in fact take the tickets from the boy and pays him slyly behind his wife.

Shortly afterwards he makes an excuse that he's going out to a sports club to watch some prize-fighting and takes himself off with his ticket to the Café Royale leaving his wife and her mother behind to spend the evening without him. He goes to the Café Royale and involves himself in a dance competition the object of which is to dance the best Charleston. His partner one Tessa McNab and he have a high old time and win the competition after which he makes his way home. However, unknown to him the whole competition has been broadcast over the wireless and when the result of the Charleston competition was announced that is to say that he was the winner, they recognised his name so they know where he was — they know he wasn't at the sports club. He tries to sneak in very quietly perhaps he hopes they would have gone to bed. However, they stay up waiting for him. He lets himself into the room, his wife rushes up to him gives him a big kiss leaving a lipstick stain over his right eye.

In their recall task the subjects were asked to watch the silent film, and then a deaf or hearing person was introduced who had not seen the film. They were then asked to recall the story they had just seen in either sign (deaf and bilinguals) or in speech (hearing people). Approximately one hour later, they were brought back to the same room and asked to retell the story again.

Transcribed stories in English and in glosses for BSL were analysed with a simple propositional analysis based on the work of Kintsch and Keenan (1973). In practice, propositions occurred in English most commonly as clauses, for example:

. . . they recognised his name. . . . (1 proposition)

or

. . . perhaps he hopes/they would have gone to bed (2 propositions)

In BSL, propositions existed where translations into English syntax, given the non-manual characteristics and contextual meaning, would produce a proposition as above. These included examples such as:

POSTMAN GAVE WIFE

ENJOYED HIMSELF DANCE

In addition there are fifteen main visual events in the story, and they are interwoven both in time and cause. The story occurs in a temporally accurate sequence so that there are quick changes of scene, i.e. 'meanwhile back at the ranch', but no flash-backs or alterations of the temporal sequence. We are therefore interested in two aspects here, the temporal order in recall and the propositional content and structure in BSL as opposed to English.

Temporal order

If Bartlett's (1932) original view is correct we ought to expect changes in the pattern of recall of events. One would predict according to Mandler and Johnson (1977) that it is the temporal order which would be altered most. In reality, the stories were recalled over only a short period of time and major event

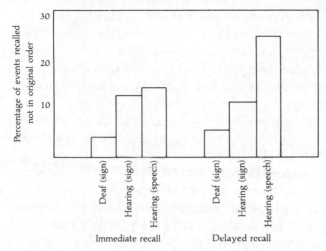

Fig. 10.5   Deaf people distort the temporal order less than hearing people.

alterations did not occur, but both deaf and hearing people recalled the main episodes equally well and there was no significant difference in the number of events recalled.

What is different is the order of events in the recalls. Hearing people distorted the temporal sequence much more than did deaf people, with bilinguals coming somewhere between. Fig. 10.5 shows the extent of the difference.

Interestingly, hearing people seemed to increase in their re-arrangement over time while there was very little difference in BSL. The fact that English tends to make these 'order errors' is not particularly surprising since its system of tenses and conditional structures allow easy reference to events out of sequence, for example:

he *makes* his way home. Unknown to him the whole contest *had been* broadcast and his wife and mother-in-law *had heard* his name . . .

The results tend to agree with Mandler and Johnson (1977) for English but not for BSL. In addition, it is not clear that the re-ordering is in the direction of simplifying the causal structure of the story. It seems more likely that the re-telling arises directly from the capabilities of the language as well as the perception of the subject as to what makes the 'good form' of a story. However, the temporal recall issue is related to the form of propositions available.

Propositional structure

The fact that Chafe (1977) has suggested that information concerning agent and recipient is not necessarily stored by the individual in a specific form is perhaps fortuitous in our comparison of English with BSL. The description of BSL as an inflecting language would allow, and indeed predict, a much more flexible approach to the construction and use of propositions. Since BSL is visual, then the feeling of being in the story must be more pronounced. If the overall recall is not significantly different, but there are differences in sequence of recall, then one must consider aspects of the surface structure as the key to the communication of the same message.

The focus of this is the language itself and, in particular, the use of 'verbs' within it. In many cases the notion of verb is not so easy to deal with in sign language. Supalla and Newport (1978) discuss ways of dealing with noun–verb distinctions in ASL, and Deuchar (1983) comments on it for BSL. Supalla and Newport (1978) maintain that nouns and verbs are separated by frequency of movement, but in BSL PILL has two movements while to TAKE-A-PILL has only one, but BRUSH has one movement while to BRUSH-UP or SWEEP has more than one; this distinction, therefore, is not simple.

It is appropriate to discuss a number of features of verb inflections. Edwards and Ladd (1983) suggest verbs do not inflect for tense or person in BSL, but though this is true for a number of verbs it is not true for some of the most frequently used verbs. Not only do these verbs inflect for person, they very often incorporate the person and/or object of the sentence. Basic verbs such as DRINK, EAT, LIVE, BUY, WORK, LOVE, CHEAT, WIN, TRY, ALLOW, ARRANGE, BREAK are not inflected in common use for tense or person: time and person are indicated by the use of adverbs or by pronouns. However, some verbs are inflected spatially in order to incorporate information on person. The verbs HAVE and AGREE vary in space according to which person 'has' the object or agrees. This is also true of COME, which indicates location as well. This links with a second category of verbs, where movement indicates both agent and recipient. Verbs such as GIVE, TEACH, HIT, SEE, HELP and TEASE fall into this category. Other verbs incorporate size into movement and provide additional meaning by their inflection. So the signs PICK-UP, PUT, THROW and PULL can indicate subject, object and size of the object. In each of these verbs the use of an additional marker of subject, object or pronoun, is optional. When they are incorporated into the verb itself it provides BSL transcription with its typically clipped appearance (see transcript 1).

Most verbs also inflect for aspect, and Klima and Bellugi (1979) describe a whole range of aspectual modulations, including (for BSL) continuative (e.g. WAITING : WAITING-FOR-AGES), frequentative (e.g. GIVE : AWAYS-GIVING) and intensive (e.g. GIVE : GIVE-AWAY). In effect, BSL (like ASL) has a colossal range of 'present tenses' and while very few verbs inflect for tense as do SEE : SAW or GO : WENT : GONE, there is an immense range of tense and aspect information available in the inflected forms.

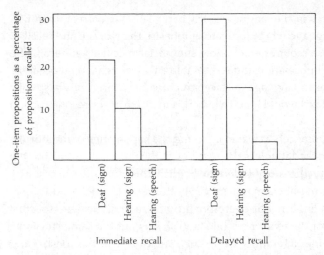

Fig. 10.6   Deaf people use more one-item propositions in recall.

One can see that BSL invites the omission of specific storage of agent and recipient, since the meaning of the proposition may be included in the verb itself. It probably constitutes a very pure form of the storage that Chafe envisages. Using only the gloss of BSL is therefore rather misleading. The three glossed signs from transcript 1 (KNOCKED, CAME, WHAT?) represent three propositions with the meaning that someone knocked at the door, the person inside came and tried to find out what it was. Stokoe (1980) has highlighted this type of one-sign sentence in ASL, where one can see the use of direction and movement to provide the full meaning. Such one-item propositions also occur in English in other commentaries:

> . . . at home/(and) realised/that . . .

> or

> she just arrived/ . . . a postman/ and he's . . .

In each case one constructs the meaning from the context and following referent or clause.

It is particularly this aspect of BSL structure which not only creates the concentration of meaning in a few glosses but is frequently brought into use by deaf people. The metric used to study this is simply the proportion of propositions in recall which are one-item propositions: fig. 10.6 shows the results.

Deaf people are much more likely to use this device in their recall, at least in the surface structure. Bilinguals come somewhere between, indicating that there may be an influence of both the language itself and the internal processing of deaf people. It must be remembered, however, that this is only, in the end, a way of reflecting differences in the languages. If Chafe (1977) is correct, then BSL would represent a language which tends to emphasise the storage and recall of events, whereas English requires much more superficial specificity in recall. BSL therefore stores story information and re-tells it in a way which would occur for all languages, but spoken language surface structure (reflecting only a specific point in time and context) would tend to hide this in its effort for reconstruction of meaning.

BSL looks imaginal; one gets a clear insight into the happenings of the story; it is impossible to understand it unless the receiver of the message enters into the perspective offered by the story-teller. In English this does not necessarily happen, although one might claim it is precisely this device which good story-tellers invoke, even in English. BSL therefore provides a great deal of aspectual information directly for the receiver, while English sets out the same story in a different way, allowing alteration of event structure without destroying meaning.

De Matteo (1977) has argued that one has to understand sign language in terms of its visual imagery and he has particularly highlighted the syntactic devices used in ASL which derive from a visual representation of events. In the stories told above, it is obvious that the richness of aspectual information comes from their visual–spatial characteristics and that there is an appeal to the visual imagery of the receiver in telling the stories. The idea that the syntax of BSL has to be understood through its visual presentation also seems reasonable and in agreement with De Matteo. The final stage of the claim, that BSL consists purely of visual images in the story-teller and that BSL functions only at the visual concrete level, however, goes beyond the information given. Even if it were true, it now seems very likely that the storage of non-verbal story material by the use of imagery is a process used in every language. Fauconnier (1981) discusses 'mental spaces' as the basic representation of all language and cites ASL as a particularly clear example of this. It seems that BSL also falls within the class of languages which demonstrate the use of imaginal processes in their construction.

In this chapter we have gone deeply into the structure of BSL from a cognitive psychological perspective. The fears that BSL consists of a limited, concrete visual language localised in the right hemisphere, can be discounted. BSL does not follow the normal rules of processing as specified by the predominantly verbal sequential tasks which psychologists have used. The realisation that those tasks usually only tap a subset of language behaviour, has come only very slowly. However, the gain to psychology, and our treatment of language, may be very great.

The idea that speech coding in memory may be only a subset of motor memory processes, including sign language behaviour, opens up a new possibility for psychological research. The fact that psycholinguists have begun to see 'deep' language processing as much in terms of images as linguistic propositions allows the incorporation of BSL work within the framework of all language work. Understanding of BSL, however, has to come first to be of value.

In chapters 11, 12 and 13 we consider the application of such an understanding. BSL processing involves sequential and spatial codes, uses direct visual representation for its syntax while displaying the same complexity of meaning as English. It is self-evident that those who use BSL professionally, given this awareness, can exploit these attributes to the full.

11. Sign language interpreting

It may appear rather odd that a book on an emerging language devotes a chapter to the process of translating meaning from that language to another and *vice versa* (especially when this second language will be, virtually always, English), but the development of BSL, and its community of users is so bound up in its treatment by hearing people that it is essential to have some discussion on the matter. While spoken language interpreting is an accepted and highly skilled profession, sign language interpreting is mainly carried out by those in a caring or managerial role with deaf people. While, for example, French–English interpreters may be either French or English nationals (or indeed from another community) BSL interpreters are drawn solely from the hearing English-speaking community. Their knowledge and use of this second language is therefore of some importance in considering BSL and deaf people's role in society.

There are some obvious prerequisites for the interpreting role if the member of a community is to be fairly represented and have the opportunity to participate fully in decision making. One expects the interpreter to influence the content, context and spirit of a message as little as possible in keeping with relaying it meaningfully in the second language. In all interpreting it is not only the technical skill of the interpreter which is important but also his attitude to the job and to the particular situation in which it has to be carried out (R.W. Anderson, 1978); also important is his awareness of the different expression of the same meaning in different cultures ('the sense' of the message; see Seleskovitch, 1978). For BSL interpreters there is often the added complication of role conflict between their social work/educational job and their impartial relay of meaning as an interpreter. If attitudes towards deaf people influence the learning and using of BSL, then they almost certainly affect BSL interpreting.

In this case interpreting is taken to mean both consecutive and simultaneous interpreting. In the first the message is received in full and is then given out to the person; in the second the message is received and is simultaneously translated into the second language. The relayed message is the source language, while the second language is the target language. As far as BSL is concerned, virtually everyone who learns some signs is at some stage called upon to interpret by a deaf person, and this is most likely to be from English into BSL. In effect this means a very broad definition of the situations where interpreting occurs, ranging from conference simultaneous interpreting to casual conversational interpreting which may be consecutive. As is the case for spoken languages, deaf people will expect and experience both simultaneous and consecutive interpreting. There has been a tendency more recently, however, for deaf people to be wary of consecutive interpreting where they may feel information is added to, or subtracted from, the message (Allsop and Kyle, 1982), even though for spoken languages it has usually been felt that consecutive interpreting is much more effective and much easier to check for the validity of the interpretation (Herbert, 1978).

The essence of discussion in this chapter is therefore the expression of meaning of one language in another language. The purpose is to compare what we know of spoken language interpreting and its effectiveness with developing awareness of the needs of deaf and hearing people in using BSL.

Spoken language interpreting

It is easily forgotten how old the task of interpreting is, but how new the profession of interpreter is. Herbert (1978) suggests that conference interpreting began only during the First World War, while before that international conferences were held in French. For most of the time this involved consecutive interpreting, i.e. making notes of what the speaker said and then at the end (of perhaps an hour's talk) repeating the speech in the target language. It was only just before the Second World War that simultaneous interpreting became possible (as well as acceptable) at conferences. With the provision of booths and sound systems, most conference interpreting is now of the simultaneous variety but, as is frequently pointed out by interpreters themselves, the most common use of interpreting is in some personal consecutive mode and not in conferences. It is also clear from Herbert's comments that the process of interpreting is generally not well understood by even those who use interpreters, and features like the interpreting lag, or the change in pace of the interpreter according to the speaker's rate, may often be mistaken for some problem in the interpreter's rendition of a message.

In practice, spoken language interpreters are highly educated and highly trained. Complete fluency in the first and second languages is taken as prerequisite for training (and one would expect a working interpreter to command at least four or five languages). The preoccupations of spoken language interpreters in discussing their task do not then concern language competence but only interpreter competence (Gerver and Sinaiko, 1978). This competence revolves around the intended meaning of the message and therefore places the responsibility of flexibility of expression and clarity of grammatical presentation on the shoulders of the interpreter. Namy suggests that simultaneous interpreting is:

the art of re-expressing in one language a message delivered in another language at the same time as it is being delivered; the re-expression should be clear, unambiguous and immediately comprehensible, that is to say perfectly idiomatic, so that the listener does not have to mentally re-interpret what reaches him through the earphones. (Namy, 1978: 26)

What is most striking in 'poor interpreting' is the lack of use of perfectly idiomatic expression in the target language (it is this particular aspect of BSL which has proved most difficult to research). This is a most basic aspect of interpreting, and requires that the interpreter fully understands the grammar and culture of the target language user. Unfortunately there is also an added complication: the distinction between *language meaning* and *message meaning* (Pergnier, 1978).

Language meaning is what is conveyed by each unit or group of units in a language, the commonly agreed meaning of a word or phrase. Unfortunately, in most languages translation of units produces ambiguity, i.e. the French word *glace* could mean in English 'ice', 'glass', 'window', 'mirror' and so on. However, the use of the unit in the language is agreed within the community because of characteristic speech habits.

Message meaning on the other hand corresponds to the intended meaning, is usually unambiguous and mostly determined by context. So the request for *une glace* in a restaurant unambiguously refers to ice-cream and it is this aspect which must be interpreted. Pergnier explains that the language user would not himself be concerned with the possible ambiguity:

Nor does the one who says, in given circumstances, 'j'attends mon frère' realise that in his language his utterance can be interpreted as meaning many different things such as: I am waiting for my brother (every day, all my life . . .); I am expecting my brother (any minute); I can't decide without my brother; I have been waiting for my brother (for several hours, days, years . . .); I look forward to seeing my brother; and so on. Whatever the French phrase may mean, the Frenchman who uses it in a given situation intends to convey one particular and unambiguous meaning. The problem for any individual who receives the message is not knowing what the *words* mean but what the *speaker* means. Such is the translator's and interpreter's problem. (1978: 201–2)

This idea is so fundamental to the principle of interpretation that it is expressed, in slightly different forms, by various writers. Seleskovitch (1978) perhaps encompasses both Namy and Pergnier in what she terms the 'keyhole' principle: the fact that language meaning through translation may not convey message meaning and the corollary that message meaning is expressed through different salient characteristics. So, in English there is a *keyhole*, but in French it is a *trou de serrure* i.e. a hole with *a lock*; in English it is a *bedroom*, but in French it is a room *for lying down* (*chambre à coucher*). It is not that English people do not lie down in the bedroom, or that French people do not have keys, but rather they choose different salient characteristics for the expression of that specific meaning. It is therefore this intention of the speaker (within the message) which has to be *interpreted*.

One can therefore extract a very simple theme in the work on spoken language interpreting: it is the intended meaning which must be first understood, and then transposed into the target language by the interpreter. It supposes complete access to the language meaning (the range of interpretations of that element of the message) and developed ability to convey the message meaning in the target language. The interpreter presents the message in the way the speaker does in his source language, and would do in the target language if he could.

Sign language interpreting

If spoken language interpreting is a young profession then sign language interpreting is in its very early infancy – in many parts of the world it has yet to be born. As with sign language research, Scandinavia and the USA have been in the forefront of developments, though each draws on different traditions, the first for the recognition of language difference needs, the second for the equalisation of society and integration of minority groups. The US has a greater experience, having had a Registry of Interpreters for the Deaf (RID) since 1964, and now has a widespread network of interpreting provision. With qualifications for interpreting provided by an assessment board and now through training at college level, and with the emergence of full-time workers, interpreters have reached professional status and have set out guidelines for their profession and for their deaf users. The use of registered interpreters is seen as sufficiently important now for Freeman, Carbin and Boese to warn:

Parents of deaf children who have some signing skills should refuse to serve as interpreters when it is against the best interests of the deaf people concerned. A certified interpreter should be demanded. If this is impossible, interpretation should be done only with a clear explanation of the reasons for using a non-professional and of the limitations involved. (1981: 279)

In Denmark, although there is assessment and provision of interpreters there is no training course but a series of starter courses to support the skills that the interpreters (usually people with deaf parents) already have (Hansen, 1980). The

219

report of Domingue and Ingram (1978), for the USA, indicates the emergence of the profession both in terms of status and in concerns for interpreter efficiency, and it is on this basis that we begin to look at the processes involved, comparing signed with spoken interpretation.

In terms of professional development the UK lags somewhat behind, having no fully recognised body of interpreters (although such an organisation may now be close to recognition) and, as far as we can make out, only one full-time interpreter in the whole country. There is no government funding for training and assessment, nor is there legislation for interpreters. Rather it is a historical fact that interpreters are provided in court (see the Jean Campbell case, 1817, referred to in chapter 3) and only recently has research to examine interpreting been undertaken. Much of our discussion in the latter part of this chapter draws on this research. As one might predict from the history of interpreting in the USA and Scandinavia, it is within the field of education that the basis of an interpreting service is laid. There is no requirement in the UK for colleges to provide any sort of support for deaf students. In effect, using BSL in further and higher education is still seen by many as part of the 'handicap of deafness' and something to be overcome in education rather than used. Interpreting in schools, colleges, courts, meetings and so on is provided by individual arrangement usually with a social worker for the deaf, though in most personal circumstances (job interviews etc.) deaf people say they prefer to use a relative or friend (Kyle and Allsop, 1982b).

In these circumstances, our developing knowledge of interpreting and language in general is critical in providing a framework for evaluating interpreter effectiveness and understanding the process in which he has to be trained.

BSL interpreting effectiveness

In an attempt to identify the component skills and abilities necessary for an interpreter to be regarded as 'good', Brasel, Montanelli and Quigley (1974) asked interpreters and deaf people to rate features of their abilities. Generally, these people rated 'accuracy in transmission of concepts', or getting the message over, as the most important, and 'fast fingerspelling' as the least important. A similar, but slightly expanded, study was carried out with British interpreters (Kyle, Llewellyn-Jones and Woll, 1979). The results of this study indicate general agreement between the hearing and the deaf subjects. The deaf group were unanimous in putting 'accuracy of transmission of concepts' as absolutely essential and, interestingly, rated 'the ability to understand all signs used, no matter which part of the country they came from', higher than did the hearing group.

The imbalance in our treatment of the two languages clearly reflects the traditional non-acceptance of sign language as an entity capable of mastery by hearing users. This same attitude is shown in existing interpreter assessment procedures; for example, that used by the American Registry of Interpreters for the Deaf, where sign language is split into articulatory features such as clear fingerspelling, lip movement and appropriate facial expression, for scoring. The fact that this is deemed necessary is probably also a reflection of the lack of formal sign language teaching and the understanding of the process itself.

Brasel (1976), in a study of fatigue, replicates Gerver's (1972) findings with spoken interpretation, that interpreter fatigue after very short periods of interpreting (30 minutes) begins to introduce an error rate which after an hour is statistically significant and unacceptable. The over-use of interpreters (e.g. interpreting all day at college for a deaf student) is probably typical of the early stages of development of the interpreting profession (Herbert, 1978) but one hopes this can be quickly overcome as better provision is made.

Murphy (1978) reports a simple study on effectiveness where interpreted information to deaf people was compared with oral lectures to hearing people. Deaf people did 16 per cent less well in a comprehension test than did hearing people, giving rise to three possibilities: that sign language is less efficient; that deaf students are less knowledgeable and able to take in less information; and that sign language interpreters are not efficient. Murphy rejects the first, accepts the second and does not actually consider the third at all! In fact it is probably the key, since in an earlier part of his discussion he opens up the possibility of interpreting not only into ASL (or BSL) but also into a manual English form. In relation to chapter 9, this means interpreting into the interlanguage, a practice which would be considered rather dubious in spoken language interpreting. The grounds for such a choice are the requirements of the deaf viewers themselves. Those with a better use of spoken and written English may prefer a sign representation more tied to English. As we will argue later, this is almost certainly what happens in most BSL interpreting and the message produced will be, at best, ambiguous.

Llewellyn-Jones (1981a) describes the assessment of interpreter effectiveness and indicates a much lower performance by interpreters than one would hope for. Taking a perfect performance as the comprehension of hearing people working from memory of an audio-recorded message, deaf people's performance after interpretation was, on average, around 60 per cent. Llewellyn-Jones (1981a) also looked at lag behind the speaker and though his concern was for individual comparison, a general conclusion is that the usual 2–3 seconds lag of the BSL interpreter behind the speaker is not sufficient for the message to be both understood and presented to the audience in a form which can be understood. The form of presentation used involved very strict adherence to English grammatical rules.

Lederer (1978) describes a similar study for spoken language interpreters, where a 3–6 seconds' lag occurs as a base level but with a great deal of interpreting occurring much further behind the speaker's words. In fact, the interpreter expects this because of his training and the need to understand the message. The shortest lag occurs where the interpreter does not understand the message and merely transposes the message from one language to the other; in BSL the transposition occurs from English to signed English, or from BSL to spoken signs.

In deaf–hearing interaction, however, it is possible to consider the interlanguage as a usable form. We have argued that much communication is English-based, and in education it constitutes a real choice since a purpose may be the teaching of specific English structures through sign. As Llewellyn-Jones (1981b) points out, interpreters frequently claim that it is audience feedback that determines which target language form is used. Experimental study fails to confirm this claim. Llewellyn-Jones (1981b) examined experienced interpreters in feedback and non-feedback situations and found no difference in target language use (in both cases they used a signed English variety). In addition, when negative feedback (i.e. lack of understanding, questioning looks) was provided there was no noticeable alteration in signing style from when positive feedback was provided. These BSL interpreters appeared to be using only a single register, and this corresponded to a signed version closely tied to the English of the original message. This would count as a very serious mistake in spoken language interpreting.

In BSL to English interpreting a strikingly similar pattern emerges. Llewellyn-Jones (1981b) compared simultaneous and consecutive interpreting situations and discovered significant differences in the same interpreters. In the consecutive mode it was much more likely that the message would be interpreted into an English form which followed all the grammatical rules, while in simultaneous translation there was a clear tendency to follow BSL structure while speaking the words. Interpreters were more likely to produce non-English sentences and omit or use incorrectly, referents in the message during simultaneous interpretation. For example, a message was interpreted as:

On Saturday I arrived – you were waiting for your friend – yes – waiting, waiting – friend came – you walked to deaf club – sitting in deaf club – waiting . . . Manchester? Waited and waited – the bus came – quickly got in the bus – quickly – the bus went quickly and they arrived in Manchester.

There is no doubt that this form of target language is unacceptable to English speakers, who might dismiss the interpreter or, more likely, assume that this was a function of the deaf person's lack of knowledge of English (and feel that the interpreter was doing a good job). If this BSL–English is unacceptable in English, one must also question the validity of interpretation in sign language forms which follow English structure. In both circumstances the deaf minority have to struggle to participate in community life if their contributions do not sound like English and if their failure to understand the interlanguage interpretation is put down to their poor general knowledge or low mental ability.

One can accept that it is a complex and difficult issue as to which target language is acceptable, but clearly deaf people's abilities are not being realised in contact with the hearing community. It perhaps is a function of the early stage of interpreter development in the UK (though there are only a very few positive indications that the situation is different in other more developed countries) and one can expect a change of provision, attitude and therefore skill. However, the *process* of interpreting is still not fully understood for BSL, and it is upon this that effectiveness of training hinges. In examining a model, the following discussion also applies to much of spoken language interpretation, and although the BSL/ signed English issue is perhaps unique, there may be a considerable amount to be exchanged between spoken and signed language models.

BSL interpreting: a process model

The features of sign language interpreting so far described, and the possible registers available, suggest something rather different from the linguistic models of Seleskovitch (1978) and others. The latter deal primarily in a currency of meaning while the former have still a conflict concerning the appropriate register for the target language. In using a cognitive approach to the task of interpreting it may be possible to find a base for comparing the language systems.

Generally speaking, psychology has concentrated on the processes involved in dealing with verbal data as it arrives in the individual. There are processes described for perception, immediate recall, attention, short-term memory, recognition and a whole range of rules whereby recall occurs. We understand that a code must be invoked in order to handle the grammatical aspect of what one person says, but the question of how we extract information from running speech remains the subject of much debate (Marslen-Wilson and Welsh, 1978). Moser (1978) typically deals with the way information is broken down in interpretation from sentences and context into meaning, and one can only presume that she proposes a similar process for the reconstruction of the message in the second language. However, it is probably this stage which separates interpreters from ordinary individuals.

Hitch and Baddeley (1978) have proposed a model of working memory, developed from what has become the basic *modal* model in psychology, which

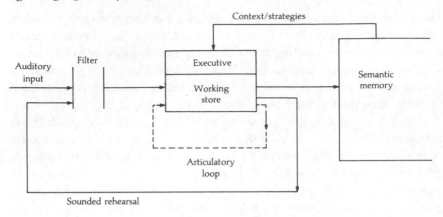

Fig. 11.1   A processing model of working memory (after Hitch and Baddeley, 1978).

gives a focus for our discussion (fig. 11.1). Auditory information in the form of one language enters the system and is filtered to reduce environmental noise. The speech left provides for an internal speech code which passes through a working memory system where it can be examined. The examining is controlled by an executive which oversees the analysis of the message and determines how it fits the context, probably discarding the surface grammar of the message by parsing in some way, and then establishes the meaning of the utterance. The system has the option of calling into action an articulatory loop, a form of silent speech rehearsing which gives the system more time either to accept more information or to examine the message in greater detail. This system links with the important child development stage of overt verbalisation of things to be remembered. Even in adulthood, difficult material may often be overtly rehearsed, giving rise to further auditory input.

Given fluent processing of first language material, the articulatory loop may never consciously intrude into the interpreter's performance. One can then envisage the model of fig. 11.2, where source language material is interpreted into meaning and this provides the instructions for translation to the target language. This calls into use a response buffer which produces articulation of the translated message. It is not clear whether this articulation makes use of the working memory system or is independent. However, it is very likely that articulating a second language interferes with the processing of the first during simultaneous interpreting.

For this reason, spoken language interpreters are specifically trained to reject the effects of their utterance of the target language. Because we are dealing with running speech, the articulatory loop should seldom be used in dealing with the source language (unless it is in an abbreviated code) – a simultaneous interpreter

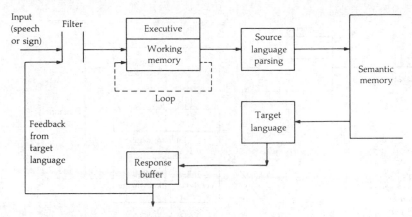

Fig. 11.2   Interpreting from one language to another.

will claim to analyse the meaning directly and have little knowledge of sound features in the source language. The technique used to train suppression of the interference is 'shadowing', whereby the listener reproduces in speech word-for-word a source language message in that source language itself. Since this creates an echo, because of the lag of a second or two, the effects of hearing the echoed message are initially disconcerting and generally cause the subjects to stop processing the source language properly. With repeated practice the interference between heard and spoken messages becomes much less and the information channelled through the response buffer should be lost at the filter as it re-enters the system.

The articulatory loop should also be seldom used since it would slow down processing of a message whose speed is beyond the control of the interpreter. The loop could act only as a monitor to be interrogated in the case of breakdown of comprehension. In spoken language interpreting it is claimed that the interpreter has to improve his memory ability and his tolerance of lag and therefore, if the loop is used at all, it must contain information specifically coded to carry language markers. This may seem rather unlikely in the very limited capacity loop in the model and may simply be a fraction of semantic memory. In either case, the articulatory loop could not be used in quite the same way as Hitch and Baddeley (1978) propose for memory, but would be more similar to its function in reading, where it is largely suppressed.

From Llewellyn-Jones' (1981a, b) findings, there must be a question as to whether BSL interpreting is actually occurring most of the time. Since the target language seems to be signs in English order in most cases, we have a situation as shown in fig. 11.3. Here the English source dominates; information is only superficially analysed and often meaning is not accessed (subjective reports of

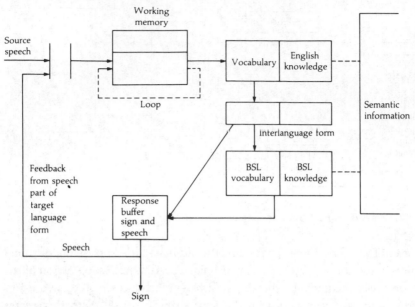

Fig. 11.3   Sign interpreting (English to BSL).

not being able to recall the material presented are not infrequent). The message to be output then simply acquires a sign vocabulary, and the response buffer has speech and sign mixed. This may arise even in circumstances where there is a knowledge of BSL and therefore some way of encoding its meaning. This could not happen in spoken language interpreting since the buffer would have two spoken codes vying for one output.

A second problem concerns the nature of analysis of the source language and its functioning in an articulatory loop system. If the task required of the listener is to shadow the message then the articulatory loop will be a useful device in establishing an appropriate lag and in maintaining information long enough for it to be recognised and repeated. It should be suppressed in spoken language interpreting, but in sign language interpreting it may not be, since speech and sign, at least on the surface, will not compete for the same articulator. The BSL interpreter can still shadow and produce the language form he expects. The preferred lag Llewellyn-Jones (1981a) mentions, of 2–3 seconds, would fit with the normally suggested duration of the loop – interpreters may simply be shadowing. The advantage in using the loop is that the message would not have to be completely understood.

Unfortunately, instead of being silent, rehearsal of this form can become overt. Sign interpreters can be seen to 'break down' under the stress of an increasing use of articulation to maintain the information in memory for it to be recalled and analysed. The interpreter in this situation becomes increasingly conscious of the lag in his articulation behind the speaker, and the increasing mismatch of messages lead to greater whispering to 'block out' the source message. He begins to hear his own voice, echoing the speaker and causing shadowing aloud effects. Inevitably that produces omissions, and may lead the interpreter to stop altogether or to ask the speaker to slow down.

The system is then being driven by working memory. As this becomes overloaded, i.e. as more information arrives in the message, an untrained interpreter tends to do one of the following:

(a) give up a slightly time consuming analysis of meaning, and simply produce word-for-sign or sign-for-word translations

(b) leave out sections of the message in order to be able to catch up, or guess at sections of a deaf signer's message

(c) stop the speaker or signer, and ask for a repeat of the information

In sign-to-speech interpreting there may be a slightly different process occurring. Although some interpreters have difficulty due to insufficient BSL knowledge there is again a tendency to incompletely process the meaning. In this instance, the grammar of BSL is rejected and the parser tends to look only at surface structure and provides word-for-sign matches. For most of the time this works imperfectly and simultaneous interpretation of BSL to English is frequently marked by the interpreter requesting repetition or further information from the deaf person. This occurs because the 'shadowed' message this time does not match the dominant language structure, i.e. English, and constant monitoring and additional concentration is required.

One can see that the task of interpreting will share similarities in its processes no matter which languages are being used. Spoken language interpreting, because it takes place only in one medium (i.e. sound), ensures that two languages cannot be mixed directly, and the use of an interlanguage is discouraged from the earliest stages of language learning. What is trained in the spoken language interpreter is the direct analysis of meaning and the active suppression of any interference effects from the production of the target language.

In BSL interpreting, at present, many of the processes seem to be active which need not be and ought not to be. The fact that the target language is not speech allows the interpreter to do something which is superficially easy: to shadow the source language without analysing it. The effort in this makes it expedient that an output form is found as quickly as possible. Under stress this becomes a simple word-for-sign or sign-for-word match which solves the immediate problem but does not give meaning. The fact that the problem recurs is inevitable given the constant shadowing and articulation.

BSL interpreting is therefore a task of some difficulty. There are a number of confounding factors in our deliberation, such as level of knowledge of BSL and the styles involved, attitudes which do not treat BSL as an adequate language code, and the pressures and difficulties of the interpreting task itself. Many of these factors appear in spoken language interpreting, but they are better understood and training aims to overcome the weaknesses of the individual interpreter.

Presenting a model of these factors gives no prescriptive power over the language analysis in BSL or speech, but it is a framework whereby we can see separate elements in the task. Attitudes to the task (R.W. Anderson, 1978), stress (Gerver, 1976), conditions (Parsons, 1978) and actual language knowledge (Longley, 1978) all have additional effects on the interpretation, and have to be taken into account over and above the actual process if we are to consider the training implications.

BSL interpreting training

As one would expect, training programmes, after an initial emphasis on ethics and aspects of the situation (e.g. court interpreting), have begun to focus on the interpreting task itself, and are much more likely to follow a pattern similar to spoken language interpreting. In the UK, and in the USA, the first step has been to try to set up an assessment procedure (Simpson, 1981); then to consider how training might best be implemented. The training, which has yet to take place in the UK in a formal way, will draw on what has been written on language techniques and the specific situation of the deaf community. Understanding the process is of considerable importance however, and it is this which has been focused on here. The considerations of language are over-riding ones, nevertheless, and it is useful to end by reviewing a number of the conditions for spoken language interpreting assessment.

Keiser (1978) reviews the selection and training of conference interpreters. He maintains that because of the highly complex activity, interpreters should be highly educated and already fluent. The basic examination should consist of: (a) an interview with frequent switching from language to language; (b) an improvised short speech in the first language on a topic chosen at random, to assess general knowledge; (c) non-technical information in one language to be rendered consecutively in a second language; (d) translation from a text off-the-cuff. These tasks are meant to be stressful and to show how well the student can use the languages in difficult circumstances. Unfortunately this constitutes only the assessment of a candidate's *suitability for entry* to an interpreters' qualifying course.

Many conclusions can be drawn from this summary. Sign language interpreting shares the process with spoken language interpreting and probably with general language comprehension but it differs in the situation of the users of the language and the community's attitude towards them. This creates additional problems of target language suitability, problems which have yet to be solved. Nevertheless, the point which comes across again and again in spoken language interpreting is that it is the meaning which is being translated. This is not the language meaning (the words or syntax of the language) but rather the message meaning or intended meaning of the speaker. Seleskovitch puts this most clearly:

Translating language meanings and obtaining the desired effect, i.e. a wording immediately intelligible to listeners, is impossible, not because there are doubts as to the intended meaning of words or phrases but because the resulting translation of such words and phrases would fail to carry sense adequately in the other language. This is why interpreters have to grasp sense and remember the ideas behind the words. (1978: 341)

BSL interpreters require the chance to develop the skills necessary to differentiate between language meaning and message meaning if deaf people are ever really to understand the sense of the interpretation.

12. Sign language in schools

As was apparent in the introductory chapters, sign language and education have historically been kept apart by those working with deaf people. Sign language was something which adult deaf people might resort to if they had failed in their education; the principal aim of education was normalisation at best, but the realisation of a child's potential at the very least. This is still valid as an educational ethos, but what comes to be questioned is the 'potential' and how it is to be measured. If we believe that the deaf child begins life as communication-handicapped, then *any* development in the ability to speak or lip-read is an education success. However, if we begin from the view that the deaf child is communicatively competent in sign language, given access to appropriate models, then all his learning goals can be reached through this language and the child becomes a second language learner in relation to English. The former view finds its sole aim in relation to communication in English, the latter sees English as part of the general educational achievements required in a shared environment with sign language.

What must be most striking to readers is how little difference there is in these two underlying premises for educational activity. Both ideals seem plausible, both effective in their own way and both derived from honest concern for the needs of children. Where the divergence has arisen is in the statement of dogma into which educators have been lured. The medical world looks for cures and, given a precise diagnosis, will set out a course of treatment which should lead to improvement in the patient's condition. Educators too have become anxious in special education to provide a 'treatment' which will lead to normalisation. Because of the nature of personal involvement in education (in a deaf school a teacher may be closely associated with the same child for a number of years) the form of treatment used relates to the personality and experience of the educator. The success achieved with children incorporates these and can become the only way of dealing with children. In publicising one's own methods it becomes only a short step to maintaining that this personal success is general success and can be achieved *only* through this personal approach. And so the doctrine is set. This happens in nearly all aspects of special education and can occur no matter from which premise we begin. Deaf education has been associated with a great deal of dogma which has had varying degrees of influence over the years. The danger is obvious: education becomes a battleground of personalities and experience; objectivity and evaluation are pushed aside.

Sadly, we still find many examples of this problem. Nolan and Tucker (1981), in writing for parents of deaf children, give no indication of the degree of language difficulty deaf children actually do face. There are no mentions of the well researched and replicated findings on reading problems, nor of the nature of the speech problems experienced. No mention at all is made of sign language in the book, even though 82 per cent of deaf young people report its use while still at school (Kyle and Allsop, 1982a). However, there is great pressure on the authors to present an optimistic view to parents:

We believe that the language learning facility possessed by normally hearing children is also possessed by hearing-impaired children and that with the exception of some with severe secondary handicaps, hearing-impaired children learn the mother tongue naturally. Of course, there will be variations in the level of functioning as there are with normally hearing children, but we know that oral language can be their tool of thought and communication. (Nolan and Tucker, 1981: 143)

One can easily understand this viewpoint since the potential of children has to be maximised and parents should be allowed to consider the ideal outcomes of their efforts. Nevertheless, the product of the optimism is greater anxiety for parent and child when these ideals are not met. The pressure is not alleviated by further statements which are over-dogmatic without consideration of their effects: 'We are convinced, and our experience supports us, that the auditory mode can be *the* mode of information transmission for hearing-impaired children' (1981: 147). This view is not supported at all in another contemporary parent's guide, Freeman, Carbin and Boese (1981). In their book, discussion ranges over many methodologies in many countries and readers are offered choices. It is this greater openness which will be required if deaf education is to assimilate the changes occurring in the community of deaf people.

While we are here concerned with the understanding and use of BSL, it is not our intention to maintain, particularly in relation to education, that this is the only method of approach. The damaging feature of oralism in the last hundred years or so in Great Britain has been its total rejection of any other method of educating deaf children. The personal elation and achievement experienced when a deaf child learns to speak recognisable words is great indeed, and has been so persuasive that many educators have perceived this experience as the only one which could possibly satisfy the deaf child as well as his teacher. The pursuit of this goal for all children, often at the expense of objective examination of results, has been misleading and is ultimately unacceptable.

The danger is that the question of methodology can easily be turned to dogma according to any premises. In deaf people's case this becomes 'BSL is the *only* method of teaching deaf children'. Certainly information can be easily conveyed in BSL and it functions to a marked degree as an effective socialisation agent in deaf children whose parents are fluent in the language. Nevertheless, there are a series of questions to be dealt with in exploring its applicability to the classroom. Even with our limited experience in the UK of signing in the classroom, there are considerable pressures already to have the 'correct' use of signs, or to find the single, standard method of teaching in sign. These pressures are valuable if they lead to early considerations of teacher skills in BSL, pupils' needs for BSL and manual English, and assessment of achievement levels as a result of the use of BSL. But the chances of these considerations occurring still seem slim.

Any consideration of deaf education should begin with the question of levels of achievement in deaf children; very often in the past, however, there have been intervening arguments proposed which have directed attention from the central purpose of all educators. Some of these points are still raised today, and it is as well to tackle them now prior to the examination of achievement.

Point 1.   Deaf children are no longer so unfortunate; technology and better methods make research findings of even recent years no longer applicable.

This is a frequent statement and is implicit in views such as those expressed by Braybrook and Powell (1980). Our quotations from the 1790s and from the *Times* in 1880 (see chapter 3) indicate that the feeling is at least two hundred years old. Bergman's (1979) comments on Sweden indicate that it is also a belief which has appeared in other countries. The fact that it constantly re-emerges suggests that the deafness problem has not been solved at all.

Kyle and Allsop (1982a) examined how recent research on deaf children tends to confirm the usual findings of poor speech and reading performance. If we consider Braybrook and Powell's (1980) surprise at finding 22 children with acceptable, natural speech abilities, and apply it to Conrad's (1979) national study of school leavers, we find that we should not be surprised at all. Taking Conrad's population and suggesting good speech as 75 per cent words in sentences correctly identified by listeners (a higher cut-off than Braybrook uses), then in the hearing loss range 80–120dB (Braybrook's range), there would be 15 children. Extending to the 6–16 years age range of Braybrook, we would predict a population of up to 150 from which the better speakers of his 22 were chosen; Conrad's figure excludes those placed in ordinary schools.

Point 2.   With the trend towards mainstreaming or integration, relatively few deaf children now need communication in anything other than speech. They will mix with hearing children from the beginning.

This is a rather curious argument about sign language. It implies that only deaf people in deaf schools who are 'isolated' need to use BSL. Not only do we have the situation in the UK where partial-hearing units (PHUs – integrated settings) are using Total Communication (e.g. Hegarty, Pocklington and Lucas, 1982), but young deaf people do not see the use of BSL as a function of their contact or lack of contact with hearing people. Young deaf people expect to use speech and lip-reading with hearing people, but at the same time want BSL as *their* language, as a medium for information (Kyle and Allsop, 1982a). The trend towards mainstreaming is an important one, but it does not alter the question of how the teacher of the deaf communicates with profoundly deaf children

Point 3. The numbers of deaf children are decreasing, and some causes such as rubella can be completely eradicated as medical prevention programmes improve. The deaf community will soon be so small as to make considerations of BSL or signing irrelevant to education.

There is an element of truth in the very first statement as it applies to the UK. There is no indication that the same is occurring in the world's most populous countries. However, the numbers are decreasing as the birth rate decreases generally. In recent years, the decrease in the number of deaf children has been greater than the general national decrease, though this is mainly in the numbers of partially-hearing children rather than deaf children. So, there is an overall decline but technology may be selectively affecting those who are partially-hearing and they are less likely to appear in the statistics for special education (DES, 1981). As far as medical intervention is concerned, 42 per cent of Conrad's national study had unknown causes, and a further 27 per cent had hereditary causes. This means that 69 per cent are not susceptible to medical intervention at least for the present. Deafness is not going to go away.

Point 4. All normal deaf children can develop in the oral system. It is only where there are additional or multiple handicaps that signing or fingerspelling should be considered, because in these cases there is an identifiable 'syndrome' preventing language acquisition

We have already seen this statement in St John Ackers' postscript to the 1890 Education Act, but it has become popular again (Van Uden, 1981). It arises from a series of acts of faith: speech is natural, language acquisition occurs naturally through audition; the oral approach incorporates this natural approach; children who do not acquire language in this way are therefore deviant, and thus defective. By this reasoning the things which they do not do well become part of the 'syndrome'. Van Uden (1981) explains at length how 'dyspraxia' and defects in intermodal integration 'endanger an education according to the purely oral way'. His description of these two conditons places them within the *normal* range of problems in profoundly deaf children:

The syndrome of dyspraxia of deaf children comprises that the child clearly suffers from dyspraxia or apraxia with dysrhythmia or arhythmia and that the child, his memory as such being normal, shows a typical profile of a strong memory for simultaneously presented visual data and a relatively weak one for successively presented visual data. (1981: 118)

The syndrome is seen as poor speech, e.g. 'omission of phonemes (*fower* instead of *flower*)' or avoidance of lip-reading by looking away. The motor-sensory integration disturbance appears 'especially in verbal behaviour, i.e. the integration of word and meaning and of the written and spoken forms of the words' (Van Uden, 1981: 120). In practice it occurs when deaf children can write a word better than speak it.

The basic premise of this approach is so startlingly simple that it is rather difficult to explain how damaging it actually is. Lack of speech development in deaf children becomes a function not of their lack of experience of spoken sound, but of additional handicap. With a simple statement we have done away with the whole concept of deafness itself. Children are either capable of speaking or not; those who are not use sign language because of their failure to speak. Handicap is defined in terms of symptoms which were traditionally attributed to hearing loss. It is a very simple denial of deafness and corrupts the most fundamental aspect of scientific investigation: the elements which are the outcome are said to be the cause.

According to the theory of dyspraxia presented above, the symptoms (poor and irregular control of articulation, better sight vocabulary than ability to speak words) become the cause of the problem. Deaf children suffer from this 'cause' and therefore the approach originally used, oralism, is not at fault in dealing with these additionally handicapped pupils. Not only is this view totally unacceptable to the deaf community as active members of society and sign language users but there is no evidence in the UK that these 'symptoms' are in any way 'causes'. The problem remains one of deafness. The developments in child language research, however, show parallel development of sign language and spoken language in young children.

The discussion of how a teacher can deal with the language capabilities of young deaf children is a lengthy one which can only be summarised. As a prerequisite, some examination of the focal achievements of deaf children in schools is required. In the UK this has been a function of the oral philosophy of education (until the last five years). The achievements we consider below, therefore, arise in non-signing environments.

Achievement levels in deaf children

For the most part we are concerned with language achievement in English, but there are grounds for concern about numeracy (Wood, Wood and Howarth,

1983), about employment prospects (Montgomery and Miller, 1977), and about behaviour and emotional development (Denmark, 1981). We have briefly discussed English speech and lip-reading skills in chapter 4; here we will be more concerned with 'formal' aspects: reading and writing. The approach of classroom testing against the hearing norms has a long tradition among educators and researchers. The findings are the same in virtually all cases: deaf children lag behind their hearing counterparts. A pattern similar to that found in the UK is found also in the USA (Jensema and Trybus, 1976), in Scandinavia (Vestberg Rasmussen, 1973), and throughout the European Community (CEC, 1979).

The pattern will be dealt with rather cursorily here, since it has occupied the attention of numerous writers who have presented lengthy explanations of the problems (e.g. Swisher, 1976; Moores, 1978; Conrad, 1979). However, it does have to be dealt with, since the effective cognitive growth of deaf children indicates a potential for educational growth which has not been realised.

The basis for this claim comes from the discovery of normal or near-normal intellectual functioning in deaf children (Vernon, 1967; Kyle, 1979). In addition, evaluation within a Piagetian framework has led Furth (1966) to claim that cognitive skills are similar in deaf children, given equivalent exposure to the task requirements. The argument is difficult to uphold in some respects since Furth's argument seems to be that deprivation of experience is at fault, but he does not provide any suggestions for an approach to maximising deaf people's performance.

However, it is in reading that the major problem of achievement lies. Reading and writing are visual and motor skills, at least superficially, and are therefore in theory directly accessible to deaf people. However, this is much too simplistic, and reading levels of deaf children are considerably depressed, as Conrad (1979) has reported in some detail. In terms of closeness to hearing children's reading, deaf children are only within striking distance between the ages of 7 and 8 years and thereafter suffer significant decline in relative performance which produces very poor performance by the time they leave school. The problem is serious. Among profoundly deaf children (greater than 85dB hearing losses) aged 16 years, more than 50 per cent will read at a level below 7 years 10 months (Kyle *et al.*, 1978; Conrad, 1979). This sort of finding is repeated again and again (e.g. Savage, Evans and Savage, 1981). Swisher (1976) in a thorough review of achievement in what she terms the 'oral deaf', found problems in speech (in word classes, in syntax and in length of utterance), in reading (whether through achievement tests, completion tasks, or direct analysis of morphology, phrases and so on), and in writing (where either limited or stereotyped production occurs). Quigley (1979) confirms this and uses it as a basis for examining alternative language environments. Wood (1981) also sees the problem in terms

235

of language environments. His suggestion is that teaching styles are related to the poor language performance. His study shows a relatively high degree of 'repair' work by teachers in conversation with deaf children. In effect, the communication interaction is disturbed by lower intelligibility, and teachers have to repeat and check utterances by their children instead of elaborating and extending conversation.

Deaf children's reading ability does increase over time, however, although it never reaches the levels of hearing children. Wood, Griffiths and Webster (1981) maintain that this development occurs in a radically different way, producing characteristic word and syntax errors. A series of papers by Quigley and his associates (e.g. Quigley *et al.*, 1976) tends to confirm these differences in syntax knowledge and handling. At least some of these can be explained by language or code interference between English and sign language (e.g. difficulties with the passive voice – BSL has no passive). Although we have seen (in chapter 9) that this interference may be interpreted as a positive intermediate strategy by a second language learner, this still leaves open the question of how to utilise it.

In terms of strategy, Ewoldt (1980) maintains that deaf children do use psycholinguistic strategies for reading, indicating a sensitivity to the rules of English. However, Goodman's (1967) view of reading, from which this is derived, is limited in its understanding of reading acquisition and, overall, the theory can be simplified to a basic strategy of 'making sense of the task' rather than being a direct help to reading progress.

The small study of children developing reading reported by Kyle (1981b) confirms the general view, but shows up the gap between vocabulary development, where progress is made throughout schooling, and sentence comprehension, where deaf children frequently reach a plateau at about the 8-year-old level. It is obviously rather dangerous to talk too generally, and the above brief survey must be interpreted as only a guide to the average performance of deaf children.

There are rather similar findings for writing. Swisher's (1976) review identifies the type of problems which occur in written work. Sentences tend to be shorter and there is a preponderance of nouns and verbs, with only gradual increase in other parts of speech as children get older. More recently there have been attempts to fit a transformational grammar framework to the written production of deaf children (Ivimey, 1976). Quigley *et al.* (1976) report on the tendency of deaf children to try to fit subject–verb–object patterns on to all sentence constructions. Quigley (1979) adds to this a tendency to interpret noun phrases as connecting to the nearest verb phrase, producing misinterpretation and limiting the range of written sentences. However, what is perhaps most striking about written productions is how often they can be disambiguated by recourse to the sign language 'rules' which would govern that meaning. Most professionals working with the deaf have had the experience of receiving letters from deaf people which need to be signed in BSL first before the meaning is apparent. As in any second language situation, the grammatical code which is relied on is the one which is already known. In the case of deaf people it relates to BSL.

One can see even from this very brief review that deaf children's learning of English does not match that of hearing children. The view that deaf children can learn through the auditory mode in exactly the same way as hearing children is not supported at all in the literature. The 'oral' approach, whether one calls it a 'natural' or 'modern' approach, has been in operation since the time educators stopped learning BSL. The technology has changed and the nature of the population in deaf school has changed, and there is no research to support the suggestion that the oral approach is viable for the deaf children in special education today. Deaf children are competent learners of language, as we have seen in chapter 4; they are cognitively able, and will progress to an effective position in working society. However, the major concern is how to maximise the effectiveness of schooling, and for this we have to examine the learning environment and subsequently the methodological considerations which have actually been presented.

The learning environment

This is one of the most difficult areas of functioning to describe effectively: it is also, perhaps, the most crucial. Much of the research and theory which has informed our educational methodology has been superseded in recent times both in psychology and linguistics. Up to the 1960s behaviourist models of learning pervaded educational practice. Not only did children have to learn by association and reinforcement, their production had to be shaped to the correct response. This was believed true of general learning and the learning of language. Deaf education also derived its inspiration from a similar source and the texts available in the 1960s and early 1970s drew heavily on learning theories (Watson, 1967; Van Uden, 1970).

Brennan (1976), in a thorough critique of these approaches, casts doubt on the actual opportunities the deaf child has to acquire language. She highlights Van Uden's insistence on imitation (and reward) as the teaching approach to language, at the expense of natural elaboration of utterances — as occurs with hearing children (this is one aspect of teaching style also taken up by Wood, 1981). The pressure of this approach on teachers produces over-zealous correction of ungrammatical utterances at the expense of interaction. Cazden's (1972) extensive analysis of hearing children interacting with parents shows how little parents actually correct children's immature syntax, yet this has been a particular bulwark of educational approaches to deaf children. Brennan puts it clearly:

Perhaps the most damaging aspect of the Van Uden model of language-learning is the assumption that it is permissible to concentrate on language structure at the cost of language function. This is completely contrary to the present recognition of the priority of function neatly expressed in Cazden's maxim 'take care of function and the structure will take care of itself'. (1976: 4)

Even though the method described by Braybrook and Powell (1980) has moved on since this time, it still does not reflect current knowledge of child language. The 'natural' approach to English acquisition draws inspiration from Chomskyan theories that the child develops his own language form through his 'language acquisition device'. In effect, this appears to be what Nolan and Tucker are proposing in the quotation given on page 231, and in:

But he will not learn language because you want him to – he will learn it *because he wants to*. This fact we believe to be fundamental to our understanding of how he will learn; he will learn language through an interaction between the efforts of his own brain and events in the outside world. (1981: 143)

Increasingly, child language research has placed the weight on interaction, not on some innate device which produces grammatical utterances in the child. Wells' extensive data (1981) indicate the critical importance of interaction. It is discourse which propels language acquisition, and it is the shared meaning in interaction which is of critical importance. It is this which is most at risk in children with limited hearing.

In one sense these findings may be seen as an argument for mainstreaming and it is appropriate to pause for a moment to consider this view. There are considerable difficulties in evaluating educational provision when placement decisions have to be made, as Cave and Maddison's (1978) review of the literature shows. Nevertheless, Hegarty, Pocklington and Lucas' (1982) exam-ination of mainstreaming case studies is particularly informative here. They consider two situations: one where unit provision is made available (on-site support in a special class) and one where children are individually integrated. Generally, children are already selected for their communication ability, but although Hegarty, Pocklington and Lucas are optimistic about the provision they describe, it is clear that in language and interaction there are problems. The presence of profoundly deaf children was viewed rather oddly in one situation:

The teacher in charge claimed that there were at least nine children who 'linguistically could be good partials' but not one was attaining anything like his or her true linguistic potential. The presence of profoundly deaf children – even though by that stage provided for in their own fairly self-contained class – was held responsible to a considerable degree. (1982: 160)

However, what is most apparent generally in the provisions described is that deaf children are unable to interact, do not contribute to class lessons through speech, are subjected to distorted and exaggerated mouthings by teachers and pupils in order to convey specific information (i.e. not natural language interaction) and are unlikely to have secure peer group friendships. There are claimed benefits in academic progress and in social and emotional maturity, but the solution to the basic problem of the language and learning environments cannot be taken to be solved in the mainstreaming option.

There have been a number of comparisons of learning environments for deaf children. None of them are completely satisfactory because of the problem of control of ability and opportunity in the different settings. The majority in recent times have favoured approaches with a sign language or fingerspelling element, though there have been studies to support written language as a most effective communication (White and Stevenson, 1975). Brasel and Quigley (1977) present a well controlled study comparing 'manual English' with 'average manual' (where little English was used by deaf parents), with 'intensive oral' (parents trained in oral method) and with 'average oral'. The achievement results in English consistently followed the order above with the 'manual English' group out-performing all the others. Brasel and Quigley's conclusion is that the early language environment offered by the use of signing improves the child's prospects in the learning of English.

This is a particular theme followed up by Conrad (1980). His interpretation of his data is that the deaf child is linguistically deprived from the very beginning and it is this early lack of language stimulation which creates the problem. He uses neurological studies of deprivation to show that early lack of speech is likely to produce later problems in speech perception and therefore production. He attacks oralism as an additional depriving agent since it insists on having no further stimulation other than speech, when it is the *language* stimulation which is most important not the *modality* of stimulation. In the logical development of this view it is the child who must choose. This does not arise because of failure, but, rather, the use of Total Communication offers both spoken and signed stimulation which provides a range of alternatives for the deaf child. From the earliest time, then, deaf children can have access to the language interaction which Wells (1981) insists is so important. While Conrad tends to minimise the task for parents and professionals in learning BSL in a way which would allow it to be used with English, the fact remains that it is the language attitude which has to be altered.

Criticisms of the view of auditory deprivation (Bench, 1979) and of bilingualism (Arnold, 1982) tend to miss the point that language acquisition occurs through interaction. Indeed, Arnold's claim that 'the main enemy is deafness' totally obscures all the previous research on the cognitive functioning of deaf children and the nature of child language. Restrictions on the interaction of children with peers and care-takers necessarily limit the language access. Both at home and at school, methodologies may fundamentally obstruct the negotiation of meaning and, in doing so, reduce the likelihood of deaf children enriching their language skills. Both Brennan (1976) and Conrad (1979) suggest that for the profoundly deaf child, oralism provides this sort of obstruction.

The examination of this issue leads both Meadow (1980) and Freeman, Carbin and Boese (1981) to similar conclusions. Meadow (1980) in particular emphasises *early* language intervention and proposes a form of Total Communication as the most effective approach. She offers this view based on her earlier research that no evidence consistently indicates the supposed negative effects of signing on speech skills. The problems of learning an additional system for parents are put to one side in stressing this need for early interaction. The delay in placing children in Total Communication programmes frequently means that they are seen as 'failures', both by parents and by themselves. The consequent problems are seen at every stage of subsequent development as the parents struggle to learn signing because their children were not 'good enough' to progress normally, and as the children have to come to terms not only with deafness but with the community of deaf people which has been shunned by their families.

Total Communication requires some explanation, both of concept and practice, and we will give this some attention in our next chapter. Nevertheless, we can already detect the influence of the research which has led to it and its appeal to educators. Garretson (1976), in considering the state of methodologies in schools in the USA, showed the tremendous acceleration in use of this approach. He reported 88 per cent of schools he sampled had adopted a Total Communication approach and these, by and large, relied on the development of sign systems which more closely reflect English syntax.

The same change appears to be happening in the UK, but there are no easily available figures. It is reflected throughout Europe, and in Tervoort's extensive study of 20 countries in Europe we can see the move toward the incorporation of signing in educational methodology: 'There is no change in favour of oralism and there is an atmosphere of change in the other direction all over Europe' (1983: 143).

In general, the move is towards supporting the spoken language so that deaf children can more easily fit into the community as a whole, but perhaps the key insight from Tervoort's study is the perception of the range of solution available to educators in different countries. Tervoort describes four stages:

There appears to be a tendency to go from oral-only to speech with speech-supportive means such as fingerspelling or cued speech; from those there is a movement in the direction of the use of sign to better disambiguate the spoken word; next comes a signed version of the spoken language either with speech or without it depending on the circumstances; and finally, the continuum develops from signed Danish, Swedish, English and so on to Danish Sign Language, Swedish Sign Language, British Sign Language etc. At that final stage the choice in favour of bilingual educational philosophy is a fact. (1983: 146)

The critical point is that the four stages are progressive: educators move along from one to the other. In any starting position, when the basis for change has been created the decision as to which stage should be contemplated is the key one. The whole question of Total Communication philosophy depends on the point of entry into these stages. We now need to consider how one makes this decision, how it is theoretically justified and whether the end point of bilingualism may be an inevitable consequence of the initial steps of educators.

13. Which sign language?

Inevitably when we reach the point of change in special education, the question is asked frequently and in different contexts and independently in different places, as to how the changes should actually occur. However, the question in the way it is posed by educators usually calls for an answer in terms of commitment rather than of attitude in school or in society and the implementation has begun by the time the thought of research arises. Action research has come about as a result of this common situation and what it tries to do is to evaluate what is already practice. It acknowledges the lack of control groups and neat experimental designs and works with perceived values of change. This type of situation does not permit classical techniques of research. The widespread emergence of 'action research' is the rationalisation of this situation. In these circumstances research monitors the extent of change and, most importantly, evaluates the degree of commitment engendered in those who participate.

The movements towards mainstreaming, towards earlier education and towards signing in schools, are of this type. They have occurred because policy makers or practitioners have judged it to be appropriate to their views and implementation has begun. This creates major difficulties for the examination of the effects of the change envisaged, but it does provide an explanation for the dramatic changes in policies which occur, most notably, in our case, the movement towards signing. This is not to underestimate the importance of the change, but rather to try to understand its power and to understand the basis on which evaluation must occur.

Unfortunately evaluation is very difficult and has seldom been done in special educational practice. Mainstreaming is a very good example of where our policies push beyond what our research has been able to show. This is not to say that the policy-making is wrong or misplaced, but rather to make clear that our questioning of research and evidence is not always simple or effective. The studies used as a basis for judgement are generally lacking in control because of the finality of educational decision making and placement (in the sense that we cannot return the child to an original or alternative placement a year later and be able to start from the same point again). Key aspects are often ignored:

Teacher variables are rarely considered. Programme variables where referred to at all are stated in gross terms. It is assumed that the fact that teachers and pupils are together in a special classroom implies the presence of an educational programme relevant to the development of children; also that the presence of a teacher provides effective educational programmes . . . in practice none of these desiderata have been met. (Tizard, 1974: 225)

Although this quotation concerns research in relation to mainstreaming, the same is obviously true of the implementation of educational methodology in deaf education. It is perhaps trite to say that the educational policy is only as good as its actual implementation *in the classroom*, but it is a point overlooked in the search for a panacea in deaf education. No method substitutes for the skill and sensitivity of the class teacher in the group interaction basis of a classroom.

A given administrative arrangement is neither good nor bad . . . what really counts is what is done with the group once it is established . . . Among the questions which must be raised are the following:
a. How competent are the teachers in each setting for dealing with the specific characteristics of the child in question? (MacMillan, 1971)

Again this draws on the subject of mainstreaming, and the subsequent questions raised, (b–e) deal with the actual level of functioning of children and other teachers in those circumstances. In summarising the factors which lead them to believe in mainstreaming, Hegarty, Pocklington and Lucas (1981) return to attitudinal variables and cite the 'enthusiasm of the headteacher' and his 'capacity to enlist the cooperation of staff' as key features.

What we can take from this contemporary debate is the realisation that although research can assess the effectiveness of signing in schools, the change to Total Communication is generally based on attitude or commitment, which minimises or ignores the teacher variable. As a result, we can begin to understand Conrad's (1981) view that there is as yet no published evidence on Total Communication producing higher *educational* standards. He relates this to the recency of developments and:

one would expect a large variation in the fluency with which teachers can instruct in sign language; many would have had no more than a relatively short course. So it will inevitably be some time before this necessary information becomes available in any meaningful way. (1981: 17)

However, we can point to a good deal of information on the effectiveness of signing in communication and in various aspects of language development (Moores, 1978; Quigley, 1979). We have set out some of this in the previous chapter; here we are concerned with what methodologies are available within the overall heading of 'signing in school'.

Types of signing available for education

The question 'which types of signing should be used in deaf schools?' is very like the question 'which food is best?'. The range of possibilities is considerable. But one would tend, in the case of food, to ask for more details. In what circumstances is the food to be produced, and what is the purpose of its use (to go on a diet, or to exclude certain elements such as meat)? In addition, the food expert would want to know more about the local conditions and the alternative sources of nourishment available. In practice the food expert would be likely to suggest a 'balanced' diet.

The same almost certainly is true of signing. Local conditions, priorities and the actual setting in which the signing is to appear will determine suitability. What is almost certain is that a range of methods is required, not a single one. What is also clear is that no approach is simpler to use, to acquire, or to maintain, than any other; teachers and parents need access and knowledge of as many varieties of signing as possible.

Having said that, we can begin to distinguish the difference in type and, therefore, the difference in application of the methods of signing available. We wish to make simple distinctions between *sign languages* (BSL, ASL and so on); *sign systems*, which will draw on sign language vocabulary but add features of the spoken language (signed English (UK), Signed Swedish, Seeing Exact English), or which have a manufactured vocabulary (Paget-Gorman Sign System); *fingerspelling*; *sign vocabularies*, which reflect the meaning of sign languages and spoken languages without necessarily adopting inflections from either (Makaton, Cued Speech); and *Total Communication* which involves a mixture of one or more of these with spoken language.

Sign language

The book so far has described what we know of BSL and its status as a natural language. Sign languages and their dialects exist in every country we have researched, though the word 'language' may not be available to deaf people to describe it. Hearing people may have had difficulty in access, but we have argued that this arises in the unequal status of the learner (hearing) and teacher (deaf). Nevertheless, knowledge of sign language is crucial to every other application of signing and we will return to this point later.

Sign systems related to sign language

In Tervoort's (1983) survey he discovered six of his responding countries had a signed spoken language form (Finland, Ireland, Norway, Rumania, Sweden and the Soviet Union), but he also discovered in a further five countries an 'unofficial' system of signs structured to reflect the spoken language. In Denmark, Hansen (1980) describes a mixed language situation:

Signed Danish is a gestural/auditive language in which Danish is spoken at the same time as signs from the Sign Language are used for all words which have a concept, and as far as possible grammatical rules [are used] from sign language. The number of pieces of information visually is equal to the number given auditively. (1980: 25)

This is perhaps the most fundamental principle of sign systems: no matter how much they are able to draw from a sign language they attempt to match their production to the spoken language which is produced simultaneously. However, this signed Danish is much further along the way to sign language than the other approaches we will describe. For example:

Spoken Danish: Where did you go to school?
Signed Danish (signs): WHERE YOU SCHOOL WHERE?

In signed Danish the words are spoken as in the upper line but only the signs in the lower line are articulated. The last sign WHERE? takes the place of intonation in the Danish question where 'school' has rising intonation. In Danish Sign Language the utterance would be: SCHOOL WHERE?

Hansen (1980) makes it very clear that signed Danish is not the same as the Signed English that has developed in the USA, and she believes it to be a more flexible and efficient natural language form. At the same time:

Signed Danish is not Danish, when you cannot hear/distinguish the words – but another type of sign language, which has the primary advantage that hearing people can use it at the same time as they use spoken language, and the secondary advantage is that some – and only some – rules applying to the spoken language are conveyed to the deaf child. (1980: 26–7)

Bergman (1979) also includes Signed Swedish under the title of a language, but her description of its history (and this history is repeated in many countries) makes it clear that the system has been *constructed* with specific aims in mind. A committee comprising deaf and hearing people began in 1970 with a Swedish word list to establish which words had sign translations. When the words had more than one sign equivalent, only one sign was used. The principle aim of the approach was standardisation. Extending this aim meant that signs had to be invented when no obvious word–sign equivalent existed. The rationale for this approach is important since we see it repeated in country after country.

There are several reasons for the adaptation to Swedish . . . all of which are connected . . . with theories about SSL [Swedish Sign Language] and its role in the teaching of the deaf. Adapting the ordering of signs to Swedish word order is supposed to result in the pupils learning Swedish with greater ease. We know that the syntactic rules of SSL turn up in their written Swedish and so by analogy, children who grow up with Signed

Swedish should instead be influenced to use the correct word order. Another advantage that Signed Swedish is supposed to have over SSL is that it is not 'abbreviated'; every word is accompanied by a sign. (Bergman, 1979: 16)

Additionally, the traditional uncertainty about sign language and its grammar was highlighted, in the need to link communication with speech and lip-reading. Last, and perhaps most significant, was the fear that SSL was too difficult for hearing people to learn: Signed Swedish would be easier. Bergman is openly critical of this emphasis:

SSL is claimed to be very difficult for (hearing) adults to learn; some go so far as to say that it is impossible. What is meant is really that it is not possible to learn to sign like a deaf person, i.e. without an 'accent'. But of what other foreign-language learning do we demand that a native speaker of the language shall not be able to discover any deviations? (1979: 16–17)

We shall return to this specific point in considering all the systems; however, we should say that Bergman's (1979) discussion of Signed Swedish is perhaps the clearest examination of a sign system in relation to the native sign language. Her conclusions are very important to our final discussion.

Distinct from Scandinavian developments have been those in the USA. Bornstein (1979) provides an extended analysis of the different systems which have been devised as a result of the same pressures described above for Signed Swedish. He picks out a number of similarly titled systems: Seeing Essential English (SEE I), Signing Exact English (SEE II), Signed English (SE). These systems share a number of characteristics. SEE I (Anthony, 1971) attempts to form compounds of base signs and signs for parts of words, affixes, prefixes and so on. SEE II (Gustason, Pfetzing and Zawolkow, 1975) takes the compounding principle further. Words like TODAY, TOMORROW and YESTERDAY become compounds because there are words/signs for TO + DAY, TO + MORROW, and YESTER + DAY. SE (Bornstein *et al.*, 1975) attempts to get round some of these problems by attempting to parallel meaning rather than form. Marker signs are invented for inflected forms of English.

Bornstein (1979), however, is able to see weaknesses in all the systems. The fact that it is impossible to borrow words from one language to another with exactly the same form and meaning means all such systems are a compromise. The use of markers, while generally insufficient to mirror the complexities of English inflection, may well be still too complex for natural fluent use by English speakers. The sign system thus involves a great learning task.

The use of signed English in the UK reflects the problems that all these systems produce both in development and use. The particular principles adopted relate to attitudes and stated priorities, so there are schools where something like the Danish approach is used, and other schools where committees have been formed to set out the principles of a formal system comparable to SEE or SE. The predominant approach in the UK can be described as Manually Coded English (MCE), i.e. the priority everywhere seems to be to support the learning of English through simultaneous use of signs and English. One problem this poses is that the Education Act (1981) specifically excludes from special educational provision children whose difficulties arise because of a non-English language background:

A child is not to be taken as having a learning difficulty solely because the language (or form of the language) in which he is or will be taught is different from a language (or form of language) which has at any time been spoken in the house. (Education Act, 1981: ch. 60, 1.4)

Deaf children of deaf parents using sign at home may come under this rule; like ethnic minority children they must then be assessed in their native language prior to any Statement or placement. This aspect of legislation has not yet been tested.

Although these systems are taught to teachers and are available for use in class, various factors appear to mitigate against full use of the systems by the teacher, and as we shall see when we discuss effects of the various approaches, something closer to the Danish system is often used.

Systems which are completely artificial. The prime example of this type of system is Paget-Gorman Sign System (PGSS) which derives from a developed set of 21 hand-postures and 37 basic signs. At times there may be an iconic overlap with BSL signs, but the system of inflection is totally different (fig. 13.1). This system, devised to help deaf people learn language, is now used with children with severe learning disabilities as well (Rowe, 1982). According to theoretical analysis by Crystal and Craig (1978), PGSS offers the greatest possibilities for accurately reflecting English. In practice, as Rowe describes, it can be used with varying degrees of grammatical marking and would in fact be introduced to mentally-handicapped children in telegraphic form, slowly building to full English linguistic structure: e.g. (1) HALL, (2) GO HALL, (3) GO TO HALL, (4) GO TO THE HALL.

There are, in practice, no more than a handful of schools in the UK still teaching deaf children with PGSS. Its use perhaps reached maximum interest in the 1970s but has declined as the move for MCE has developed. However, there is still considerable use among children with severe learning disabilities. Kiernan, Reid and Jones (1982), in a survey of special schools using some form of signing, claim 34 per cent of schools responding have a PGSS programme and 33 per cent of children had some PGSS in their education. These children included educationally-subnormal, physically-handicapped and autistic children. It is

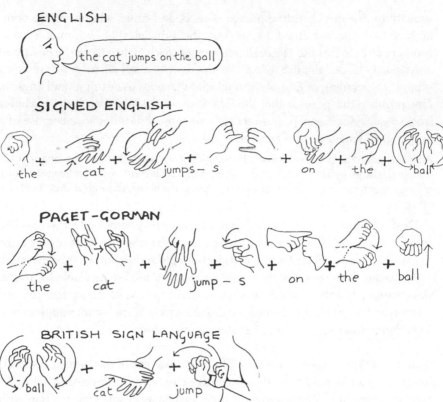

Fig. 13.1 Systems of communication.

probably within these groups that systems like PGSS, which do not rely on contact with native signs, can be most effective. The prime aim is spoken language and the system is meant as a stimulus and a support.

Because these systems are not 'natural' their structure is complex and even the knowledge of English can prove to be unhelpful when markers represent meaning and not form.

Fingerspelling

The origins of fingerspelling are rather difficult to trace, though there are better records than for signs. In most languages with writing systems alphabetic fingerspelling has been available for over two hundred years. The use of finger shapes to convey meaning can be seen even further back in Christian art where 'secret' signs were available for God, the Trinity, and so on. Fingerspelling as it

248

exists today consists of a direct alphabetic representation of the language as it would be written down. In BSL this is two-handed but in most countries the system used is one-handed (see fig. 6.12, page 125).

As far as can be made out, systems of fingerspelling have always come about by hearing invention. *Digiti lingua* (1698) is the earliest published system which seems comparable to currently used fingerspelling in the UK, and this was written by a 'friend to the deaf'. However, alphabets were often designed for use among hearing people (Dalgarno, 1661) as a sort of linguistic exercise to show speech was not the only communicative agent.

Fingerspelling requires an unambiguous representation of each letter of the alphabet in order that words from the spoken language can be produced on the hands letter by letter. Its concept is more or less universal, although its implementation is not. In China, although a system has been proposed and taught, it is still not used by deaf people. The same is true in Israel. Both these countries indicate that the spoken language base is unnecessary for the specification of places and people (a particular use which hearing users make of fingerspelling), since fingerspelled names are not used. A comparison of the UK and USA also indicates a difference in function and use of fingerspelling. In both countries fingerspelling has become incorporated into sign language communication and deaf people will use fingerspelling with one another. This produces a 'borrowing' from English which has been described by Battison (1978) for ASL, and Woll (1981) for BSL. The descriptions indicate differences in use of fingerspelling such that BSL fingerspelling occurs primarily in place names and people's names, while in ASL initialisation of signs is a primary aspect of borrowing. Initialisation involves a change of handshape to represent the first letter of the English translation of the sign (see chapter 6). An important aspect of fingerspelling borrowing is the adoption of the fingerspelled representation, or part of it, as a sign. We have described this process earlier (chapter 6), and it seems to occur in every case where fingerspelling has been available for some time and there has been a strong hearing influence.

Fingerspelling does not, therefore, stand alone as a system but has in most cases become part of sign language for adult deaf people. There are educational approaches where it has been used as a method. The 'Rochester' method of fingerspelling with speech and lip-reading has been in use in the USA for over a hundred years (Savage, Evans and Savage, 1981). Interestingly, this system was initially supported by the oralist lobby (Bell, 1887). More detailed description of the approach has been set out by Savage, Evans and Savage (1981) and an evaluation of its effectiveness within a Total Communication programme in the UK is provided, which we will examine in the context of all the systems.

Which sign language?

Systems as partial support

We wish to examine two approaches under this heading: Cued Speech and Makaton Vocabulary. The former is a system superficially like a support for lip-reading, but potentially of value in all communication. The latter is a developmental vocabulary primarily used with deaf children with learning difficulties.

Montgomery (1981) classifies Cued Speech as a phoneme transmission system similar to the Danish Hand–Mouth system (Forchhammer, 1903). The latter was used as a support within the oral method, while Cornett (1975) would identify Cued Speech as a manual method. The system involves classifying lip-patterns which look alike and providing cues to disambiguate them. The cues require eight hand patterns and four hand positions, all executed by the dominant hand somewhere close to the side of the face. They are therefore expected to be within the visual focus when children watch the teacher's face and lips.

The system has been taken up in many countries, including the USA, UK and Australia, but effective evaluation has still to be done. Certainly added visual information helps lip-reading, but, since Cued Speech is based on spoken phonemes to which deaf children may not have access, it is difficult to see how it affects language development as a whole.

The Makaton Vocabulary was devised as a 'language enabling device' for people with learning disabilities (Walker and Armfield, 1982). It was originally used with deaf mentally-handicapped patients. It consists of a developmental sequence of signs taken from a BSL dialect and carries a simple formal system of teaching the signs to children and adults. The approach used is simple reward-based learning. The basic vocabulary of around 350 signs can be combined in sentences as the child develops the ability to use and understand signs. This latter aspect has developed without knowledge of BSL and has led to an uninflected form of signing which has been slow to change.

The system is now in widespread use. Kiernan, Reid and Jones (1979) indicate its use in over 80 per cent of schools for children with severe learning disabilities. Its use is greater than BSL or MCE (children with severe learning disabilities are eight times as numerous as profoundly deaf children). Its prime value is with those with severe learning disabilities where communication growth is likely to be limited. Nevertheless, the principle is that the 350 signs learned should be overtaken by the 'release' of spoken words, such that spoken English becomes the means of communication. As Montgomery (1981) points out, the Makaton Vocabulary is not suitable for the general population of deaf children due to its limited vocabulary size. The originators of the system claim its use with young deaf children in the normal range (Walker and Armfield, 1982), but would tend to agree about its ideal application to severe communication and learning disabilities.

Total Communication

Total Communication involves the simultaneous use of one or other of the systems described above, together with oral language. It was first adopted by Denton (1970) to describe practice at the Maryland School for the Deaf. It is a description of a logical response to impaired communication in any 'channel' by the use of additional channels. In itself it is not a new idea, and it shares much with the combined method which was the basis for deaf education in the UK in the 19th century. Savage, Evans and Savage (1981) describe it as a revivalist term for a philosophy. Montgomery defines it as follows:

> mention should be made of *Total Communication* which is often wrongly equated with 'simultaneous' methods of speaking and signing 'Siglish' at the same time. More accurately, however, the Total Communication Approach is a philosophy rather than a method and as such is in contrast to 'the oral-way-of-life' oral-onlyism, or any restrictive, prohibitive, Limited Communication Approach. The TC approach uses all communication channels available to children, without the counter-productive forceful insistence on the use of more defective channels. An encouraging, positive, relationship is part of the philosophy. (1981; 4)

This philosophy offers the children more. It fits the principles set out by Conrad (1980) in allowing language stimulation by making available a number of forms of code. Unfortunately, it does not carry with it a directive as to which code or system is to be involved, or indeed whether any code is actually usable internally by the children who experience it. The only thing in practice it excludes, at least in simultaneous mode, is BSL (even though the philosophy will allow it).

Evaluating the approaches

Given our general theme, that it has been attitudes which determine methods, it is perhaps not surprising for the reader to discover that the amount of research on the effects of the systems of signing is very small indeed. There are, of course, major problems in evaluating programmes, as we have already discussed, but one could perhaps have expected more concern about the amount of information transmitted by each method and about how each works in the classroom.

PGSS and Makaton have received perhaps the least evaluation. Kiernan, Reid and Jones' (1982) review concludes that any evidence available is weakened by poor methodology and/or ineffective description of what was measured. Fenn and Rowe (1975) found PGSS use with deaf multiply-handicapped children produced some combining in sentences. Inglis (1978) found some evidence of PGSS coding in memory in multiply-handicapped individuals.

There has been slightly greater interest in Cued Speech, but again the findings have mainly consisted of case studies or unsubstantiated claims. Ling and Clarke (1975) found some limited evidence of better performance with Cued Speech as compared with speech-reading on its own, but performance in both was poor.

Clarke and Ling (1976) studied only eight children and conclude that Cued Speech produces better performance than speech-reading. A more detailed, longer-term study by Mohay (1983) followed three children through early language development stages both pre- and post-Cued Speech programmes. The Cued Speech programmes varied between 6 months and just over 2 years. Her findings indicate many difficulties with Cued Speech and her conclusions do not support the proposal that Cued Speech aids spoken language development:

With the introduction of Cued Speech, the frequency with which the children used communicative gestures dropped dramatically without a corresponding increase in speech production. Consequently the overall frequency of their communication was depressed. (1983: 25)

The evidence for these systems is generally personal and tends to reinforce our view that it is attitude of the teacher or parent which determines adherence to a given system rather than any objective verification. There is very little objective reason for choosing among these approaches at the present time.

Fingerspelling has been available longer and there have been studies of it. Savage, Evans and Savage (1981) show that adding fingerspelling to lip-spoken messages increases comprehension significantly; unfortunately, this increase results in only 50 per cent understood at 14 years of age. Moores, Weiss and Goodwin (1973) had slightly better findings with increase in comprehension of up to 61 per cent. In general the gap between lip-reading with fingerspelling, and lip-reading alone is greatest for comprehension of larger units such as sentences, and least for single words. These findings are similar to those of Klopping (1971) and Montgomery and Lines (1976).

Bornstein (1979), however, points out the problems of using fingerspelling which is meant to follow spoken language exactly. A maximum of around five letters per second (very fast) gives only 60 words per minute transmission, when a normal spoken rate would be about 150 per minute (and that would include pauses). To accompany fingerspelling, speech would therefore need to be slowed down considerably, or parts of the fingerspelling would need to be omitted. This is what tends to happen (Reich and Bick, 1976). Bornstein (1979) also suggests that fingerspelling would not be useful for young children since it involves fine perceptions and handshapes which they themselves may not be able to form. However, we have already seen that deaf adults use fingerspelling with infants (Maestas y Moores, 1980), and it is an important part of the Russian fingerspelling approach described by Moores (1978).

The most significant finding is that when signing is added to fingerspelling, communication level increases further. Savage, Evans and Savage (1981) show that fingerspelling comprehension of 55 per cent increases to 76 per cent if signing is added. Moores, Weiss and Goodwin (1973) similarly found comprehension to increase from 61 per cent to 71 per cent with the addition of signing. Klopping (1971) produced the same pattern.

White and Stevenson (1975) offer further support for signing as part of Total Communication over oral methods, though their study was relatively small and involved an interpreter presenting information. Sorensen and Hansen (1976) show that deaf children using Danish Sign Language for communication in pairs produce 70 per cent levels of comprehension.

The major question, of course, concerns educational effects of signing systems and these sorts of effects are most difficult to trace. Savage, Evans and Savage (1981) could find no effects on reading performance of having introduced a one handed fingerspelling system, though, not surprisingly, part of the difficulty arose in the methodology of the comparisons made. Quigley (1969) did find the Rochester Method (fingerspelling with lip-reading) better than the oral method and also better than signing for producing success in English. Brasel and Quigley (1977) reversed this finding in favour of signing producing the best English development. The Manual English group (who had parents who were 'language competent' deaf persons) were better than the average manual group (whose deaf parents' written language was 'grossly deviant from standard English'). There is, however, some problem in this last comparison, since family income in the first group was $15,972, while in the latter it was only $9,300. That is, although a socioeconomic factor weighting was used in statistical tests, the 'class' difference between the two groups is sufficient to explain the difference in outcomes in performance.

Gustason (1983) reports progress in reading performance, as measured in a test of syntactic abilities after a period in a programme using Signing Exact English, as compared to the norms for deaf children. There was, however, no control of length of exposure or parent/teacher fluency and so the effects may be an underestimate of what can be achieved. Gustason indicates that this may relate to attitude and shows further evidence on positive attitudes towards both ASL and Manual English among teachers. The problem which arose among deaf teachers was whether it was possible for teachers to use ASL in teaching. It is this last uncertainty which influenced both Conrad (1979) and Meadow (1980) in suggesting that an MCE form of signing is most likely to satisfy deaf children's needs.

Which sign language?

We are left with a picture of general support for the use of signing. The evidence which exists is not comprehensive, nor does it adequately differentiate between different systems in terms of educational progress. The least favourable reports are on systems which only partially embrace signing or fingerspelling, and systems based on fingerspelling alone are not possible unless speech is slowed down considerably. This leaves signed English systems as the most likely candidates for success in education, but it is also appropriate to introduce the 'bilingual' possibility of sign language. The purpose in doing so is to examine how signs can, in psychological and linguistic terms, actually form part of the cognitive system.

Signing for cognition

A major problem arises in the adoption of a signing approach, and that is its effectiveness, not from the teacher or parent's point of view but from the child's point of view, as a device for carrying the cognitive processes. Educators might argue, as did Alexander Graham Bell, that although sign language could be a vehicle for thought it was not the 'right' vehicle, nor did it produce the 'right' thoughts'. Given our current state of knowledge of sign languages, it is obvious that these comments are no longer appropriate and that BSL can be treated as an effective cognitive component in development. We have, therefore, two possibilities to offer at this stage of our thinking: a simultaneous approach offering a mixture of BSL and English presented concurrently by teacher and pupil, or a bilingual approach where both BSL and English are accepted and used as separate languages.

The latter, which seemed so strange even a few years ago, is now available as a result of our understanding of sign languages and of the developments in foreign spoken language learning. Even ten years ago the idea that English-speaking children should be educated completely in a foreign language for every subject, including science, without actual specific prior tuition or without reinforcement at home, would have been considered strange to say the least. Yet throughout Canada there are total immersion schools where children forego their parents' mother tongue to be taught wholly in French. This has been the practice in many countries internationally, but our sudden realisation of its effectiveness in creating bilingualism has made it the major discovery in language acquisition.

The first point is that educating through a language which is not the parents' own, does not produce a deviant development. Secondly, there is nothing to suggest that using two languages detracts from either one of them or that it produces continued interference. Thirdly, the ease with which children can switch from one language code to another has astonished educators. We can therefore suggest that bilingualism is an acceptable concept within education.

There are differences for deaf children. To have BSL in school we would need to have native users as teachers, i.e. deaf people or teachers whose parents were deaf. The first is virtually impossible in the UK because of government legislation, and there are relatively few teachers with a native knowledge of BSL who have not been told in the past that it is an impoverished way of communicating. A further difference is that the other language, English, is not learned naturally and probably has to be 'taught' rather than simply acquired through access. For this the school has twin responsibilities for the presentation of both languages; it would need to be bilingual itself.

It is this approach which Sweden has begun to adopt. Ahlgren (1982) describes the beginnings of this bilingualism where a 'formal description' of written and spoken language is being found through sign language. That is, written and spoken language have to be taught through an awareness of Swedish Sign Language and the perspective this creates for the learning task. This adds greater pressure to the bilingual setting, but is the first real attempt to consider the implications of bilingualism for deaf children.

We then find ourselves with these two approaches: the simultaneous and the bilingual. Which offers the most effective cognitive code? The first should create English-like codes, while the latter a natural language code different from English. Virtually no work exists on this critical topic. All that is available is simple theorising.

Baddeley's (1979) work on speech coding as basic to reading development has direct application in studies of dyslexic children, where speech coding can be shown not to occur. Conrad (1979) shows deaf children do not develop speech coding easily and do not read well. The purpose of MCE or BSL in education has to be to create a code upon which the processes for reading can develop. As we have seen, however, sign codes, although they can be shown to exist and function as language codes (see chapter 10), do not behave in exactly the same way as speech codes. The notion that MCE somehow models the speech code by allowing the child to see English word order, which can then be internalised, is not theoretically viable. If one were to suggest that in order to learn French we should first practise and watch sentences such as 'He makes of the sun' in order to prepare the way for the sentence 'Il fait du soleil', it would be ridiculed by modern language theorists.

In addition, the stated view that in MCE or Total Communication children receive bimodal or multi-modal stimulation, has to be examined very carefully. From the hearing teacher's point of view what occurs is a mixture of modes: the oral/aural (through which verbal information passes for the teacher), the non-verbal (facial expression etc., through which emotion is conveyed), and the manual (through which sign language passes). From the profoundly deaf child's point of view the non-verbal is part of BSL, so the last two 'channels' are the same, and since the child does not hear effectively, the oral/aural 'channel' is also primarily visual. So, from the child's point of view what is experienced is visual and, thereby, *unimodal*. The child is not choosing from modes but accepting this visual mixture.

Quite apart from this we can show that MCE is not performed consistently or accurately enough to provide effective codes even in this unimodal situation. Teachers using simultaneous communication have been shown to present deficient models of English syntax in their signing (Marmor and Petitto, 1979; Kluwin, 1981). The teachers are not untypical in their problems with two language codes. Wickham (in press), in a study of teachers and children in the UK, shows the same problem of the 'drop-out' of information in teachers' use of simultaneous communication. Maxwell (1983), in a direct attempt to examine the effect of simultaneous communication using MCE on deaf children's writing, produces the results one might predict from the above and from our preceding discussion of BSL. The children do not make a direct transition from structured signs into English written grammar; in fact, they rely on structures in ASL they already know, and this forms the basis of their task solution of writing down English from sign users. The errors which occur could be explained in this way. It seems likely that access to signing in school prompts the development among children of a 'natural' sign language which forms the language code, and that this occurs independently of the visual mixture offered by teachers. This view receives support from the work of Livingston (1983).

None of this, of course, says that MCE *cannot* be effective. We are presenting a view only that educational effects cannot be interpreted without a full understanding of sign language. Parents, teachers and those professionals around deaf children need to understand the significance of sign language development and its emergence from what, in the past, they have often classified as playground gestures. If on close inspection, educators can begin to understand the great importance of these supposed 'gestures' in portraying the syntax and semantics of sign language communication, then a more effective view of the children's needs in language will emerge. The possibilities of Total Communication are colossal if the practitioner really understands what the children actually perceive when they see teachers using it. The full range of information available in Total Communication is only available to the hearing teacher; deaf children have to piece together what the visual mixture actually represents. Not surprisingly, when we asked deaf people to examine videotapes of teachers using simultaneous communication, their rating of effectiveness closely matched their rating of the teachers' use of facial expression. The information available is primarily on a *single dimension* and it is evaluated in sign language terms.

We therefore return to our original view. In choosing systems of educating deaf children with signs, it is attitude which has determined the choice. The evidence is not sufficient for any protagonists of particular approaches to feel satisfied. The theory of MCE is inadequately thought out and would not be supported in language learning fields. At the same time, we have still a great deal of development work to do to make the bilingualism which has become so accepted in other language fields directly applicable to deaf education.

At least the beginnings of the attitude development are there. Gustason's (1983) findings on positive views of ASL by teachers is augmented by Stewart's (1983) finding of attitudinal change towards ASL being part of deaf children's bilingualism. While this is seen within Total Communication programmes in education, there is no doubt that acceptance of BSL, ASL and so on offers the greatest hope for the development of effective education for deaf children. Only through awareness of, and agreement on, the value of each aspect of communication can we hope that educational methodology will progress. The key is the understanding of deaf children's processing of their own language, and it is this which requires our immediate and continued attention.

14. Developments for sign language

Our entry into the field of study which encompasses the language of deaf people came about in searching for an educational solution for deaf children. The swings of attitude so clear in the historical analysis of deafness had once again created a climate of opinion where the predominance of one methodology could be questioned. The simplicity of our initial beliefs about how signs might be used to alleviate the plight of deaf pupils was quickly overwhelmed when we realised the extensiveness of sign language itself. The motivation for our search was to see how signs might support the spoken message in schools, how deaf children could be given the benefit of the happy accident which allowed two modalities to be used simultaneously to present two languages. Right from the first evening of video recording, when we realised that BSL (or deaf people's signing) was not only a manual language, because of its animated involvement of the deaf person, it became clear that the key to understanding the learning task for deaf people lies in the examination of the language itself. BSL is fundamental to the cognitive and linguistic representation which deaf people use.

This awareness was a growing one, not a sudden flash of illumination, not a conversion at all but rather a slow, painful, at times embarrassing progress towards competence in communicating with deaf people. The more video recordings we collected, the more we talked to hearing professionals, the greater appeared the gulf between what hearing people told us about deaf signing and what deaf people were actually doing. The direct questions we needed to ask of deaf people could not be asked adequately, since we were only language learners. In the end, the understandings we have offered here came about indirectly from the actual learning process itself and contact with the deaf community as much as from the direct questioning we felt necessary at the initial stage. The fact that these understandings are incomplete or ineffectively explained arises because of our intermediate stage of knowledge.

To expect a full grammatical statement of BSL after a research history which can be traced only to the mid-70s, would have been optimistic in the extreme. All we have attempted is to provide the groundwork for expanding our comprehension of the structure of BSL and its relationship with other languages.

Perhaps that should be our first and major point: that BSL should be researched and evaluated as a language, and that this language, though apparently different in medium, shares similar grammatical processes with many spoken languages.

The sequence of studies we have carried out have derived from the tools available to us in the context of psychological and linguistic expertise. These tools have often proved to be too language-specific and have often highlighted our need to re-evaluate concepts of language and communication. The simple search for a solution to deaf children's educational needs had to be set in the broader context of the internal representation which BSL obviously offered to deaf people. It became clear that we needed more time and more study before we could support both Conrad's (1979) and Meadow's (1980) conclusions that deaf children need the early support of speech-based signing. As it turns out, our long way round through the deaf community, its history, sign language, memory and interpreting has given us an understanding of the concept of Total Communication and of how it might fit into the world of deaf people. The priorities for the deaf community will have to come from deaf people themselves but the effective use of Total Communication by deaf and hearing people offers a way towards a sharing of views. This is still an unbalanced sharing since spoken language drives the interaction between deaf and hearing; but it is a beginning.

It appears from Tervoort's (1983) work that Total Communication is an inevitable beginning for most countries. Simultaneous combination of signs and speech usually confirms the dominance of the spoken language and its predominance as the target for the deaf in hearing society. This may be vital for education but in adult life it can become a great barrier to deaf people's attempts to have access to information.

The language dominance case should not be overplayed, however. Deaf people are in a situation which many minority cultures share. Their chosen language is undervalued by the community at large and does not carry the technological information and knowledge that society's official language has come to have. Minority groups under pressure change, and do so in a few generations: they become bilingual and accept the culture of the larger society. But it is here that the difference re-emerges. Deaf people have changed in the past, and continue to change as other minority groups do; they adapt and accept the broader society. They establish their national identity with hearing people, and live and work with hearing people. Deaf people's integration and acceptance of hearing society is constantly underestimated in extent and in the effort involved. The one aspect of minority groups' change which is at present unavailable to deaf people is the adoption of spoken language: that is, unlike other groups, they do not acquire a substitute mother tongue for their own language. If one accepts this, even if only for the present and not as an inevitable fact for the future, then a responsibility lies with hearing society to meet not only the communication requirements of deaf people but also to understand and be able to work with this group in their language. This has been recognised periodically since the 17th century. Hearing society, however, has not taken up this responsibility nor seen that all society's members have a right of access to society's knowledge.

Statements on the supposed needs of deaf people can in turn be questioned by members of the deaf community themselves. Their efforts to meet society's linguistic and cultural priorities have been immense. The fact that these efforts go unrecognised has been a major element in the 'failure' labels attached to many deaf schoolchildren. The deaf community might well attach the label 'failure' to much of hearing society's attempts to provide services to meet their needs. The principal component, as always, is lack of language proficiency. Nevertheless, recognition of the primacy of both languages under consideration would lead to more adequate performance at every level.

In suggesting that minority groups change and are integrated into society, we do not see this as a subtle attack on the deaf community. BSL is not under threat in this sense. Its status, once ensured, not only in theory but in practice, offers opportunities for increasing involvement for deaf people and ready access to accumulated knowledge. Through the provision of proficient BSL interpreters in employment, further education and in law, an enormous range of choice is offered to deaf people. BSL would be enhanced by this recognition and use.

When we apply these views to early childhood we begin to have a clearer picture of deaf children's future. The educational problems we began with can be interpreted in a more realistic and systematic way. The 'fatal' choices offered to parents and teachers at every stage of the child's schooling can thus be examined in the light of development, not as part of a race against failure. Throughout, our view has been that it is teachers who are closest to children, and together with parents they are responsible for deciding how to use the tools at hand. We have argued strongly that BSL is one of those tools and a very powerful one for language growth. It is also a desirable one for the profoundly deaf young person and should be recognised for this positive value rather than for the negative one of its non-Englishness. BSL will always be present in deaf schools despite the continued denial, in some circles, of its existence.

The choice of method within deaf education is obviously a major one and the lack of positive research to inform the choice is an added problem. The purpose of our work has been to try to look at all aspects of sign language which might help those who make choices. It would be foolish to see the outcome as additional pressure, or as a thesis that only a single method should be available. Our view is that knowledge of BSL is a key to the curriculum and to the teacher's function but that unless it is supported by appropriate methods the teacher's role will be limited. Schools use methods to produce specific skills in children; these methods and the skills of teachers can be separated from the language of interaction.

Just as people can be educated in Welsh, or in immersion schools in Canada in French, so we can predict situations where BSL might be the sole medium. One could propose BSL as appropriate in a class learning politics, or economics, or geography and in the same school find a signed English form in the teaching of English or science, or foreign languages. One might quibble with these distinctions, but the proposal is simple: BSL is a language for conveying information and will be optimal where accurate and immediate knowledge is the goal; methods imposed on this medium will be tailored to specific educational goals and these will be a function of the priorities of teachers, parents and society. The realisation of this will be a major step for progress in the deaf community.

In the last analysis, the study of BSL offers real insights to educators, psychologists, sociologists and linguists. It is a newly discovered (or perhaps re-discovered) complex, natural language, linked to a cognitive representation which carries all the information of a society with limited sound. At every level, it allows the test of theories. Through research on this and other natural signed languages, greater understanding of the universal features of language, of how languages are created and learned and of how minority language groups relate to majority culture will be achieved. We are only beginning to work out these implications and our chapters of research can only be a base for others to examine in greater detail how our theories work. BSL research has only just begun and a great deal more will emerge in the coming years. The prospects of interchange at the research level between deaf and hearing people are very good. If acceptance can be achieved at this level, then there is great scope for development.

In the sections where we have dealt with the psychological aspects of sign language we can see a great deal of information of relevance to psychological theories themselves. Just as spoken language was seen as central to education, so cognitive theories have relied on speech coding as a key process. The fact that some deaf people appear to use a completely different form of coding just as effectively, makes it essential that some re-assessment of the models be made. In the same way, second language learning approaches and applications such as interpreting have all drawn on spoken languages from communities which have

261

separate cultural and geographical identities. The needs of people to learn the language which is not speech, and to use it to interpret for members of the deaf community, test these theories to their limits.

In each case, our conclusions have been tentative and we are content for the present to have made the links between these diverse disciplines and the study of sign language. There remain a great many questions to answer for psychological and linguistic theories. The way they are answered will benefit both hearing and deaf communities alike.

APPENDIX 1

Growing up in the deaf community

This section is based on a true account given to us by a deaf person. It is unique in many respects, since it reflects the feelings and goals of the community, but is written in English. The English used owes something to the writer's use of sign language, but is presented here in its original form, since it conveys much more of the force and conviction of being deaf and having to cope with the hearing community. It represents a view of education from the 1950s in one area of England and one hopes that many of the attitudes and practices have changed. However, it is important to understand the background of being deaf in the current deaf community and we do not feel that these experiences are untypical for this period of our recent history.

I was born deaf, my parents are deaf too, also other family are deaf too. My family accepted me as deaf because they knew that I shall be normal when I grow up, not the same as hearing parents who found out about their child's deafness. I learned in signings in normal ways, but I had some different signing from them. They accepted until I get older and realised the different signings then changed my signings same as them. My father and uncles taught me to fingerspell because they think it is important for me to learn; my grandparents used fingerspelling all the time. I was able to fingerspell when I was 4 years old and able to spell my name, animals' names etc., when I was 5 years old. I started school when I was $4\frac{1}{2}$ years old. I find different between at home and school because the teachers don't use sign, but my family use signs. Then I started find problem in school and realised my deafness because I never thought myself in deafness in my family. The teachers had lot of problem with me because I signed a lot in school which other children to tried to copy my signs. I had lot of punishments for using my signings and the teachers forced me to use oralist which wasn't interested to me. Then very often I was caught using my signings in classroom and at playground. The teachers reported me to headmistress many times, then one morning at assembly I was caught again, then ordered me to stand in front of the children, then the headmistress announced that I looked like a monkey from the zoo, waving my hands everywhere. She thinks she will put me into a cage in the zoo so the people will laugh at a stupid boy in the cage. They tried lot of different things and treat other children against me, but it haven't cured at all, but very often I hate in school. My parents visited school often, and received complaint about my signings, but they argued with them, but no one can help, and the headmistress understood my mother and still not accepted signing in school.

The teachers always says that I am lazy in speech, but I did try hard but unable to use properly. I goes to speech lesson more than some of the children. One or two of the teachers showed their sympathy and tried to help me, but I felt failed in school.

The teachers were puzzle that I always done homework very well, but one day the teacher gave me different homework and haven't explained how to do this homework, and said that I must find out how do it. It never worried me because if I have some words which I don't understand I always asked my parents, and my parents always explained me fully better than in school, because they signed in BSL and I understood BSL easy. Then the teacher visited my house to have a good talk with my parents about my homework, so after that the teacher realised how I understood better from my parents.

I was moved in top class when I was 11 years old and in some years I felt bored with my work in school, then the teacher find problem I have, and my parents asked about my problem then told the teacher – but it haven't improved. I loves Maths but not interested in English; Geography and History are my favourite. I can carry on working on my own quietly and always have top marks for them, but English are worst mark in school. I can't understand why my English are terrible because I always felt the sentence seem right but I used BSL and wrote in my own language. The teacher tried to improve my English, but I never improve. When I was in teens, the headmistress asked me to help her in her study and I realised there was a deaf mother waiting there (which I met her often in Deaf Club with my family). The headmistress asked me I can understand her signings, then they need me as interpret between signing and speech after solve their problem. The headmistress gave me a praise then I felt wonderful which I never felt it in my school life, and it gave me a wrong idea because when I saw the headmistress walking and I started to sign to other girl in front of the headmistress so I had told off for using signing. I don't understand why she praised me a couple of hours ago, then I realised that she used me, and my feeling was bitter toward the headmistress.

When I was about 15 years old, the headmistress was retired. I was over the moon because I thought the other will able to sign, but we had a headmaster and I felt settle down better because he don't give me a strict warnings about my signings, only always explained that I can use my signings outside schools and the speech are important for me to learn because I shall mix with hearing people when I leave school, but often he signed me when we were alone. My behaviour had started improve, but the other teachers picked on me.

I left school in 1959 and had a job in a factory. I was very nervous and realised so many people working there which my communicate was problem, then I had lot of help from my parents and they gave me lot of example how to cope the communication problem. Then I realised that it is my deafness's problem, then I made some friends there and I went out with them to dancing, but still go to deaf club.

I had some friends in deaf club and join the youth club and drama in deaf club; then other deaf adults encouraged me to join the sports. Tennis was my first interested in sports – then swimming. After some years, I joined all events in sports. The social club opened twice a week, and I never miss a night because I felt that I am belong to deaf community, I had lot of interested there then I was elected committee for the club and continue for many years, then I realised that I had lot of work, but they encouraged me to continue.

When I was 20 years old and got married, but not to deaf. But our communicate has not problem because she learned to sign and join the member of the deaf club and able to mix other deaf. I gave up as committee for the deaf centre because I was elected to a sports council which I find lot of work.

The deaf people meet other deaf people in these sports events and deaf people meet their friends at deaf club and are able to enjoy themselves without feeling suspect by hearing people. The reason the deaf people feel relax without having hearing around them because the deaf people works with hearing people every day and some hearing people are misunderstood the deafness. Some of them gave their sympathy toward the deaf people which the deaf people don't need the sympathy. Other hearing people don't agree that the deaf people to use signing. Few of them has change their mind toward the signing and realised how important to have their sign language which these use in communicate without problem. They are able to forget to use English which they find problem to communicate in English with hearing people. The strain of their feelings vanish in the deaf community they felt at home with their language and forget all the other English. The deaf adult feel settle down towards the deaf people – their problem and same interest hold them together. It may be said that communicative barriers are holding them away from hearing world but really, deaf people do mix with hearing. Most of the deaf have warm friends among the hearing – from familial contacts, acquaintances with their hearing friends. However very few of these deaf adults really find it possible and enjoyable to integrate with their hearing friends and devote all their social life to them. No normal self-respecting deaf adults likes to find his rapport with his hearing friends repeatedly cut off when they turn to their other hearing friends and resume their ordinary conversation, which the deaf persons usually finds to be very difficult and upsetting to follow. The deaf people always go to deaf clubs which place are for them. There are no problem in communicate in deaf community. They feel normal people which in hearing community they looks up to the hearing people and feel themselves lower but now the time has change slowly, so they are able to look at them at level.

The deaf people invite each other to the parties at their homes and always have big numbers to invite. The average deaf community is so closely-knit that is usually very difficult for deaf persons to draw line when they wish to plan for a private occasion. Whenever a deaf couple is given a house warming party at their new home, a crowd of 50 or more are not uncommon. A deaf twosome are very lucky if they can limit attendance of their wedding 150 to 200. The twosome arrange a big hall for these big numbers also have two separate parties on the same day, e.g. during the day the families and close friends attended then in the evening all their deaf friends attended. Very often they arrange a coach for the transport to the wedding or other parties outside their area.

Some deaf adults feel sorry for the deaf children because the hearing people force them to use the aid all the time. This is alright for some but not for profound deaf as there are some different stories about it, e.g. a deaf child in an ordinary classroom with his hearing the worst in the class. So in the class there are music. The teachers put the record player on and the other children who are able to understand the songs so this deaf child feel sad because the teacher always tell him to listen careful etc. so the deaf child went home and ask his family to help him to learn the song so lucky his sister knew that song and wrote down on the paper and after that he learned the words until the next music lesson. Lucky the teacher kept the same record and he is able to speak all the song then the teacher was pleased with his hearing as the teacher asked him if he understand the song, but it wasn't true because he felt odd out in the classroom. So one day the teacher asked all the children to say every sentence in their turns so this deaf child find more problem but he was able to manage it by watching others to say each sentence then when his turn came and able to know what to say. Then later the teacher put another record on but his family was unable to help him then the teacher realised what he had been doing and he was punished for cheating in music class. We feel that if they are unable to cope the hearing level so they should put out of hearing test and learn more other things which we often thinks it is waste of time for those who are profound deaf to learn to hear the words. But others who are able to hear are right to use these.

The deaf children has some problem about understanding about their deafness. Some children thought they will become hearing when they left school. This problem are because the deaf children haven't met the deaf adults. If they allow the deaf adults works in schools and they will able to explain them about outside the deaf school – deaf sports etc. The deaf adults understand different problem in hearing people at work etc. These will encourage the deaf school leavers to build their confidence to mix the hearing people as without meeting the deaf adults the school leavers will not prepare to build their confidence.

When my daughter was born, the doctor in the hospital said that her hearing are normal. I can't believe it because in my family always have a first child to be deaf. Few months later, I noticed it was rather strange because other babies acts different because when a little noise and they jumps easy, but not Emma. Also her eyes are very sharp; then I told my wife about it but she wasn't worry at all, so I checked with noises, but Emma didn't turn round straight away which the normal babies will do.

At last I decided to take her to family doctor and explained about it, the doctor was very understanding and arranged our visit to Hearing Clinic. The Hearing Clinic wasn't sure at first and asked why I believe her as a deaf, then I explained about my background of deafness. After some visited the Hearing Clinic they found out she is deaf, but I already know it before.

When Emma was about $2\frac{1}{2}$ years old, she went to Deaf School. She was very happy there and we felt that she went to right school. Years later she showed us that she done very well in school, but had some problem with her signing but she lip-reads very well and friendly child and ready to mix anyone. We were not worried at all because she done well.

When Emma reached nearly 7 years old, the headmaster arranged to see us one day. We met the headmaster in school and had a long talk about Emma good progress in school and her teacher was very pleased with her school-work, and she lip-read so well and understand while two teachers talked together and asked question which she should not. The teachers realised that she was too good to be kept in the Deaf School. The headmaster explained us about PHU which we never heard of it before. Then we visited the PHU which Emma will attend, but we were not sure if it is best for her to attend. Then meet the headmaster again and were told it is best for Emma to go to PHU which she will be better off there than a Deaf School, and it was agreed to give it a trial for six months to see if she can cope; if not she can go back to Deaf School. I was worried because I understand it may face some problem because I had my deafness' experiences, but I thought better for Emma to see how she can.

At first, Emma found lot of problem in her classroom and playground, because she still use her signings which the hearing children thinks they look funny and made lot of fun of her. Emma was very upset and told us. Then I said I preferred her to return to Deaf School, but my wife says don't give up too easy, then helped Emma to understand how to stand on her two feet.

A couple of months later we were invited to open evening in her school and met her teacher and saw her school work, but it shown same but no improve, but the teacher says that she is quite settle down but need give her more time. Also the teacher found that Emma had difficult with hearing children because the hearing children became afraid of her because of her heavy-handed which harmed them, but we explained that we believe that she should do something if other children makes fun of her. The teacher said that she must not use her signings in school if it didn't so it won't happen, but we don't agreed.

Before six months was due, the PHU was closed so the children transferred to other PHU, then Emma became settle down quick and cope it well. The teacher of PHU was very pleased with her, and her school work shown very good and we were very pleased with it; and her behaviour toward the hearing children are better. She become a bright child in her PHU and cope everything well there.

She reached 11 years old and moved to Lower School. Emma changed, and we tried to help her to find out why she changed and thought it may be difficult for her to change schools so she do all over again. About one year later, she became settle down in school but not her school work. We begin to noticed that her maths became weak and talked with her teacher but the teacher says that her other school work are very good, only maths and need help, but nothing to worry because the child must find one subject not good enough. But my wife believed maths are important so each evening we helped Emma to improve by lot of explaining how it works. Then realized Emma's frustration quickly in maths and hate in learning in maths which she used to love learning maths before. I can't understand why she changed. Then we allowed her every half hour each evenings for maths.

When the reports came, it showed that she cope everything very well except maths, so I thought well, if she done well others so I can't grumble about maths. So we had another idea; so we asked her to go to shops to pay something and gave her £1, then, when she came back and we asked her how much is this item cost, but she has no clue at all. We taught her how to, then we went to school for open evening and talked with her teachers but we can't do much because the teacher gave lot of praise for her hard work in school and mixing with other children very well, and using her voice well, etc. So we accepted her poor maths.

Every year we received her school reports and visited her school. The teacher always praised her hard work and all the reports shown very good.

When Emma moved to Middle School it happened the same, then moved to Upper School and we still received all her wonderful reports and praised from the teachers; then we became suspected there must be something wrong somewhere. We always asked Emma lot of questions what happened in school etc. The answers always the same, that Emma always find problem in classroom, which one or two deaf in classroom of more numbers of hearing children, and the teachers tried to talk to all at the same time. Also, the teacher sometimes forgot that a deaf child in this classroom which the teachers moved around at the same time talking, also sometime the teacher wrote things on the blackboard and talked at the same time, and it makes more difficult for deaf child to lip-read. Then she asked other girl who sat beside her to help her so we were not satisfied and went to school to talk about this problem, but the PHU teacher explained that if the other teacher noticed if there is difficult so report to PHU teacher to help the children to catch up. Then we realised that Emma's English are getting worse and complained about it, but the teacher said that Emma always does well in school. We can't do much about it so we leave it.

When Emma reached her final year and we read all her reports, these showed very well and should be enough to take her exams for CSE and 'O' levels, but realized that

Emma said she is not having any exams, so we thought it is unfair to have no exams after had wonderful reports. Then we went to see the Education Officer and talked about this problem and showed all the reports which were received, also why she can't have her exams. There must be mistake somewhere. So he explained to us about PHU etc; then my wife want Emma to taken out and put in Deaf School, but was told it is too late, also other children in Deaf School may notice strange to have her back in last year of school. Then we were furious about it and argued with them but we felt strongly that Emma should not be taken out from Deaf School in the first place. We were mad because we want to know the truth about her school work in her reports, but not trying to make it look good because Emma tried hard; but we felt if they put the truth in her reports so we can put into action a long time ago.

Then we went to PHU and saw the teacher and explained about this problem. The teacher said because Emma is deaf they gave her a good report because she always tried hard. The teacher explained the problem in the classroom, the problem is that you have thirty-plus children, perhaps one or two deaf children with them that the teacher has not got the time to make sure the deaf children understand what is going on. The result is seven or eight years' waste because the teacher hasn't got the time and knowledge to teach the deaf children.

Emma left school with beautiful reports but no knowledge. The PHU were more worried about Emma's mixing with hearing children and using her voice (speech). The education came bottom of the list.

When Emma left school, she found problem because of her poor education, her knowledge of English and maths were so low that she was lost when by herself; she has to fill up the application forms, i.e. *surname? present address?* This gives the wrong impression to any future employer and it gives the hearing people that the deaf children are backwards.

So you see now my children are integrated, but still education isn't right for deaf people because they didn't accept our language. The education looks into English etc., but they tries to avoid our language which they have no knowledge of this language. If the education accept our language and use it in the schools then their education will improve.

There are some different ways to provide by hearing people, but still not valuable for deaf children; but if the people in education meets the deaf and ask about their education so this may improve this problem. We, the deaf, want to help but never been asked.

With those deaf parents with deaf children, they understand the problem because of parent's experience in the past, so they are able to help their children, but we are worried about those other parents who have a little knowledge about deafness. They sometimes find difficult to understand why their child has difficulty in English.

It is obvious that there is a strong sense of solidarity among the members of the community and a reliance on the language as a key feature. This account of deafness, for those people who understand a little of sign language, will have conjured up a set of very rich images. The account informs us more deeply of the feelings of deaf people in the community than much of our questioning and research.

Teaching sign language

Out of the research described in this book, we have developed and tested a specific approach to BSL teaching. It is not unique, nor idiosyncratic, and has begun to be used elsewhere in the UK (*British Deaf News*, 1983). However, what is important is that it primarily derives from the strengths of deaf people as tutors of their own language and takes largely from the direct approach to language learning. Grammatical approaches will be possible in future as research on BSL progresses. For the moment we wish only to describe the factors behind this BSL teaching and, very briefly, what it actually involves. Neither the materials used nor the sequence is crucial, and the method can be adapted to suit the needs of other tutors of BSL.

Background

Much of what follows comes from the very simple contention that BSL is a language and many of the principles of teaching and learning apply to other subjects as well as languages. In developing the principles which psychology and education use we are doing nothing new, but in applying them to the learning of the language of deaf people we are exploring a completely different methodology for BSL instruction.

The famous comment that learning a language is learning a new culture is not an overstatement; to deal adequately with a second language we need to understand how the people use the language in their lives. Perhaps in order to understand the people we need to know their language, and it becomes something of a circular argument. But what is clear is that in order to use fluently and to understand a language one must first identify to some degree with the users of that language. It is not uncommon for native English people who become fluent in French to develop an attachment to France and its culture, and this is a common experience among anthropologists in their search for an understanding of culture. But is it acceptable to identify with deaf people in order to learn their language? Society has, in the past, usually said 'No'. Those who have identified with 'handicapped groups' have been regarded with some suspicion. Society's goal is to educate, to 'raise' the handicapped groups to the 'level of normal participation'; someone who goes 'down to their level' fails to meet society's requirements. This attitude is fundamentally wrong. The goal of integration is not to raise up but to accept, not to educate but to share knowledge with. There is no doubt that there is now a much greater international awareness of these ideas, and perhaps that explains our interest in sign language. Some degree of acceptance for deaf people is fundamental but how can one identify with deaf society?

Unlike foreign spoken language learning where the language can be experienced totally by going to that community and living there, the deaf community offers no such focus. There is no environment where one is surrounded by sign language and where all sound is excluded. There are no learning conditions which match the opportunities allowed to spoken language learners. It is therefore much easier for sign language to be treated differently, as a language of a non-cohesive community, as a language which can be accessed more conveniently through someone who shares one's own language in the first place. It is this which generally has happened. The vast majority of sign language learning has been through hearing tutors, and has taken place outside the community of deaf people. Although this is not considered ideal, it is also widespread in spoken language learning. The difference, however, is that the tutor has had a period of immersion in that community, usually of at least one year. Very few tutors of sign language have lived and worked as a deaf person for one year.

Hearing people with deaf parents do, however, meet this requirement and may often be highly skilled in BSL. These are people who do have the experience; they are bilingual from an early age. Again, however, there is an important difference. Spoken language bilinguals will often have a language environment where two languages are seen as almost equal, where the language is not experienced solely through parents (there are newspapers, books, and even films in that language) and where later in life one can choose to join either society without sanction. Only a small proportion of those with deaf parents can do this. Our access to sign language is not ideal: the community is not available for immersion, and bilinguals do not have the same background as spoken language bilinguals.

Learning rarely takes place in ideal settings, however, and the basis of education is to give knowledge without first-hand experience, to teach the principles which might be applied. Spoken language education recognises this, and has developed methods of teaching language (without the culture) and most important, has insisted that its educators be trained specifically in the methodology available. It is this last point which is the final difference for BSL tutors. There is little methodology for sign language teaching, and there is no training programme for the tutors of BSL which would allow them to adapt foreign spoken language methods to their particular needs, nor which would allow them to develop a picture of the learning needs of their students. To produce a BSL course we do need to use as much of the available information as possible.

Developing a course

The most apparently obvious field of knowledge is first language learning. Since every potential language teacher has experienced this there is a tremendous intuitive knowledge to draw on in language learning. There are disadvantages too. First languages are learned at the same time as concepts are learned. Although a child goes through stages of using one-word utterances and so on, this does not suggest that he is learning single words at a time. Not only can we show that children may use a one-word utterance to convey entirely separate meanings, but it is also clear that the language of those around the child does not proceed at the same pace as the child's. Rather it is much more complex. The most used published instructional material in BSL consists of a dictionary-like listing of pictures of single signs (RNID, 1981). This problem is highlighted in the foreword to the first linguistic examination of sign language teaching:

As sign language teachers, the two of us look back upon those days when we first began. We remember clearly that we were teaching simple sign equivalents for common English words. We remember noticing that our students could sign quite neatly but could hardly understand anything we signed . . . From time to time, we told ourselves '. . . there must be a better way than this. But this is all I know how to do and, besides, everyone else is doing the same.' (Carter and Leutz' foreword to Baker and Cokely, 1980).

We must, therefore, consider very carefully how we use first language knowledge in second language teaching. Probably the first thing to consider is the major point that children learn to speak their language in an environment which they cannot control. All the speech is much more complex than the level at which they function. They learn by abstracting parts of the message, by trying out certain parts of the heard speech and then by noting the sort of response they get. They very actively generate new sentences/ words in order to satisfy themselves that they are beginning to pick up the language. Very often what they say is wrong and does not fit the language's grammar. These errors are not things which are copied from adults around, but rather these constitute active processing by the child. Another major point is that the child does not have to learn all the vocabulary before he can make sentences and communicate: in fact quite the opposite. The last point about first language acquisition which we want to use here is that *language understanding is always in advance of production* – the child always understands more of what his parents say than he can reflect in his own speech.

Most of these points can also be applied to second language learning except that the second language learner already has a language to 'think in' and to relate all his new learning to. This has particularly important implications in the early stages of learning. Just as the child needs to express himself at a stage beyond the one he is at (in order to progress), the second language learner has to adopt a strategy for putting together the language utterances. He has to 'try out' sentences and words and pronunciations in a way which is novel for him and will often be slightly inaccurate. The most obvious strategy is to fall back on the knowledge already available on language, i.e. the learner's own first language. In school learning we get 'Franglais' as an intermediate for English learners of French, and we can see the same thing happening in every other second language situation. Although these are technically errors (as we have seen in chapter 9) they represent very positive steps on the way to learning a language and need not be 'punished' – they should rather be supported by providing a more useful, natural (and correct) version.

These are the major points for BSL learning too (if we adapt Krashen's 1981 model):
(a) Learning occurs when the material presented is at a stage beyond the current one of the learner but this will not always just consist of *one* stage beyond the learner's stage.
(b) The learner acquires the languages not by copying or acquiring vocabulary, but by 'trying out' the language in the context of communication.
(c) Language understanding will always precede language production in a natural context of communication.
(d) The carry-over of first language into second language production is a normal feature of the early stages of learning. The interlanguage, though it occurs, should never be allowed to become the target language.
To expand these points in the context of BSL learning has various implications:

271

Teaching sign language

(1) In the early stages of a course on BSL, it is often felt that a very simplistic setting must be used, for if the students 'do not understand' they will somehow 'not learn'. At times this has meant tutors have used 'readiness activities', i.e. taken out supposed components of the language and presented these for learning. Most commonly this is the use of mime activities. The nearest comparison in second language learning would be to teach 'sounds' or 'intonation rhythm' – which would clearly be unhelpful. The use of mime is only practical where it fits with a clear indication of how it is used in BSL.

The alternative approach is that conversations used as stimuli for language use need not be graded exactly for difficulty, but it ought to be clear that certain points are focussed on and it should be possible for the learner in the context of the class to achieve a personal level of understanding of the materials (some will understand all of a conversation, others only part).

(2) Each session of BSL teaching should allow the learner access not only to a deaf model but also to a BSL tutor on whom the student can try out his communication. Even though this initially may be faltering and full of errors, it is the base on which the language learning will be built.

(3) It is relatively easy to reach BSL vocabulary in a way which will allow a measure of fluent articulation but in the end this may be counterproductive if it has not been learned in the context of communication. Often students come to our courses with articulation skills in BSL which may be highly fluent but which have to be re-learned in the face of their inability to understand a deaf adult or child. The complex grammar of BSL means that production needs to be based on an awareness of, or an overt attempt to understand, the signed message. For BSL learners we can expect the tutors and conversations to be understood at a higher level than they themselves can produce.

(4) An important issue has arisen, firstly in the USA and now more clearly in the UK, concerning whether the sign language or some interlanguage form of Manual English (signed English) should be used with deaf people (see chapters 12 and 13). Many people have claimed that hearing people can only acquire the interlanguage anyway, because BSL is too difficult. If BSL is a language there is no reason to accept this as an inevitable fact, but there is a reason for examining our attitudes and our methodology. Hearing people will, like all second language learners, naturally use their own native language to probe the meaning and structure of the second language. Deaf people in the past have accepted this as understandable communication and it has been possible for hearing people to 'get by' with an incomplete grasp of BSL rather than be corrected as one would in a foreign country. The BSL learner has to be given the continued opportunity to see BSL as the target if acceptable communication is to be possible. (The educational/ therapeutic use of signing is not dismissed by these claims, rather it is emphasised that adequate use of any form of signing will come from thorough knowledge of the language. Particularly in deaf education, where deaf children may already use BSL, the teacher must understand the language even though the teacher's specific aim in any one lesson is to teach English and to use a form of signing which more closely reflects English grammar and word order.)

These fairly simple points about language learning have provided the framework for our course development. Some of the points may lead other tutors to different conclusions or different ideas, but they are set out here as explanations of the particular approach adopted. We believe these are consistent and hope that it will provide a base for progress towards the goal of giving more people access to BSL.

Practical aspects

There are a number of principles which have governed our use of videotaped materials. They may not be central to the learning of the language, but we have found them effective.

(1) Deaf tutors do as much sign teaching as is possible. This usually means they lead sessions involving the videotapes and only spoken language sessions on the theory of sign language are handled by hearing tutors. Both are given equal weighting in our courses but the two languages are kept separate throughout. When the aim is to improve signing skills, then BSL is used with deaf tutors. When the aim is to build up understanding of BSL and its principles and uses, then hearing tutors teach through speech.

(2) The use of deaf tutors has a number of advantages:

(i)   there is less likelihood of English being used in BSL sessions

(ii)   there is more awareness of the communication situation and the need to convey meaning in BSL

(iii)   there is less likelihood that English-based fingerspelling will be used since deaf tutors will usually prefer BSL signs

(iv)   there is less chance of becoming tied to the individual vocabulary items – questions such as 'what's the sign for X?' cannot be used unless the student can explain or communicate the meaning of X without English, i.e. in BSL

and, most important of all,

(v)   the students are provided with a valid, living model of the language they are attempting to learn

Deaf people may need initial induction to this type of teaching situation but we have found that we can introduce new deaf people to this approach within a few hours and we have experienced only a very, very small number of deaf people who could not act as tutors.

A typical session

Each session is introduced by the principal tutors as another BSL session where the students should not use voice and preferably where they should avoid 'silent English' where all the words are mouthed. (If there are deaf tutors in this situation there is no way of ensuring this happens, since they are deaf, but most students are happy to adhere to this ruling.) The aim of every session is to take a previously unseen piece of conversation and make it understood to the group of students. There is no ideal size of group though there is probably an ideal ratio of one deaf tutor to four students, so that if there are twenty people wishing to learn signing then ideally there should be five tutors. Increasing the ratio of student-to-tutor weakens the learning in the long run.

There are probably three stages to a single session:

(1) *Initial presentation of a conversation either 'live' or from videotape with repeated viewing as thought appropriate.* At the end of each showing, the group is asked in BSL what they have 'picked out'. It is important to emphasise before the course starts that this request does not necessarily mean 'What did you understand?' The tutor should reward every

273

Teaching sign language

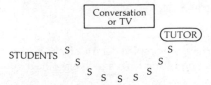

STUDENTS

Fig. A.1

correct suggestion from the group, but never say 'No, that's wrong'. Any inaccurate suggestion should have a response of 'Well, perhaps . . .', or 'does everyone agree?' from the tutor. The purpose is to encourage production by students, to build up confidence and to increase their awareness of their already developed visual skills. In this part of the session it is obviously very important that each student can see every other, so the lay-out should be that shown in fig. A.1. There is often a problem of students looking in the wrong direction! Some students feel that the tutor is the only person who can make a valid contribution and so spend all their time watching the tutor and not their fellow students. They need to be specifically directed to follow the conversation as they would a tennis match — from signer to signer.

The purpose of this part of the session is to give the tutor feedback on the amount of knowledge of the students, but it must never turn into a test session. There should *never* be a 'round the class' questioning where each student in turn has to produce something. This will not work, especially in the early stages: it builds up tension in the class and makes people more sensitive to their weaknesses. They need to be gently encouraged to contribute, but it should be remembered that any foreign language situation involves a 'silent period' where the learner has difficulty in producing even though he understands a little.

Given some basic knowledge (and the tutor can reinforce and elaborate parts of the conversation) the tutor should then split the group into subgroups.

(2) *Subgroups for dissecting the conversation.* The subgroups should be arranged as in fig. A.2. In this case each tutor will work through the conversation from memory explaining each part in BSL (using paraphrasing and mime or gesture). The aim is to give each student closer contact with the BSL used by having a model with whom to work each part out. As the course progresses this will be more of a question and answer session where the tutor asks the groups to produce the meaning for one another. In the very first session the tutor will provide more information than later in the course. It is important that the tutor should not become 'bogged down' by one student's lack of understanding. The varying rate of understanding and learning will have been explained prior to the course. Tolerance in novice students of all backgrounds is very high, and the fact that more is understood at the end of a session than at the beginning acts as a sufficient reinforcement.

If a session is going well individual students should be prepared to re-tell the conversation in whole or in part and should be encouraged to do so towards the end of *this part* of the lesson; if each lesson is an hour in length, this should be approximately forty minutes. Again, in these subgroups students may need to be reminded to watch each signer in turn and to accept that it is a group solution to the comprehension problem which is required: that is, students who are ahead of the others in the subgroup should be allowed and encouraged to explain their understanding to the others (but always in BSL, *not* by whispering!)

274

Fig. A.2

(3) *The final examination of the conversation and discussion or teaching of the particular points it illustrates.* For this the group should again be arranged as in the first part. The conversation should be shown again at least once to confirm the students' own understanding of the conversation. Particular questions can be asked of the whole group as seems appropriate by the tutors if a specific problem seems to have arisen. This part has to boost the student's view of himself as a learner because he will understand considerably more of the conversation than he did at the beginning even if it is only the gist of the conversation. It will be possible at a later date to come back to analyse it again.

The tutor should then pick out and work through *grammatical* points in relation to the conversational material and should use this as part of a constructive framework for BSL knowledge. It is again important to avoid being drawn into a discussion of individual signs, as tutors' variations in signs will be wrongly emphasised by students. The gist and meaning are the target.

Course topics

There are a great many possibilities for sign language teaching materials and the themes we have used were chosen for their simplicity rather than their grammatical convenience. The approach at this stage involves only conversation and is designed to create awareness of BSL as a living language. Topics we have used include:

(a) *Placement.* The particular conversation chosen has a great deal of placing of objects and shows how space is used to locate items precisely so that their relation to other items can be explained. Through this we can illustrate the use of pronouns in BSL.
(b) *Direction.* In this instance the conversation emphasises the spatial aspects of verbs. In this we see the first aspect of modulation whereby verbs change according to the items already located in space.
(c) *Emotion* The conversation used in this instance shows how change in meaning occurs as a result of non-manual features such as facial expression. It picks out what is often a severe problem for hearing students: to remember to use their faces and bodies accurately, while at the same time using the manual aspects.
(d) *Modulation.* At this stage the whole question of change in meaning is set out for students. The conversation involves inflection of the form described by Klima and Bellugi (1979) and, particularly, shows temporal modulation. Students are encouraged to generate their own rules for modulation and try them with deaf tutors.
(e) *Time.* This follows directly on the above, showing how time is expressed through space. Brennan (1983) has described 'time-lines' and these are provided to students as a framework for specifying the temporal nature of events.
(f) *Mime.* To introduce mime it is important to show clearly how mime differs from BSL. Generally we have used accurate mimed descriptions by deaf people followed by the same 'story' in BSL. Students are encouraged to pick out differences, but

then in future conversations to see how mime has a role and how it complements features such as direction and placement.

Obviously, these topics are only a simple guide to what has become practice in some courses. Grammar teaching and structural courses will follow as our research knowledge becomes more specific.

The problems which arise in this sort of course are typical of direct methods of language teaching. The fact that students do not take away a list of items which they have learned, or a book to study, may seem to them as if they are not able to specify exactly what they have learned. There is no easy answer except to show in conversation how much they are learning. In general, we have done this by including a 'test' at the beginning of the course where students write down a translation of a simple piece of BSL conversation. Mid-way through the course, the same conversation is shown and the students' scripts returned. In the vast majority of cases their improvement in understanding is strikingly displayed to them.

Language teaching develops all the time and clearly the above notes are designed to help suggest a structure for BSL teaching. They are not prescriptive and we would expect them to be modified to suit individual tutors and groups of students. The central principle remains of 'access to BSL through deaf tutors' and it is this more than anything which makes the teaching effective.

BSL notation

Introduction

In order to begin the study of any new field it has usually been a prerequisite that some way be found to write down the phenomena encountered. This has also been a pressing need in the study of sign language. When it was first attempted by Stokoe (1960) his primary concern was an analysis of manual elements in signs and the production of a dictionary. What he produced has become the model for most attempts at describing national sign languages. One-handed fingerspelling handshapes are used to describe the signs even when this is an alien system (for example, in the UK a two-handed system is used).

It has become obvious that non-manual activity plays a vital role in describing the language of deaf people – but that should be seen as complementary to the system we describe here rather than invalidating it. The study of the manual elements remains an intriguing and complex area. We have described in detail (in chapter 6) the components of signing in BSL and our task here is to elaborate that and indicate how it has been implemented on a microcomputer.

From the outset, a computer-based dictionary of signs was felt to be a necessary complement to the work being carried out at Bristol. Initially used as a kind of 'sign language typewriter', the system has been added to and improved so that it can be a valuable and time-saving resource. Signs can be entered, edited and added to the database; the database can be searched for signs corresponding to particular criteria, subsets of the data can be created, and any or all of the signs can be printed out on a graphics printer.

The collection, handling and analysis of linguistic data poses problems which lend themselves well to solution by established data-processing principles. The bulk and the complexity of data produced by even a simple exercise in sign analysis makes processing by hand a time-consuming task. However, it must be borne in mind that existing commercial implementations of data processing procedures (database management systems) can only work on raw data which is highly structured and predictable. Data of the type considered here is anything but that. Nevertheless, certain techniques can be used to good effect. Once a 'library' of procedures has been built up, it is generalisable to other studies and other linguistic systems. Other advantages of computer analysis include: speed and repeatability of analyses; ease of changing important parameters, and ease of constructing 'user-friendly' operating procedures for naive or casual users.

The two most important activities to be carried out (assuming the data have been collected) are, firstly, the matching of patterns supplied by the investigator to those possibly present in the data and secondly, the calculation of the frequency of occurrence of those patterns in any context determined by the investigator. By use of these techniques it is possible to answer such questions as 'what is the frequency of occurrence of a sign where the non-active hand is used as Tab? Print out the corresponding gloss'. For this, some form of pattern matching is required.

In its simplest form, a pattern matching procedure scans a file of signs looking for an occurrence of a given string of characters. Generally, the procedure returns a 'true' condition if a match is found, and a 'false' one if not. For example, a procedure to match 'quire' within a file of words will return a 'true' value upon encountering the word 'requirements'. Matching a simple text pattern is hardly adequate for our purposes, however. The data file is not homogenous; it contains records from different occasions, subjects, etc., and it is necessary to identify the correct segment. More importantly, we need to specify in much greater detail the context in which a pattern is to be matched. The construction used is known generally as the 'wild card' pattern. For example, the pattern:

c?t

will match 'cat', 'cot', and 'cut'. The pattern specified is now an ambiguous pattern which will match any three-letter word beginning with 'c' and ending with 't'. A more powerful construction is the asterisk or 'wild card' (*). Thus:

c*t

will match to 'cat', 'cart', 'connaught', etc. Finally, the concept of a 'character class' has been implemented. Thus the search mask:

c[a,o,u]t

will match 'cat', 'cot' and 'cut' but no other middle letter. These techniques can be combined, so:

c[a-z ~x]*t*

will search for any word beginning with c, followed by any combination of the letters a to z (but not x), followed by t, and finally any combination of the letters a to z.

The types of character developed for the notation system can be intermixed freely, so that patterns of arbitrary complexity can be searched for. Additionally, the patterns can be named and generated automatically. This is of particular utility when searching for minimal pairs.

The BSL database and the accompanying suite of programs have been designed to be compact and portable, and can be implemented on any 64k microcomputer running the CP/M operating system. The current implementation is on a BBC Model B microcomputer with the Torch second processor.

The activities may be grouped into data entry, selection and editing and indexing. Our major philosophy has been to keep the procedures as flexible as possible, in order to avoid forcing the data into an unsuitable form. For example, the decisions on indexing and grouping the data do not need to be taken until just before an indexing operation. The procedures will be discussed in their natural order. All the operations are carried out using the following equipment: a BBC Model B microcomputer with a Z80 second processor, 2 minifloppy disk drives, a Logitek 5000 graphics printer and (*via* a Local Area Network) a Qume Sprint 9 daisywheel printer.

The software is written in a combination of FORTRAN IV and machine code, with the exception of the input routines on the BBC Micro which are written in BBC Z80 BASIC to take advantage of the graphics handling capability of this particular machine. The machine code routines are used where speed is essential, such as in character string matching. The system is currently being rewritten in Pascal/MT +, and later routines are coded in this language.

Data entry

A program is run which prompts the operator for the desired operation, *via* a menu, and formats the screen appropriately. The operator can control a cursor which indicates where the next character will be displayed. The gloss is input using normal alphabetic characters, while the sign is coded in the form of a special character set. This is obtainable by striking a special key, whereupon the notation characters are displayed directly. When the operator has finished with a sign it is read from the screen and added to a file disk. After data entry, the file produced can be named and saved. Once the file has been saved, it can be edited if neccessary before further work is carried out on it.

When a file is reviewed, either on the video display or from a printout, errors may be noticed in the gloss or sign. Using a prompting technique, the offending record is read in from disk, modified and rewritten. When the contents of the file appear satisfactory, they are ready for analysis or printing on the graphics printer.

Further activities

This covers the basic activities of sorting, merging and indexing. It is evident that the data as it is arranged in a raw file is not suitable for rapid access. In the worst case, in the absence of any indexing scheme, accessing a record at the end of a file means a serial search through all the other items. The first operation, therefore, is to sort the file so that the gloss field is alphabetically arranged. This is so that, if access is required to a sign by gloss, the appropriate sign can be extracted using a 'binary chop' technique in which the database is halved at each search until the appropriate sign is found.

All the files input by the operator, after sorting, are ultimately added to one large file (the database proper) by a merge procedure. This reads both files (the master file and the update file) and writes the records in alphabetical order to a third file, the output file. The old files are then deleted.

Clearly there are many other applications for such a system and it is still in the development phase. To provide a more concrete illustration of the type of database handled by the system, the following sections show a subsample of the basic dictionary held by the microcomputer, on the basis of which an analysis in chapter 6 was presented.

BSL entries used

A

ALLOW

Index fingers extended, pointing towards each other and palms to body, move up and down in neutral space.

ANGRY   [ ]   E ┳ ‹

Clawed hand on centre of chest, palm towards body and fingers left. Fingertips touch chest then hand moves upwards rapidly.

ASHAMED   ꝫ   A ‹ ∧

Fist, palm facing cheek, fingers up; hand moves up and opens to spread hand.

AUNT   U   H ┳ ∧

Index and middle fingers extended and together, palm towards body, fingers up, tips of extended fingers touching chin. Hand moves down.

B

BAD   ØI ‹ ∧

Hand in neutral space, little finger extended from fist, palm left, fingers up. No movement.

BALLOON   ꝺ   O › ∧   O ‹ ∧

O hands at lips, palm facing each other, fingers up. Hands move away from mouth, opening to curved and spread fingers.

BEAR   [   ]   A ┳ ›   A ┳ ›

Hands in fists, crossed at upper chest, palms facing chest. Hands touch chest.

BECAUSE   B ›   B ⌄ ‹   ⁝⁝   B ›   B ┳ ‹

Left hand, fingers extended and together, thumb extended. Palm left, fingers away. Right hand, fingers extended and together, touches thumb side of hand, then turns so that the palm faces the body and touches the left thumb.

BEG　　　　ØB ∧ ⌐

Right hand, curved with thumb alongside fingers, palm up and fingers away, in neutral space. No movement.

BLUE　　　　B ∨　B ∨ ‹　(× ☺)

Left hand, fingers extended and together, palm down. Right hand, fingers together and angled, rubs back of left hand with fingertips in counter-clockwise circle.

BOOTS　　　⨆Ĥ ⊤ ∨ Ĥ ⊤ ∨

Both hands in 'capped' fists at left thigh. Hands move up, then to right thigh and repeat upwards movement.

BORN　　　[ ]　B › ∨　D ‹ ∨　(⊥ ∧)

Flat hands, fingers extended and together at hips, palms facing each other, fingers down. Hands move up and away from the body.

BOY　　　∪　G ⊤ ∧　(× ∨)

Index finger extended from fist, palm towards body, finger pointing up, grazes chin in a downward direction.

BROTHER　　Ø　A › ⊥　A ‹ ⊥　(× N) ~

Both hands in neutral space, fists with palms facing each other and fingers facing away from the body, graze each other as they move up and down alternately.

C

CAREFUL　　∪　X ⊤ ∧　X ⊤ ∧

In front of eyes, index fingers extended and crooked, palms to face, fingers up. Hands move down.

CLEVER $\quad$ ∩ A‹ ⊥

At forehead, fist with thumb extended, palm left, thumb towards forehead. Hand moves leftwards.

CLOTHES $\quad$ [ ] 5⊤› $\qquad$ 5⊤‹

Hands on chest, fingers extended and spread, palms towards body, fingers towards centre. Hands move downwards, grazing chest.

COME $\quad$ ØX⊤∧

Neutral space, index finger extended and crooked. Hand moves towards body.

COPY $\quad$ ØC∨⊥

Flattened C hand in neutral space, palm away from body, fingers up. Hand moves towards body and closes to flattened O.

COW $\quad$ ∩ Y⊥∧ $\qquad$ Y⊥∧

Hands on forehead, thumbs and little fingers extended from fists. No movement.

D

DEAF $\quad$ ⊃ H‹∧

Hand at ear, index and middle fingers extended and together, palm left, fingers up. Fingertips touch ear.

DENMARK $\quad$ ØV⊤‹

Neutral space, thumb, index and middle fingers extended and spread, palm towards body, fingers left. Hand moves up and down and rightwards.

DISAPPOINTED $\quad$ π Y⊤∧

Index and middle fingers extended and spread from fist, palm towards body, fingers up. Fingertips touch neck.

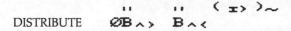

DISTRIBUTE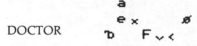

Neutral space. Hands with fingers together and curved, palms up, fingers facing. Hands move to and fro alternately while moving rightwards.

DOCTOR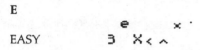

'F' hand, palm down and fingers left. Thumb and index finger touch left wrist.

E

EASY   ∃   Ӿ_{<} ∧

Index finger extended and crooked, palm left and fingers up, touches cheek repeatedly.

F

FED-UP

Flat hand, fingers extended and together, palm downwards and fingers left, moves upwards to touch under-chin with back of hand. Head moves up when contacted.

FEEL

Middle finger bent towards palm, other fingers extended and spread, palm towards body, fingers left. Middle finger grazes chest, moving upwards.

FEW

'O' hand in neutral space, palm upwards, fingers away from body. Fingertips make crumbling motion.

FOOD

'O' hand, palm towards body, fingertips towards mouth. Hand moves repeatedly towards mouth.

FUTURE [ ] B ⊥ ∧

Hand at right shoulder, fingers together and angled, palm away from body, fingers up. Hand moves away from body.

G

GIVE ØB ∧ <

Curved hand, fingers together, palm up and fingers left in neutral space. Hand moves away from the body.

GLASS ØC < ⊥

'C' Hand in neutral space, palm left, fingers away from the body. No movement.

GOOD ØA < ⊥

Fist with thumb extended, palm left, fingers away from the body in neutral space. No movement.

GUN ØH < ⊥

Index and middle fingers extended and together, thumb extended at right angles, palm left, fingers away from the body. No movement.

H

HEAVY Ø5 ∧ ⊥   5 ∧ ⊥

Neutral space, fingers spread and curved, palms up, fingers away from body. Hands move up and down slowly.

HERE ØG ∨ ⊥

Neutral space. Index finger extended and angled, palm down, fingers away from body. Hand moves down.

HIKE

Hands on upper part of chest, fists with thumbs extended, palms to centre, fingers away from body. Hands remain still while shoulders move alternatively.

HOLIDAY

Middle finger extended from fist, palm towards body, fingers up. Hand moves counter-clockwise in neutral space.

HOT

Fingers curved and spread, palm towards body, fingers left, in front of mouth. Hand moves right.

K

KEY

'Capped' fist, palm down, fingers away from body, in neutral space. Hand supinates and repeats.

KING

'Clawed' hand on top of head, palm down, fingers left. No movement.

L

LAZY

Right hand, fingers together and extended, palm up and fingers left, touches left elbow and repeats.

LITTLE
(height)

Fingers extended and together, palm down, fingers away from body. No movement.

285

LITTLE
(object)

Thumb and index finger extended and parallel, palm away from body, fingers up, in neutral space. No movement.

LIVE
(to live)

Middle finger bent towards palm, other fingers extended, palm to body, fingers left. Middle finger grazes right side of the chest, moving up and down.

LONDON

Extended index finger points to ear, palm towards body and fingers pointing left. Hand circles clockwise.

LUCKY

Index finger and thumb extended at right angles, palm towards body, fingers left. Hand moves left.

M

MEET

Index fingers extended, palms facing, fingers up, in neutral space. Hands approach.

MILK

'C' hands, palms facing, fingers away from body, in neutral space. Hands move up and down, opening and closing alternately and repeat.

MY

Fist, palm facing body, fingers facing left, touches the chest.

N

NAME   ∩   H⊤<

Index and middle fingers extended and together, fingertips touching forehead, palm towards body and fingers left. Hand moves down and away, pronating.

NOISE   ɔ   G⊤<

Extended index finger points to ear, palm towards body, fingers pointing left. Hand moves clock-wise.

NOSEY   U G<∧

Extended index finger points to nose, palm facing left, fingers up. Index finger touches nose and repeats.

NOTHING   ØF⊥∧ F⊥∧

'F' hands, palms away from body, fingers up in neutral space. Hands move side to side, separating and approaching repeatedly.

NOW   Ø5∧⊥ 5∧⊥

Fingers extended and spread, palms up and fingers away from body in neutral space. Hands move down.

O

OFFICER   ～ V⊤<

Tips of spread and bent index and middle fingers, palm towards body and fingers left, tap shoulder.

OLD   Ꙍ V⊤∧

Index and middle fingers, extended and spread, in front of eyes, palm towards body and fingers up. Hand moves down and closes to bent fingers.

R

READ

Left hand flat, thumb extended, palm up. Right index and middle fingers extended and spread, palm down, fingers away, move side to side above left palm.

RUBBISH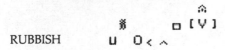

'O' hand at nose, palm left, fingers up, opens to 'angled thumb V' with thumb, index and middle fingers extended and angled.

S

SAD ⟶ O B‹ ⌃

Flat hand, palm facing left, fingers pointing up, thumb side of hand next to face, moves down.

SALT Ø0⌄⌐

Palm down, fingertips and thumb touching in neutral space. Fingertips make crumbling motion.

SCOTLAND [ ]› A⊤‹

Right hand in fist at right side of body. Hand remains still while elbow moves to touch side of body and repeats.

SEE ᴜ› G‹ ⌃

Index finger extended, fingertip at right eye, palm left, fingers up. Hand moves away from body.

SERGEANT ～ W⊤‹

Index, middle and ring fingers extended and spread, palm towards body, fingers left. Fingers touch upper arm.

288

SHOE   ⊔   ⟨₍☉⟩
         C∧B⌄<

Left hand curved in 'C', palm up, right hand flat, palm down, fingers left. Right hand moves left and enters space in palm of left hand.

SIGN   Ø5>⊥   5<⊥   ⓡ⌐

Hands in neutral space, fingers extended and spread. Hands move in clockwise circles, alternately.

SLEEP   ⊔   ø
         ϶ B<∧

Flat hand at cheek, palm left, fingers up. Hand remains still while head bends towards hand.

SLOW   ⌐   ⊔   ⟨ ×⊤⟩ₗₗ
         B⌄ B⌄<

Left hand flat, palm down, right hand flat, palm down, fingers left. Palm of right hand strokes back of left hand, slowly.

STAND   ⊔ ▓ ×   ø
         B∧   V⊤⌄

Fingertips of extended index and middle fingers, palm towards body, fingers down, touch palm of flat left hand.

SUCCESS ∂ ▪   ∂ ▪   × ⊚÷
         Ø A⊤>   A⊤<

Extended thumbs touch, then twist and separate in neutral space.

T

TABLE   L   L   ÷   ⊔   ⊔   ⌄
         Ø B⌄⊥ B⌄⊥ ⁞⁞ Ø B>⊥ B<⊥

Flat hand, palms down, fingers away from body in neutral space, separate sideways, then hands turn so that palms face each other and hands move down.

TALK   L   ‒   × ˙
         G⊤ G<⊥

Both hands with index fingers extended, little finger edge of right hand above thumb edge of left hand. Right hand taps left hand and repeats.

THICK   ⌒   ∅
       ∅C ⊥ ∧

'Angled C' hand in neutral space, palm away from body, fingers up. No movement.

TROUBLE   ⊓   ⁑ ⌒   × ·
       B ⌣   B ⌣ <

Angled hand, fingers together and facing left, palm down, taps the back of flat, palm-down left hand and repeats.

TUBE   L   L   ÷
      ∅ C ⊥ ∧   C ⊥ ∧

'C' hands, side-by-side, palms away from body, fingers up, move apart.

W   ' '
          > ⊓   (⌣#) [W]
WALES   [ ] W ⊥ ∧

Hand in front of right shoulder, index, middle and ring fingers extended. Hand moves down and fingers bend.

WHEN   ⁑   ℺
       3̌   5 < ∧

Fingers extended and spread, pointing up, fingertips at cheek, palm left. Fingers flicker.

WHICH   z
      ∅Y ⌣ ⊥

Palm down, thumb and little finger extended, fingers away from the body, in neutral space. Hand moves side-to-side.

WISH   ∅
      ∅R ⊥ ∧   R ⊥ ∧

Index and middle fingers of both hands crossed, palms away from body, fingers up, in neutral space. No movement.

WOMAN   e   (× <) ·
       3̌ G ⊥ ∧

Extended index finger, palm away from body, fingers up, strokes cheek and repeats.

WONDERFUL   <   > ⊓   ⊓   (⊥÷□) [5]
       [ ] O ⊥ ∧   O ⊥ ∧

'O' hands in front of shoulders, palms away from body, fingers up. Hands move away from body, separating and opening to extended and spread fingers.

References

Ackers, B. St J. 1880. Advantages to the deaf of the German system in the after life. Paper from the international congress in Milan. Pamphlet. London: RNID Library.

1890. Postscript to Education Act – Education Act for the deaf and blind. London: HMSO.

Addison, W.H. 1899. *Glasgow Society for the Education of the Deaf and Dumb*. Glasgow: Blackie.

Ahlgren, I. 1982. Sign language and the learning of Swedish by deaf children. *Newsletter School Research, 2*. Stockholm: National Board of Education, Division of Research and Development.

Allsop, L. and Kyle, J.G. 1982. Deaf people and the community. *British Deaf News, 9*: 331–4.

Anderson, L.B. 1978. A comparative typological analysis of sign language vocabulary. Unpublished paper. Gallaudet College Library.

1979. Sign language typology. Paper presented at the first international sign language symposium, Stockholm.

Anderson, R.W. 1978. Interpreter roles and interpretation situations: cross cutting typologies. In Gerver and Sinaiko (1978).

Anthony, D. 1971. *Seeing Essential English*. Anaheim, California: Educational Services Division, Anaheim Union High School District.

Arnold, P. 1982. Oralism and the deaf child's brain: a reply to Dr Conrad. *International Journal of Pediatric Otorhinolaryngology, 4*: 275–86.

Arnold, T. 1883. Lip reading. In *Conference report* (1882).

Australian council for educational research 1962. *ACER speed and accuracy test*. Victoria, Australia: ACER.

Babbini, B.E. and Quigley, S.P. 1970. *A study of the growth patterns in language, communication and educational achievements in six residential schools for deaf students*. Urbana: Ill. Institute for Research on Exceptional Children, Illinois University.

Baddeley, A.D. 1979. Working memory and reading. In P.A. Kolers, M. Wrolstad and H. Bouma (eds). *The processing of visible language*. New York: Plenum Press.

Baddeley, A.D. and Hitch, G. 1974. Working memory. In G.A. Bower (ed.) *The psychology of learning and motivation, vol. 8*. New York: Academic Press.

Baker, C. 1980. On the terms verbal and non-verbal. In I. Ahlgren and B. Bergman (eds). *Papers from the first international symposium on Sign Language research*. Stockholm: Swedish National Association for the Deaf.

Baker, C. and Cokely, D. 1980. *American Sign Language: A teacher's resource text on grammar and culture*. Silver Springs Md.: T.J. Publishers.

References

Baker, C. and Padden, C. 1978. Focusing on the nonmanual components of American Sign Language. In P. Siple (ed.). *Understanding language through sign language research*. New York: Academic Press.

Baker-Shenk, C.L. 1983a. Non-manual features of ASL. Paper presented at the third international symposium on sign language research, Rome.

1983b. A Microanalysis of the non-manual components of questions in ASL. Unpublished Ph.D thesis. Berkeley: University of California.

Bartlett, F.C. 1932. *Remembering: a study in experimental and social psychology*. Cambridge: Cambridge University Press.

Bates, E., Camaioni, L. and Volterra, V. 1975. The acquisition of performatives prior to speech. *Merrill Palmer Quarterly, 21*: 205–26.

Batkin, S., Groth, H., Watson, J.R. and Ansberry, M. 1970. The effects of auditory deprivation in the development of auditory sensitivity in albino rats, *EEG Clinical Neurophysiology, 28*: 351–9.

Batson, T.W. and Bergman, E. 1976. *The deaf experience*. South Waterford: Merriam Eddy.

Battison, R. 1978. *Lexical borrowing in American Sign Language*. Silver Springs Md.: Linstock Press.

Battison, R. and Jordan, I.K. 1976. Cross-cultural communication with foreign signers: fact and fancy. *Sign Language Studies, 10*: 53–68.

BDA (British Deaf Association) working party. 1974. *Review of developments in welfare services for deaf people*. Carlisle: BDA.

Bell, A.G. 1887. Newspaper report in *Union and Advertiser*, 18 March, Rochester, New York. Quoted in Z.F. Westervelt (1893) *Histories of American schools for the deaf, vol. II*. Washington DC: Volta Bureau.

Bell, E.G. 1955. Inner-directed and other-directed attitudes. Unpublished Ph.D dissertation, Yale University.

Bellugi, U. 1980. Clues from the similarities between signed and spoken language. In U. Bellugi and M. Studdert-Kennedy (eds) *Signed and spoken language: biological constraints on linguistic form*. Berlin: Verlag Chemie.

Bellugi, U, and Klima, E.S. 1972. The roots of language in the sign talk of the deaf. *Psychology Today, 6*: 61–76.

Bellugi, U., Klima, E.S. and Siple, P. 1975. Remembering in signs. *Cognition, 3*: 93–125.

Bench, J. 1979. Auditory deprivation – an intrinsic or an extrinsic problem? *British Journal of Audiology, 13*: 51–2.

Berger, P.L. and Luckman, T. 1966. *The social construction of reality*. London: Allen Lane.

Bergman, B. 1979. *Signed Swedish*. Rosenludstrychunit: National Swedish Board of Education.

1983. Verbs and adjectives: morphological processes in Swedish Sign Language. In Kyle and Woll, (1983).

Bonvillian, J.D., Orlansky, M.D. and Novak, L.L. 1983. Early sign language acquisition and its relation to cognitive and motor development. In Kyle and Woll (1983).

Booth, E. 1878. Thinking in words and gestures. *American Annals of the Deaf, 23*: 223–5.

Borges, S. and Berry, M. 1976. Preferential orientation of stellate cell dendrites in the visual cortex of the dark reared cat. *Brain Research, 112*: 141–7.

Bornstein, H. 1979. Systems of sign. In Bradford and Hardy (1979).

Bornstein, H., Hamilton, L., Saulnier, K.L. and Roy, H. 1975. *The Signed English dictionary for pre-school and elementary level*. Washington DC: Gallaudet College Press.

Boyes, P. 1973. Visual processing and the structure of sign language. Unpublished paper, obtainable from Centre for Sign Language Research, University of Zurich.

Bradford, L.J. and Hardy, W.G. (eds) 1979. *Hearing and hearing impairment*. New York: Grune and Stratton.

Bransford, J.D. and McCarrell, N.S. 1975. A sketch of a cognitive approach to comprehension. In W.B. Weimar and D.S. Palermo *Cognition and the symbolic processes*. Hillsdale, N.J.: Lawrence Erlbaum.

Brasel, B.B. 1976. The effects of fatigue on the competence of interpreters for the deaf. In H.J. Murphy *Selected readings in the integration of deaf students at CSUN*. Centre on Deafness series (No. 1). Northridge: California State University.

Brasel, B., Montanelli, D.S. and Quigley, S.P. 1974. The component skills of interpreting as viewed by interpreters. *Journal of the Rehabilitation of the Deaf*, 7, 3: 27–8.

Brasel, K. and Quigley, S.P. 1977. The influence of certain language and communication environments on the development of language in deaf individuals. *Journal of Speech and Hearing Research*, 20: 95–107.

Braybrook, D. and Powell, C. 1980. 1980 – one hundred years after Milan. In *Papers presented at the triennial congress of BDA, Scarborough 1980*. Carlisle: British Deaf Association.

Bronnan, M. 1976. Can deaf children acquire language? *Supplement to the British Deaf News*, February.

1983. Marking time in British Sign Language. In Kyle and Woll (1983).

Brennan, M. and Hayhurst, A.B. 1981. The renaissance of BSL. In C. Baker and R. Battison *Sign language and the deaf community*. Silver Springs, Md.: National Association of the Deaf.

Brennan, M., Colville, M.D. and Lawson, L.K. 1980. *Words in hand: a structural analysis of the signs of British Sign Language*. Edinburgh: Moray House Publications.

Brill, R.G. 1969. The superior IQ's of deaf children of deaf parents. *The California Palms*, 15. 1 4.

British Deaf News. 1983. New way of BSL teaching given a test. *British Deaf News*, 14, 8: 4.

Broca, P. 1861. Perte de la parole, ramolissement chronique et destruction partielle du lobe anterieur gauche de cerveau. *Bulletin of the Society of Anthropology of Paris*, 2: 235–8.

Brown, H.D. 1980. *Principles of language learning and teaching*. Englewood Cliffs NJ.: Prentice Hall

Bulwer, J.B. 1644. *Chirologia: or the natural language of the hand*. London: R. Whitaker.

1648. *Philocophus: or the deafe and dumbe man's friend*. London: Humphrey Moseley.

Bunting, C. 1981. *Public attitudes to deafness*, OPCS Social Survey Division. London: HMSO.

Burstall, C. 1975. *Primary French in the balance*. Slough: NFER.

Carter, M. 1980a. *Some issues involved in attempting a linguistic analysis of BSL*. Bristol University, School of Education.

1980b. *Noun phrase modifications in BSL*. Bristol University, School of Education.

Caselli, M.C. 1983. Communication to language: deaf children's and hearing children's development compared. *Sign Language Studies*, 39: 113–44.

Cattell, R.B. 1973. *Culture fair intelligence tests*. Illinois: Institute for Personal Assessment and Testing.

Cave, C. and Maddison, P. 1978. *A survey of recent research in special education*. Slough: NFER.

References

Cazden, C.B. 1972. *Child language in education.* New York: Holt, Rinehart and Winston.
CEC. 1979. *Childhood deafness in the European Community.* Brussels: CEC.
Chafe, W.L. 1977. The recall and verbalization of past experience. In R.W. Cole *Current issues in linguistic theory.* Indiana University Press.
Clarke, B.R. and Ling, D. 1976. The effects of using Cued Speech. *Volta Review, 78:* 23–34.
Cohen, G. 1977. *Psychology of cognition.* London: Academic Press.
Cokely, D.R. and Gawlik, R. 1974. Childrenese as pidgin. *Sign Language Studies, 5:* 72–81.
Collins-Ahlgren, M. 1975. Language development of two deaf children. *American Annals of the Deaf, 120:* 524–39.
Condillac, 1746. *An essay on the origin of human knowledge.* Reprinted 1971. Gainsville, Fla.: Scholars Facsimiles and Reprints.
Conference Report 1882. Conference of headmasters of institutions and of other workers for the education of the deaf and dumb, London 1881. London: Allen.
Conrad, R. 1971. The chronology of the development of covert speech in children, *Developmental Psychology, 5:* 398–405.
  1977. Lipreading by deaf and hearing children. *British Journal of Educational Psychology, 47:* 60–5.
  1979. *The deaf school child: language and cognitive function.* London: Harper and Row.
  1980. Let the children choose. *International Journal of Pediatric Otorhinolaryngology, 1:* 317–29.
  1981. Sign language in education: some consequent problems. In B. Woll, J.G. Kyle and M. Deuchar (1981).
Conrad, R. and Rush, M.L. 1965. On the nature of short-term memory encoding by the deaf. *Journal of Speech and Hearing Disorders, 30:* 336–43.
Conrad, R. and Weiskrantz, B.C. 1981. On the cognitive ability of deaf children of deaf parents. *American Annals of the Deaf, 126:* 995–1003.
Cornett, O. 1975. What is Cued Speech? *Gallaudet Today, 5:* 28–30.
Cox, D., Davis, C., Kennedy, M., Thomas, A. and Wordley, T. 1979. The introduction of Total Communication into a primary school for the deaf. *Teacher of the Deaf, 3:* 92–5.
Crutchfield, R.S., Woodworth, D.G. and Albrecht, R.E. 1958. Perceptual performance and the effective person. Lackland Airforce Base, Texas: Wright Air Development Centre, TN-58-60. Document No. AD151039.
Crystal, D. and Craig, E. 1978. Contrived sign language. In I.M. Schlesinger and L. Namir (eds). *Sign language of the deaf: psychological, linguistic and social perspectives.* London: Academic Press.
Curran, H.V. 1980. Cross cultural perspectives. In G. Claxton (ed.) *Cognitive psychology: new dimensions.* London: Routledge and Kegan Paul.
Curtiss, S. 1977. *Genie: a psycholinguistic study of a modern day 'wild child'.* New York: Academic Press.
Dalgarno, G. 1661. *Ars signorum, vulgo character universalis philosophica et lingua.* London: J. Hayes.
Dawson, E. 1981. Psycholinguistic processes in prelingually deaf adolescents. In B. Woll, J.G. Kyle and M. Deuchar (1981).
De Ladebat, L. 1815. *A collection of the most remarkable definitions and answers of Massieu and Clerc.* London: Cox and Bayliss.

De Lemos, M.M. 1974. The development of spatial concepts in Zulu children. In J.W. Berry and P.R. Dasen (eds) *Culture and cognition: readings in cross-cultural psychology.* London: Methuen.

De Matteo, A. 1977. Visual imagery and visual analogues in ASL. In Friedman (1977).

Denmark, J.C. 1981. A psychiatric view of the importance and early use of sign language. In B. Woll, J.G. Kyle and M. Deuchar (1981).

Denmark, J.C., Rodda, M., Abel, R.A., Skelton, U., Eldridge, R.W., Warren, F. and Gordon, A. 1979. *A word in deaf ears. A study of communication and behaviour in a sample of 75 deaf adolescents.* London: RNID.

Denton, D.M. 1970. Remarks in support of a system of Total Communication for deaf children. *Communication symposium.* Frederick, Md.: Maryland School for the Deaf.

DES. 1981. *Education Act.* London: HMSO.

Deuchar, M. 1983. Is British Sign Language an SVO language? In Kyle and Woll (1983).
    1984. Sign language and universal grammar. Paper presented at the Linguistics Association of Great Britain Silver Jubilee Meeting, Hull.

Dickens, C. 1865. Dr Marigold's prescription. In vol.7 (Christmas stories) of *Works of Charles Dickens.* London: Merrill and Baker.

Diderot 1751. Letter on the deaf and dumb. In R.L. Caldwell 1971 Structure de la lettre sur les sourds et muets. *Studies on Voltaire and the 18th Century,* 84: 109–22.

Digby, K. 1644. *Treatise on the nature of bodies.* Paris.

Digiti lingua. 1698. Pamphlet available from the RNID library, London.

Domingue, R.L. and Ingram, B.L. 1978. Sign language interpretation: the state of the art. In Gerver and Sinaiko (1978).

Dornic, S., Hagdahl, R. and Hanson, G. 1973. *Visual search and short term memory in the deaf.* Reports from the Institute of Applied Psychology, No. 38. University of Stockholm.

Dulay, H. and Burt, M. 1977. Remarks on creativity in language acquisition. In M. Burt, H. Dulay and M. Finnochiaro *Viewpoints on English as a second language.* New York: Regents Press.

Edwards, V. and Ladd, B. 1983. British Sign Language and West Indian Creole. In Kyle and Woll (1983).

Eicholz, A. 1932. *A study of the deaf in England and Wales.* London: HMSO.

Elizabeth, C. (c. 1830) *Memoir of John Britt, the happy mute.* Pamphlet. London: RNID Library.

Ellenberger, R. and Steyaert, M. 1978. A child's representation of action in ASL. In P. Siple (ed.) *Understanding language.*

Elliott, R. 1882. The Milan Congress and the future of the education of the deaf and dumb. In *Conference Report* (1882).
    1907. The present state of deaf-mute education in England. In *Proceedings of the international conference on the education of the deaf, Edinburgh 1907.* Edinburgh: National Association of Teachers of the Deaf.

Erting, C. 1982. *Deafness, communication and social identity: an anthropological analysis of interaction among parents, teachers and deaf children in a pre school.* Ph.D thesis. Ann Arbor Mich.: University Microfilms International.

Esam, S. 1981. A proposed new notation. *Edinburgh Working Papers in Linguistics.* University of Edinburgh.

Evans, J. 1981. Hemispheric differences for temporally salient signs. *Research on Deafness*

References

and BSL. vol.III. Bristol: School of Education, University of Bristol.

Ewing, A. and Ewing, E.C. 1964. *Teaching deaf children to talk.* Manchester: Manchester University Press.

Ewing, I.R. and Ewing, A. 1938. *The handicap of deafness.* London: Longmans.

Ewoldt, C. 1980. Psycholinguistic processes in reading in deaf children. Paper presented at the International congress on the education of the deaf, Hamburg.

Fathman, A. 1975. The relationship between age and second language productive ability. *Language Learning*, 25: 245–66.

Fauconnier, G. 1981. Pragmatic functions and mental space *Cognition, 10.* 85 0.

Feldman, I I., Goldin-Meadow, S. and Gleitman, L. 1978. Beyond Herodotus: the creation of language by linguistically deprived children. In A. Lock (ed.) *Action, gesture and symbol: the emergence of language.* London: Academic Press.

Fenn, G. and Rowe, J.A. 1975. An experiment in manual communication. *British Journal of Disorders of Communication*, 10: 3–16.

Ferreira Brita, L. 1983. Time reference in two Brazilian sign languages. Paper presented at the third international symposium on sign language research, Rome.

Fischer, S.D. 1973a. The child's acquisition of verb inflection in ASL. Paper presented to the annual meeting of the Linguistic Society of America, San Diego.

1973b. Two processes of reduplication in American Sign Language. *Foundations of Language*, 9: 469–80.

1974. Sign language and linguistic universals. *Actes du colloque Franco-Allemand de grammaire transformationelle.* pp. 187–204.

1975. Influences on word order change in American Sign Language. In C.N. Li, (ed.) *Word order and word order change.* Austin: University of Texas Press.

1978. Sign language and creoles. In P. Siple (ed.) *Understanding language.*

Flint, R.W. 1979. History of education for the hearing impaired. In Bradford and Hardy (1979).

Forchhammer, G. 1903. *On nodvendigheden af sikra meddelelsmidler dovstumme under ervisingen,* Copenhagen: J. Frimodts, Fortag. Translated version in RNID Library, London.

Freeman, R.D., Carbin, C.F. and Boese, R.J. 1981. *Can't your child hear?* London: Croom Helm.

Friedman, L.A. 1976. The manifestation of subject, object and topic in American Sign Language, in C.N. Li (ed.) *Subject and topic.* New York: Academic Press.

(ed.) 1977. *On the other hand.* New York: Academic Press.

Furth, J.G. 1966. *Thinking without language.* London: Collier, Macmillan.

Gardner, R.C. and Lambert, W.E. 1972. *Attitudes and motivation in second language learning.* Rowley, Mass: Newbury House.

Garretson, M.D. 1976. Total Communication. In R. Frisina (ed.) *A bicentennial monograph on hearing-impairment trends in the USA.* Washington DC: Alex. G. Bell Associates.

Gerver, D. 1972. *Simultaneous and consecutive interpretation and human information processing.* London: SSRC report, HR 566/1.

1976. Empirical studies of simultaneous interpretation: a review and a model. In R. Brislin, *Translation: applications and research.* New York: Gardner Press.

Gerver, D. and Sinaiko, H.W. (eds) 1978. *Language interpretation and communication.* New York: Plenum Press.

Glasgow Herald 1817. Extract, 26 September. Glasgow: Glasgow Herald Newspapers.

Goldin-Meadow, S. 1977. Structure in a manual communication system developed without a conventional language model: language without a helping hand. In H. Whitaker and H.A. Whitaker, (eds.) *Studies in Neurolinguistics 4.* New York: Academic Press.

Goodman, K. 1967. Reading: a psycholinguistic guessing game. *Journal of the Reading Specialist,* 6: 126–36.

Green, F. 1783. *Vox oculis subjecta.* London: B. White.

Green, W.B. and Shepherd, D.C. 1975. The semantic structure of deaf children. *Journal of Communication Disorders,* 8: 357.

Gregory, S. 1976. *The deaf child and his family.* London: George Allen and Unwin.

Gregory, S. and Mogford, K. 1981. Early language development in deaf children. In B. Woll, J.G. Kyle and M. Deuchar (1981).

Griffiths, P. 1979. Speech acts and early sentences. In P. Fletcher and M. Garman (eds) *Language acquisition.* Cambridge: Cambridge University Press.

Gustason, G. 1983. Manual English and ASL: where do we go from here? In Kyle and Woll (1983).

Gustason, G., Pfetzing, D. and Zawolkow, E. 1975. *Signing Exact English.* Los Alamitos, California: Modern Signs Press.

Halliday, M.A.K. 1975. *Learning how to mean.* London: Edward Arnold.

Hansen, B. 1975. Varieties in Danish Sign Language and grammatical features of the original sign language. *Sign Language Studies,* 8: 249–56.

1980. *Aspects of deafness and Total Communication in Denmark.* Copenhagen: Center for Total Communication, Kastelsvej 58.

Haycock, G.S. 1933. *The teaching of speech.* Stoke on Trent: Hill and Ainsworth.

Hegarty, S., Pocklington, K. and Lucas, D. 1981. *Educating pupils with special needs in the ordinary school.* Slough: NFER-Nelson.

1982. *Integration in action.* Slough: NFER-Nelson.

Herbert, J. 1978. How conference interpretation grew. In Gerver and Sinaiko (1978).

Hewes, G.W. 1976. The current status of the gestural theory of language origin. In S.R. Harnad, H.D. Steklis and J. Lancaster. *Origins and evolution of language and speech.* New York: New York Academy of Sciences.

Higgins, P. 1980. *Outsiders in a hearing world.* New York: Sage.

Hitch, G. and Baddeley, A.D. 1978. Working memory. In *Cognitive psychology D303 OU text.* Milton Keynes: Open University.

Hockett, C.F. 1958. *A course in modern linguistics.* New York: Macmillan.

1960. The origin of speech. *Scientific American,* 203, 89–96.

Hodgson, K.W. 1954. *The deaf and their problems.* London: Watts.

Hoemann, H. 1978. *Communicating with deaf people.* Baltimore: University Park Press.

Hoemann, H. and Lucafo, R. 1980. *I want to talk: a child model of ASL.* Silver Springs, Md.: American Society of the Deaf.

Hoffmeister, R.J. and Moores, D.F. 1973. The acquisition of specific reference in the linguistic system of a deaf child of deaf parents. *Research Report 5* Minnesota University: Resource, Development and Demonstration Center in Education of Handicapped Children.

Hume, D. 1829. *Commentaries on the law of Scotland.* Edinburgh: Bell and Bradfute.

References

Inglis, A.L. 1978. A pilot investigation into the memory coding strategies used by multi-handicapped children learning the Paget Gorman Sign System. *Australian Journal of Human Communication Disorders, 6*: 32–42.

Itard, J.M.G. 1821. *Traité des maladies de l'oreille et le l'audition*. Paris: Mequignon-Marvis.

Ivimey, G.P. 1976. The written syntax of an English deaf child: an exploration in method. *British Journal of Disorders of Communication, 11*, 2: 103–20.

Jensema, C.J. and Trybus, R.J. 1976. *Communication patterns and educational achievement of hearing impaired students*. Series T2. Washington DC: Gallaudet College, Office of Demographic Studies.

Jensema, C.J., Karchmer, M.A. and Trybus, R.J. 1978. *The rated speech intelligibility of hearing-impaired children*. Series R, No.6. Washington DC: Gallaudet College, Office of Demographic Studies.

Jordan, I.K. and Battison, R. 1976. A referential communication experiment with foreign sign languages. *Sign Language Studies, 10*: 69–80.

Karchmer, M.A., Trybus, R.J. and Paquin, M.M. 1978. Early manual communication, parental status, and the academic achievement of deaf students. Paper presented at American Education Research Association annual meeting, Toronto, Ontario, Canada.

Keiser, W. 1978. Selection and training of conference interpreters. In Gerver and Sinaiko (1978).

Kelly, R.R. and Tomlinson-Keasey, C. 1977. Hemispheric laterality of deaf children for processing words and pictures visually presented to the hemifields. *American Annals of the Deaf, 12*: 525–33.

Kerr-Love, J. and Addison, W.H. 1896. *Deaf mutism*. Glasgow: Maclehouse.

Kiernan, C., Reid, B. and Jones, L. 1979. Signs and symbols: who uses what? *Special Education Forward Trends, 6*: 32–5.

    1982. *Signs and symbols: use of non-vocal communication systems*. London: Heinemann Educational Books for University of London Institute of Education.

Kintsch, W. and Keenan, J. 1973. Reading rate and retention as a function of the number of propositions in the base structure of sentences. *Cognitive Psychology, 5*: 257–74.

Klima, E. 1975. Sound and its absence in the linguistic symbol. In J.F. Cavanagh and J.E. Cutting (eds.) *The role of speech in language*. Cambridge, Mass.: MIT Press.

Klima, E. and Bellugi, U. 1966. Syntactic regularities in the speech of children. In J. Lyons and R. Wales (eds) *Psycholinguistic papers – proceedings of the Edinburgh Conference*. Edinburgh: Edinburgh University Press.

    1972. The signs of language in child and chimpanzee. In T. Alloway, (ed.) *Communication and affect*. New York: Academic Press.

    1979. *The signs of language*. Cambridge: Harvard University Press.

Klopping, H. 1971. Language understanding of deaf students under three audio-visual stimulus conditions. Ed.D thesis, University of Arizona.

Kluwin, T. 1981. The grammaticality of manual representations of English in classroom settings. *American Annals of the Deaf, 127*: 417–21.

Kohl, H. 1966. *Language and the education of the deaf*. New York: Center for Urban Studies.

Krashen, S.D. 1978. Individual variation in the use of the monitor. In W. Ritchie (ed.) *Principles of second language learning*, New York: Academic Press.

    1981. *Principles and practices in second language acquisition* Oxford: Pergamon.

Krashen, S.D., Long, M.A. and Scarcella, R.C. 1979 Age, rate and eventual attainment in second language acquisition. *TESOL Quarterly, 13*: 173–83.

Krashen, S.D. and Seliger, H. 1975. The essential contributions of formal instruction in adult second language learning. *TESOL Quarterly, 9*: 173–83.

Kruse, 1863. Quoted G.F. Stout. *A manual of psychology.* London: University Correspondence College Press. See also Tylor (1874).

Kyle, J.G. 1978. The study of auditory deprivation from birth. *British Journal of Audiology, 12*: 37–9.

1979. Measuring the intelligence of deaf children. *Bulletin of British Psychological Society, 33*: 30–2.

1980s. Auditory deprivation: a clarification of some issues. *British Journal of Audiology. 14*: 30–2.

1980b. Sign language and internal representation. In I. Ahlgren and B. Bergman, *Papers from the first international symposium on sign language research, Stokholm.*

1981a. Signs and memory: the search for the code. In B. Woll, J.G. Kyle and M. Deuchar. *Perspectives on BSL.*

1981b. Signs of speech, *Special Education Forward Trends, 8*: 19–23.

1981c. Reading development in deaf children. *Journal of Research in Reading, 3*: 86–97.

1982. Signs of English: some clues to thinking in sign. Paper presented to British Psychological Society conference, cognitive psychology section, Brunel University.

1983. Meaning in sign: recalling events in BSL and English. In D. Rogers and J. Sloboda (eds) *Symbolic skills.* London: Plenum, Press.

Kyle, J. G. and Allsop, L. 1982a. *Deaf people and the community: final report to the Nuffield Foundation.* Bristol: School of Education, Bristol University.

1982b. Communicating with young deaf people. *Teacher of the Deaf, 6*: 89–95.

Kyle, J.G., Carter, M. and Maddix, F. 1981. Analysing sign structure by computer. In *Research on deafness and British Sign Language.* Centre for the Study of Language and Communication, University of Bristol.

Kyle, J.G., Conrad, R., McKenzie, M.G., Morris, A.J.M. and Weiskrantz, B.C. 1978. Language abilities in deaf school leavers. *The Teacher of the Deaf, 2, 2.*

Kyle, J.G., Llewellyn-Jones, P. and Woll, B. 1979. The qualities of interpreters. *British Deaf News, 10*: 62–3.

Kyle, J.G., Pullen, G., Wood, P.L. and Allsop, L. 1984. BSL in the British deaf community In V. Volterra and W.C. Stokoe, *Proceedings of the third international sign language symposium.* Silver Springs Md.: Linstock Press.

Kyle, J.G. and Woll, B. (eds). 1983. *Language in sign: an international perspective on sign language.* London: Croom Helm.

Kyle, J.G., Woll, B., and Carter, M. 1979. *Coding British Sign Language.* University of Bristol, School of Education Research Unit.

Kyle, J.G., Woll, B. and Llewellyn-Jones, P. 1981. Learning and using BSL. *Sign Language Studies, 31*: 155–78.

Kyle, J.G., Woll, B., Llewellyn-Jones, P. and Pullen, G. 1981. *Sign language learning and use. Final report to DHSS.* Bristol: School of Education, Bristol University.

Kyle, J.G. and Wood, P. 1983. *Social and vocational aspects of acquired deafness. Final report to MSC.* Bristol: School of Education, Bristol University.

Lane, H. 1977. *The wild boy of Aveyron.* London: Allen and Unwin.

References

Lawson, L. 1981. The role of sign in the structure of the deaf community. In B. Woll, J.G. Kyle and M. Deuchar (1981).

1983. Multi-channel signs. In Kyle and Woll (1983).

Layne, C.A. 1982. The deaf way: an ethnography of a deaf adult. In P. Higgins and J. Nash (eds) *The deaf community and the deaf population. Working Papers 3.* Washington DC: Gallaudet College.

Lederer, M. 1978. Simultaneous interpretation-units of meaning and other features. In Gerver and Sinaiko (1978).

Lewis, M.M. 1968. *The education of deaf children: the possible place of fingerspelling and signing.* London: HMSO.

Li, C.N. and Thompson, S.A. 1976. Subject and topic: a new typology of language. In C.N. Li, (ed.) *Subject and topic.*

Liddell, S. 1980. *American Sign Language syntax.* The Hague: Mouton.

Ling, D. and Clarke, B.R. 1975. Cued Speech: an evaluative study. *American Annals of the Deaf, 120:* 480–8.

Livingston, S. 1983. Levels of development in the language of deaf children. *Sign Language Studies, 40:* 193–286.

Llewellyn-Jones, P. 1981a. Simultaneous interpreting. In B. Woll, J. Kyle and M. Deuchar (1981).

1981b. BSL interpreting. Paper presented to the Third international sign language interpreters conference, Bristol. London: RNID.

Llewellyn-Jones, P., Kyle, J.G. and Woll, B. 1979. Sign language communication. Paper presented at the International conference on social psychology of language, Bristol.

Locke, J. and Locke, V. 1971. Deaf children's phonetic visual and dactylic coding in a grapheme recall task. *Journal of Experimental Psychology, 89:* 142–6.

Loncke, F. 1983. The specific situation of the Flemish deaf people and their attitudes towards sign language. In Kyle and Woll (1983).

Long, J.S. 1918. *The sign language: a manual of signs.* Iowa City: Athens Press.

Longley, P. 1978. An integrated programme for training interpreters. In Gerver and Sinaiko (1978).

Lubert, B.J. 1975. *The relation of brain asymmetry to visual processing of sign language.* Unpublished Masters thesis, University of Western Ontario.

Lyons, J. 1977. *Semantics.* Cambridge: Cambridge University Press.

Lysons, K. 1977–8. The development of local voluntary societies for adult deaf persons in England. *British Deaf News, 10–11* (serialised).

McDonald, B. 1983. Levels of analysis in sign language research. In Kyle and Woll (1983).

McDonough, S.H. 1981. *Psychology in foreign language teaching.* London: George Allen and Unwin.

McIntire, M.L. 1977. The acquisition of American Sign Language hand configurations. *Sign Language Studies, 16:* 247–66.

McKeever, W.F., Hoemann, H.W., Florian, V.A. and Van Deventer, A.D. 1976. Evidence of minimal cerebral asymmetries for the processing of English words and ASL stimuli in the congenitally deaf. *Neuropsychologia, 14:* 413–23.

MacMillan, D.L. 1971. Special education for the retarded: servant or savant? In R.L.

Jones (ed.) *Problems and issues in the education of exceptional children.* Boston: Houghton Mifflin.

McNeil, D. 1966. Developmental psycholinguistics. In F. Smith and G.A. Miller (eds) *The genesis of language: a psycholinguistic approach.* Cambridge, Mass: MIT Press.

Maestas y Moores, J. 1980. Early linguistic environment: interactions of deaf parents with their infants. *Sign Language Studies, 26:* 1–13.

Mallery, G. 1881. *Sign language among North American Indians.* Washington DC: Govt. Printing Office.

Mandler, J.M. and Johnson, N.S. 1977. Remembrance of things parsed: story structure and recall. *Cognitive Psychology, 9:* 111–51.

Manning, A.A., Goble, W., Markman, R. and Labreche, T. 1977. Lateral cerebral differences in the deaf in response to linguistic and nonlinguistic stimuli. *Brain and Language, 4:* 309–21.

Markides, A. 1970. The speech of deaf and partially hearing children with special reference to factors affecting intelligibility. *British Journal of Disorders of Communication, 5:* 126–40.

Markowicz, H. and Woodward, J.C. 1975. *Language and maintenance of ethnic boundaries in the deaf community.* Washington DC: Linguistics Research Lab. Gallaudet College

Marmor, G.S. and Petitto, L. 1979. Simultaneous communication in the classroom: how well is English grammar represented? *Sign Language Studies, 23:* 99–136.

Marshall, J.C., Caplan, D. and Holmes, J.M. 1975. The measure of laterality. *Neuropsychologia, 13:* 315–21.

Marslen-Wilson, W. and Welsh, A. 1978. Processing interactions and lexical access during word recognition in continuous speech. *Cognitive Psychology, 10:* 29–63.

Maxwell, M.M. 1983. Simultaneous communication in the classroom. *Sign Language Studies, 39:* 95–112.

Mayberry, R.I. 1978. French Canadian Sign Language: a study of inter-sign language comprehension. In P. Siple (ed.) *Understanding language.*

Meadow, K.P. 1980. *Deafness and child development.* London: E. Arnold.

Michaels 1923. *A handbook of the sign language of the deaf,* Atlanta Ga.: Southern Baptist Convention.

Mills, C.B. and Jordan, I.K. 1980. Timing sensitivity and age as predictors of sign language learning. *Sign Language Studies, 26:* 15–28.

Milner, B., Branch, C. and Rasmussen, T. 1964. Intracarotid sodium amytal for the lateralisation of cerebral speech dominance. *Journal of Neurosurgery, 21:* 399–404.

Mohay, H. 1982. A preliminary description of the communication systems evolved by two deaf children in the absence of a sign language model. *Sign Language Studies, 34:* 73–90.

1983. The effects of Cued Speech on the language development of three deaf children. *Sign Language Studies, 38:* 25–49.

Montgomery, G. 1981. *The integration and disintegration of the deaf in society.* Edinburgh: Scottish Workshop for the Deaf.

Montgomery, G. and Lines, A. 1976. Comparison of several single and combined methods of communicating with deaf children. *Proceedings of the seminar on visual communication.* Newcastle upon Tyne: Northern Counties School for the Deaf.

References

Montgomery, G. and Miller, J. 1977. Assessment and preparation of deaf adolescents for employment. *Teacher of the Deaf, 1*: 167–76.

Moody, B. 1979. La Communication internationale chez les sourds. *Rééducation Orthophonique, 17*: 213–24.

Moores, D.F. 1978. *Educating the deaf: psychology, principles, and practices.* Boston: Houghton Mifflin.

Moores, D., Weiss, K. and Goodwin, M. 1973. Receptive abilities of deaf children across five modes of communication. *Exceptional Children, 39*: 22–8.

Moser, B. 1978. Simultaneous interpretation: a hypothetical model. In Gerver and Sinaiko (1978).

Murphy, H.J. 1978. Research in sign language interpreting at California State University, Northridge. In Gerver and Sinaiko (1978).

Myklebust, H.R. 1964. *The psychology of deafness: sensory deprivation, learning and adjustment.* 2nd edn. New York: Grune and Stratton.

Naiman, N., Frohlich, A. and Stern, H. 1975. *The good language learner.* Ontario: Modern Language Center, Curriculum Dept, Ontario Institute for Studies in Education.

Namy, C. 1978. Reflections in the training of simultaneous interpreters: a metalinguistic approach. In Gerver and Sinaiko (1978).

Nelson, K. 1973. *Structure and strategy in learning to talk.* Monograph 38, Society for Research in Child Development.

Nevins, J.B. 1895. *The sign language of the deaf and dumb.* Literary and Philosophical Society of Liverpool.

Newmark, L. 1966. How not to interfere with language learning. *International Journal of American Linguistics, 32*: 77–83.

Newmark, L. and Riebel, D. 1968. Necessity and sufficiency in language learning. *International Review of Applied Linguistics in Language Teaching, 6*: 145–61.

Newport, E.L. and Bellugi, U. 1978. Linguistic expression of category levels in a visual gestural language. In E. Rosch, and B.B. Lloyd (eds) *Cognition and categorization.* New Jersey: Lawrence Erlbaum.

Nolan, M. and Tucker, I.G. 1981. *The hearing impaired child and the family* London: Souvenir Press.

O'Connor, N. and Hermelin, B. 1973. Short term memory for the order of pictures and syllables by deaf and hearing children. *Neuropsychologia, 11*: 437–42.

Oller, J., Baca, L. and Vigil, A. 1977. Attitudes and attained proficiency in ESL. *TESOL Quarterly, 11*: 173–83.

Oyama, S. 1976. A sensitive period for the acquisition of non-native phonological systems. *Journal of Psychological Research, 5*: 261–4.

Parsons, H. McI. 1978. Human factors approach to simultaneous interpretation. In Gerver and Sinaiko (1978).

Payne, A.H. 1903. The mental development of the deaf. In *Proceedings of the eighth biennial congress of the British Deaf and Dumb Association.* Blackburn: Muir.

Penfield, W. and Roberts, L. 1959. *Speech and brain mechanisms.* Princeton: Princeton University Press.

Pergnier, M. 1978. Language meaning and message meaning: toward a sociolinguistic approach to translation. In Gerver and Sinaiko (1978).

Peter, M. and Barnes, R. (eds) 1982. *Signs, symbols and schools.* London: National Council for Special Education.

Petitto, L. 1983. *From gesture to symbol: the acquisition of personal pronouns in ASL.* Unpubished paper, McGill University, Montreal, Canada.

Phippard, D. 1977. Hemifield differences in visual perception in deaf and hearing subjects. *Neuropsychologia, 15:* 555–61.

Poizner, H. 1979. Hemispheric specialization in the deaf. In B. Frokjaer-Jensen (ed.) *Selected papers of the NATO ASI: sign language research.* Special Issue, LOGOS. Copenhagen: Audiologopedic Research Group.

Poizner, H. and Lane, H. 1978. Discrimination of location in American Sign Language. In P. Siple (ed.) *Understanding language.*

Poizner, H., Battison, R. and Lane, H.L. 1979. Cerebral Asymmetry for perception of American Sign Language: the effects of moving stimuli. *Brain and Language, 7:* 351–62.

Poizner, H., Bellugi, U. and Tweney, R.D. 1981. Processing of formational, semantic and iconic information in ASL. *Journal of Experimental Psychology: Human Perception and Performance, 7:* 1146–59.

Powell, C. and Braybrook, D. 1981. Deafness and living language. Paper presented at the British Association of Teachers of the Deaf conference, Blackpool, October.

Quigley, S.P. 1969. *The influence of fingerspelling on the development of language, communication, and educational achievement in deaf children.* Urbana: University of Illinois, Institute for Research on Exceptional Children.

1979. Language and communication in the language development of deaf children. In Bradford and Hardy (1979).

Quigley, S.P., Wilbur, R.B., Power, D.J., Montanelli, D.S. and Steinkamp, M.W. (1976). Syntactic structures in the language of deaf children. Urbana, Illinois: Institute for Child Behavior and Development.

Rainer, J.D. and Altshuler, K.Z. 1968. *Psychiatry and the deaf:* being the report of the workshop for psychiatrists on extending mental health services to the deaf, New York, 1967. Washington, DC: Social and Rehabilitation Service, Department of Health, Education and Welfare.

Ravem, R. 1974. The development of Wh-questions in first and second language learners. In J. Richards (ed.) *Error analysis: perspectives on second language learning.* New York: Longmans.

Ray, L. 1848. Thoughts of the deaf and dumb before instruction. *American Annals of the Deaf, 1:* 149–57.

Reich, P. and Bick, M. 1976. An empirical investigation of some claims made in support of Visible English, *American Annals of the Deaf, 121:* 573–77.

Remvig, J. 1969. *Three clinical studies of deaf-mutism and psychiatry.* Copenhagen: Munksgard.

RNID (Royal National Institute for the Deaf). 1981. *Sign and say.* London: RNID.

Rosch, E. 1973. On the internal structure of perceptual and semantic categories. In C. Moore (ed.) *Cognitive development and the acquisition of language.* New York: Academic Press.

Ross, P., Pergament, L. and Anisfeld, M. 1979. Cerebral lateralization of deaf and hearing individuals for linguistic comparison judgements. *Brain and Language, 8:* 69–80.

Rowe, J. 1982. The Paget-Gorman Sign System. In Peter and Barnes (1982).

Royal Commission. 1889. *On the education of the blind, deaf and dumb.* London: HMSO.

Ruben, R.J. and Rapin, I. 1980. Theoretical issues in the development of audition. In L.T.

References

Taft and M. Lewis (eds.) *Symposium in developmental disabilities in the preschool child.* New York: Spectrum.

Samarin, W.J. 1967. *Field linguistics.* New York: Holt, Reinhart and Winston.

Sasanuma, S., Itoh, M., Mori, K. and Kobayashi, Y. 1977. Tachistoscopic recognition of Kana and Kanji words. *Neuropsychologia, 15*: 547–53.

Savage, R.D., Evans, L. and Savage, J.F. 1981. *Psychology and communication in deaf children.* Sydney: Grune and Stratton.

Schein, J.D. 1979. Society and culture of hearing impaired people. In Bradford and Hardy 1979.

Schein, J.D. and Delk, M.T. 1974. *The deaf population of the United States.* Silver Springs, Md.: National Association of the Deaf.

Schlesinger, H. 1978. The acquisition of bimodal language. In I.M. Schlesinger and L. Namir (eds) *Sign language of the deaf: international perspectives.* New York. Academic Press.

Schlesinger, H. and Meadow, K. 1972. *Sound and sign: childhood deafness and mental health.* Berkeley Ca: University of California Press.

Scholes, R.J. and Fischler, I. 1979. Hemispheric function and linguistic skill in the deaf. *Brain and Language, 7*: 336–50.

Schontheil, S. 1882. My experience in the classroom. In *Conference Report* (1882).

Schroedel, J.G. and Schiff, W. (1972). Attitudes towards deafness among several deaf and hearing populations, *Rehabilitation Psychology, 19*: 59–70.

Schumann, J.H. 1977. Second language acquisition: the pidginisation hypothesis. *Language Learning, 26*: 391–408.

Scott Hutton 1882. In *Conference Report.* (1882)

Scott, W.R. 1870. *The deaf and dumb.* London: Bell and Daldy.

Scroggs, C. 1983. Communication interactions between hearing-impaired infants and their parents. In Kyle and Woll (1983).

Seidel, J.V. 1982. The points at which deaf and hearing worlds intersect: a dialectical analysis. In P. Higgins and J. Nash *The deaf community and the deaf population. Working Papers 3.* Washington DC: Gallaudet College.

Seleskovitch, D. 1978. *Interpreting for international conferences.* Washington DC: Pen and Booth.

Seliger, H., Krashen, S. and Ladefoged, P. 1975. Maturational constraints in the acquisition of 2nd language accent. *Language Sciences, 36*: 20–2.

Selniker, L. 1972. Interlanguage, *International Review of Applied Linguistics, 10*: 201–31.

Shand, M.A. 1982. Sign based short term coding of ASL signs and printed English words by congenitally deaf signers. *Cognitive Psychology, 14*: 1–12.

Shand, M.A. and Klima, E.S. 1981. Non-auditory suffix effects in congenitally deaf signers of ASL. *Journal of Experimental Psychology: Human learning and memory, 7*: 464–74.

Shapin, S. 1978. The politics of observation: cerebral anatomy and social interests in the Edinburgh phrenology debates. *Sociological Review Monograph,* ed. Roy Wallis.

Shapira, R.G. 1978. The non-learning of English: case study of an adult. In E.M. Hatch (ed.) *Second language acquisition: a book of readings.* Rowley, Mass.: Newbury House.

Sicard, R.A. 1803. *Cours d'instruction d'un sourd-muet de naissance.* 2nd edn. Paris: Le Clère.

Simpson, T.S. 1981. Council for the Advancement of Communication with Deaf People. *British Deaf News* (supplement), July.

Siple, P. 1978. Visual constraints for sign language communication. *Sign Language Studies, 19*: 97–112.

Siple, P., Brewer, L., and Caccamise, F. 1980. The influence of language knowledge on the form of the memory code for sign language users. Paper presented at the annual meeting AERA, Boston, Mass., April.

Siple, P., Fischer, S.D. and Bellugi, U. 1977. Memory for non-semantic attributes of ASL signs and English words. *Journal of Verbal Learning and Verbal Behaviour, 16*: 561–74.

Sisco, F.H. and Anderson, R.J. 1980. Deaf children's performance on the WISC-R relative to hearing status of parents and child-rearing experiences. *American Annals of the Deaf, 125*: 923–30.

Snow, C.E. 1972. Mothers' speech to children learning language. *Child Development, 43*.

Snow, C.E. and Hofnagel-Höhle, M. 1978. Age differences in second language acquisition. In E.M. Hatch (ed.) *Second language acquisition*. Rowley Mass: Newbury House.

Sorensen, R.K. and Hansen, B. 1976. *The sign language of deaf children*. Copenhagen: Doves Center for Total Kommunikation, Kastelsvej, 58.

Stein, B.E. and Shuckman, H. 1973. Effects of sensory restriction upon the responses to cortical stimulation in rats. *Journal of Comparative Physiology, 63*, 182–7.

Stewart D. 1815. Some account of a boy born blind and deaf. *Transactions of the Royal Society of Edinburgh, 7*: 1–78.

Stewart, D.A. 1983. Bilingual education: teachers' opinions of signs. *Sign Language Studies, 39*: 145–67.

Stokoe, W.C. 1960. *Sign language structure: an outline of the visual communication system of the American deaf*. Studies in Linguistics Occasional Paper 8. University of Buffalo.

1972. Classification and description of sign languages. In T.A. Sebeok (ed.) *Current trends in linguistics 12*. The Hague: Mouton.

1980. The study and use of sign language. In R.L. Schiefelbusch (ed.) *Non-speech language and communication*. Baltimore, Md. University Park Press.

Stokoe, W.C. and Kuschel, R. 1979. *A field guide for sign language research*. Silver Springs, Md.: Linstok Press.

Stokoe, W.C., Casterline, D. and Croneberg, C. 1965. *A dictionary of American Sign Language*. Washington DC: Gallaudet College Press.

Storer, R.D.K. 1977. The vocational boundaries of deaf and partially hearing adolescents and young adults in the West Midlands. *Teacher of the Deaf, 1*: 134.

Story, A.J. 1905. *Language for the deaf*. Hanley: Wood Mitchell.

Stout, G.F. 1899. *A manual of psychology*. London: University Correspondence College Press.

Supalla, T. and Newport, E. 1978. How many seats in a chair? The derivation of nouns and verbs in American Sign Language. In P. Siple (ed.) *Understanding language*.

Swayne, A.B. 1934. The teaching of language. In *Proceedings of the twelfth conference of teachers of the deaf*. Liverpool: Hadley.

Swisher, L. 1976. The language performance of the oral deaf. In H.A. Whitaker and H. Whitaker *Studies in Neurolinguistics Vol.2*, New York: Academic Press.

TALK. 1982. An oral approach: the answers of the staff of St John's, Boston Spa to some questions asked by parents. *TALK, 102*: Spring: 12–15.

Teacher of the Deaf. 1946. Letter *Teacher of the Deaf, 44*: 50.

Tervoort, B.T. 1961. Esoteric symbolism in the communication behaviour of young deaf children. *American Annals of the Deaf,* 106: 436–80.

1979. What is the native language of a deaf child?, *Studies in honour of Prof. B. Siertsema* Amsterdam: Institute for General Linguistics.

1983. The status of sign language in education in Europe. In Kyle and Woll (1983).

TIMES. 1798. Extract, 4th May 1798. London: Times Newspapers.

TIMES. 1880. Extract, 13 September 1880. London: Times Newspapers.

Tizard, J. 1974. Longitudinal studies: problems and findings. In A.M. Clarke and A.D.B. Clarke *Mental deficiency: the changing outlook.* 3rd edn. London: Methuen.

Tuckfield, H. 1839. *Education for the people.* London: Taylor and Walton.

Tylor, E.B. 1874. *Researches into the early history of mankind.* London: Murray.

1878. *Researches into the early history of mankind.* 2nd edn. London: Murray.

1895. *Anthropology: an introduction to the study of man and civilisation.* London: Macmillan.

Ulfsparre, S. 1979. Panto-signs. Paper presented at the first international symposium on sign language research, Stockholm.

Van Uden, A. 1970. *A world of language for deaf children.* Rotterdam: Rotterdam University Press.

1981. Early diagnosis of those multiple handicaps in prelingually profoundly deaf children which endanger an education according to the purely oral way. *Teacher of the Deaf,* 5: 112–27.

Vernon, McC. 1967. Relationship of language to the thinking process. *Archives of General Psychiatry,* 16: 325–33.

Vestberg Rasmussen 1973. Evaluation of reading achievements of deaf children. In E. Kampp *Evaluation of hearing handicapped children.* Denmark: Ebeltoft.

Vogt-Svendsen, M. 1983. Lip movements in Norwegian Sign Language. In Kyle and Woll (1983).

Volterra, V. 1983. Gestures, signs and words at two years. In Kyle and Woll (1983).

Walberg, Hose and Raster. 1978. Cited in S.D. Krashen and T.D. Terrell (eds.) 1982. *The natural approach: language acquisition in the classroom.* Oxford: Pergamon.

Walker, M. 1976. *The Makaton Vocabulary.* London: Royal Association for the Deaf and Dumb.

Walker, M. and Armfield, A. 1982. What is the Makaton Vocabulary? In Peter and Barnes (1982).

Warnock, H.M. 1978. *Special educational needs: report of the Committee of Enquiry.* London: HMSO.

Warr, P., Cook, J. and Wall, T. 1979. Scales for the measurement of some work attitudes and aspects of psychological well-being. *Journal of Occupational Psychology,* 52: 129–48.

Watson, J. 1809. *Instruction of the deaf and dumb.* London: Darton and Harvey.

Watson, T.J. 1967. *The education of hearing-handicapped children.* Manchester: Manchester University Press.

Wells, C.G. 1981. *Learning through interaction.* Cambridge: Cambridge University Press.

Wernicke, 1874. *Das aphasische SymptomenKomplex.* Breslau.

White, A.H. and Stevenson, V.M. 1975. The effects of Total Communication, manual communication, oral communication and reading on the learning of factual information in residential school deaf children. *American Annals of the Deaf,* 120: 48–57.

Whorf, B.L. 1956. *Language, thought and reality*. Cambridge Mass.: MIT Press.

Wickham, C. in press. Modulation of BSL signs in children exposed to manually coded English. Ms. Bristol School of Education.

Witkin, H.A. 1950. Individual differences in ease of perception of embedded figures. *Journal of Personality, 19*: 1–15.

Woll, B. 1981. Processes of change in BSL. Paper presented at LAGB autumn meeting, York.

Woll, B. 1983. The comparative study of different sign languages. In Loncke, LeBrun and Boyes-Braem (eds). *Comparing sign languages: recent research in European sign language*. Ca. Lisse. Swets.

Woll, B., Kyle, J.G. and Deuchar, M. (eds) 1981. *Perspectives on BSL and deafness*. London: Croom Helm.

Wood, D. 1981. Some developmental aspects of prelingual deafness. In B. Woll, J.G. Kyle and M. Deuchar (1981).

Wood, D., Griffiths, A.J. and Webster, A. 1981. Reading retardation or linguistic deficit. *Journal of Research on Reading, 4*: 148–56.

Wood, D., Wood, H. and Howarth, P. 1983. Language, deafness and mathematical reasoning. In D. Rogers and J. Sloboda (eds) *The acquisition of symbolic skills*. London: Plenum.

Woodward, J. 1973. Some characteristics of Pidgin Sign English. *Sign Language Studies, 3*: 39–46.

Woodward, J. 1976. *Historical bases of ASL*. In P. Siple (ed.) *Understanding language*.

Worswick, C. 1982. Interrogatives in BSL. Edinburgh: Moray House College of Education. BSL Project. Pamphlet.

Subject index

Subject index

Index of signs in the text

Index of signs in the text